CW01507183

Cockaigne

Essays on Elgar 'In London Town'

Lectures given to the Elgar Society, London Branch

edited by

Kevin D. Mitchell

 Elgar Editions

Published in Great Britain by

Elgar Editions

the publishing imprint of

Elgar Enterprises
20 High Street, Rickmansworth, Herts WD3 1ER
(e-mail : editions@elgar.org)

© individual contributors, 2004

First Published : November 2004

British Library Cataloguing in Publication Data
A Catalogue record for this book
is available from the British Library

ISBN 0 9548553 0 2 (Elgar Editions)

Printed and bound in Great Britain by
Antony Rowe Ltd,
Bumper's Farm, Chippenham, Wiltshire

Contents

In Memory of
Edward Wulstan Ivor Atkins (1904-2003)

Acknowledgments

I must thank all the contributors who kindly provided essays for this book. In particular I thank Michael Kennedy, who specially prepared his essay on Elgar and Strauss at my request. Unhappily, Michael Oliver died before reading the transcription of his taped lecture, which would undoubtedly have been revised by him before publication. I am most grateful to Michael Downing and Michael Oliver's family who approved the text and agreed to its appearance.

The initial idea for this volume emanated from Relf Clark, London Branch Secretary. I am hugely indebted to him for his careful reading of the majority of the contributions and I have benefited greatly from his knowledge and wisdom, which has been invaluable. It is with pleasure that I thank Martin Passande, London Branch Chairman, Stephen and Professor Jenny Harrow and Jane Owen, for their insightful comments on the essays they have read and who encouraged and sustained me when my light was low. I thank Philip and Helen Petchey for their advice and support; Paul Rooke for preparing the musical illustrations; Ann Vernau and Janet Norris for their help in preparing the index; and all my colleagues who have served on the London Branch committee since the book's inception and who authorised funding to enable it to appear.

I thank Cathy Sloan and Christopher Bennett for their assistance at the Elgar Birthplace Museum and for access to the photographic archive. I thank Arthur Reynolds and Raymond Monk for kindly providing photographs from their collections and to David Bury for the cover photograph and others from his collection. I am grateful to the Masters and Fellows of Magdalene College, Cambridge for permission to reproduce the portrait of A.C. Benson. I am indebted to the Elgar Will Trust for permission to quote from the music and writings of Edward and Alice Elgar and to the editor of the *Elgar Society Journal* for permission to reproduce, albeit after revision, two essays that originally appeared there.

Finally, I thank John Norris for his help, patience and skill, which has been indispensable in processing the material and for his superb guidance in all aspects of the production process.

Chislehurst, Kent: September 2004

Introduction

Kevin D. Mitchell

The London Branch of the Elgar Society was created in October 1971. It was the first branch outside the West Midlands. Initially, meetings were held at the British Institute of Recorded Sound, but the Branch later settled on Imperial College, where an annual, October – June series of lectures has been maintained ever since. Many distinguished musicians have been invited to address the Branch including Yehudi Menhuin, Paul Tortelier, Norman Del Mar, Bernard Keefe, Vernon Handley, Lady Barbirolli, Dame Joan Hammond, Jean Rigby, Margaret Harrison and Dame Janet Baker among others. Elgar scholars and biographers who have spoken include Diana McVeagh, Michael Kennedy, Percy Young, Jerrold Northrop Moore, Wulstan Atkins, Christopher Kent, Robert Anderson, John Pickard and Relf Clark. There have been visits by Sir Malcolm Sargent's son and Christopher Finzi. Singers, pianists, organists, string quartets and instrumentalists have presented plenty of live music and there have been two presentations by pianola players. Broadcasters and those from the record industry have given lectures, as have the historian Asa Briggs and the biographer Michael Holroyd. Many Society and Branch members have shared their wisdom and love of Elgar with members, to acclaim and looking back over the history of the Branch the array of names and subjects is truly astonishing.

It was with that in mind that the committee decided to preserve in a more permanent form some of the lectures given, to show a small part of what had been achieved in London over more than thirty years. Unhappily, many presentations were beyond recall as notes were no longer preserved and speakers no longer alive. Others were simply not structured to be transformed into print. The choice was restricted also in that it was decided to print lectures on subjects – so far as possible – which were not already covered in the Elgarian literature. Obviously the nine given here represent a very small proportion of the presentations that have been given since the Branch's formation.

Over two seasons from 1983 to 1985, the Branch gave a symposium 'Aspects of Elgar': some of the lectures were recorded and the earliest given here is that by the late Michael Oliver, on Elgar's Legacy. Two important friendships are considered, one from the middle of Elgar's life, with Strauss; and the other which blossomed at the end, with Shaw. Michael Kennedy a biographer of both Elgar and Richard Strauss, is admirably suited to shed light on Elgar's important friendship with a great European contemporary. Similarly, Michael Holroyd with his multi-volume study of Shaw is equally qualified to portray Elgar's relationship with the greatest dramatist of the time. A number of individual works are considered: David Bury has produced a detailed study of the *Coronation Ode* and the important role in it of Arthur Benson, using much material that has not appeared before. John Kelly has been studying the Violin Concerto for twenty years and has written a wide-ranging study of the prospective sources for and background to that work. The music for the masque *The Crown of India* has long been a subject of fascination for Dr Robert Anderson and the lecture given here is a foretaste of what is to come when the volume on the masque, edited by Dr Anderson, is published in the *Elgar Complete Edition*. Arthur Reynolds has provided an original study of *Falstaff* and has fascinatingly traced the history of some rogue pages of the manuscript score, which were missing for many years. Andrew Neill has given a detailed history of the Elgar Birthplace Museum, showing how important it was to the composer, how it was created and how it has developed. His use of the diaries of Carice Elgar Blake and other material published for the first time, adds to this unique history. Elgar's place in history is the focus of Carl Newton's iconoclastic study, which considers from a new perspective the cultural climate of Elgar's life, his finances, political views and whether he was a 'nationalist' composer.

Shaw stoutly declared that 'Elgar is alone for Westminster Abbey' [1] but that was not possible in 1934. Thirty-eight years later, Elgar was recognised in the Abbey when a Memorial Stone was unveiled in the presence of the Society's President, Sir Adrian Boult, its Chairman and Vice-Chairman, A.T. Shaw and Frank Greatwich, together with the Prime Minister, Edward Heath, and the Master of the Queen's Musick, Sir Arthur Bliss. The city of London, Edward Elgar and the Society formed to honour him were thus brought together in this ceremony - as they are again with this book.

Notes and References

1   Shaw, George Bernard: 'Sir Edward Elgar' in *Music and Letters,* I, No.1 [1920] in Redwood, C. (ed): *An Elgar Companion* [Ashbourne: Sequoia Press, 1982] 250.

Elgar the Londoner

Kevin D. Mitchell

Many nineteenth-century creative artists from the provinces were attracted, to a greater or lesser extent, to London. Jane Austen often passed through the capital on her journeys to and from Kent and stayed a night or sometimes longer, but she was uneasy there: 'Like most country-dwellers she regarded London as a threatening presence, an evil allurement, which was surprisingly enjoyable when one was actually there, but in prospect and retrospect an abomination.' [1]

Thomas Hardy, at the age of twenty-two, left his native Dorset and ventured to London to further his career as an architect, but after five years, ill-health forced him to return, little headway having been made with his literary ambitions. After his marriage in 1874, he lived again in London for a few months, and from 1878 to 1881 took a house near Wandsworth Common. But London still oppressed him, being 'a monster whose body had four million heads and eight million eyes'.[2] A serious illness made him retreat once more to Dorset, and he found 'that residence in or near a city tended to force mechanical and ordinary productions from his pen'.[3] London therefore henceforth became 'a place of sojourn for a few months only … each year'.[4]

Escaping from Dublin in 1876, George Bernard Shaw encountered 'a London of primitive streets with clinging red mud, miserably treated animals, dark unventilated basements and an atmosphere malodorous with soot and dust',[5] yet he was to make it his home for many years and only relinquished his Whitehall Court flat in 1949. J.M. Barrie, too, became a life-long Londoner after arriving from Kirriemuir in 1885; yet Rudyard Kipling, who arrived in London in October 1889, after leaving India earlier in the year, spent only two unhappy winters at Embankment Chambers, Villiers Street, before ill-health and mental exhaustion necessitated recuperative travel. After his marriage he sailed to Vermont and, on his return to England in 1896, found that Sussex answered his needs, living first in Rottingdean, and then at 'Batemans' near Burwash. He never lived in London permanently again.

1 - Notes and references for this chapter appear on pages xxii-xxiii.

Like these people Elgar was drawn to London, his first recorded stay being in 1877; but his feelings for it were, to say the least, ambiguous. Of his many facets one dichotomy has long stood out, namely the countryman versus the city dweller; the rural Ted Elgar and the metropolitan Sir Edward; the cyclist and walker in Worcestershire and the London sophisticated clubman. The countryman has been viewed as the quintessential Elgar, the lover of fields, lanes and trees who was content 'in the solitude of his own sanctuary',[6] while the London Elgar was a mechanical, stiff and possibly pompous decorated figure. There was a tension between retreat and social engagement, which was never fully resolved. The division was reflected in his moods: 'It is significant that those who remember his happiness, his affection, his gaiety, knew him as a countryman: those who found him moody, crusty, discontented, knew him as a Londoner.'[7] The division has even affected, to some extent, the critical evaluation of his works, in that it is argued the 'rural' Elgar produced his best work, the 'city' Elgar wrote lesser pieces. One is the true composer, the other false.

This is at least arguable, but it does not tell the whole story. Elgar propagated the concept of rural sources of inspiration – 'the trees are signing my music';[8] his injunction to 'play it like something we hear down by the river'[9] – and these pantheistic spurs to his imagination cannot, and should not, be denied or ignored. They were vital to his creativity, but if music was 'in the air' there is no reason why he could only pluck ideas when walking on the Malvern Hills and not in Marylebone.

He found a country life to be important and told one interviewer that he could not live in the capital as ' … London is too noisy for me: one cannot formulate any peaceful thoughts and can work even less',[10] and he knew that this was important to his art. This was recognised by a critic of *The World* after hearing the first London performance of his cantata *King Olaf* in April 1897: 'Perhaps if he had settled in London he would by now be a professor giving eighty lessons and dining out seven times a week and scribbling royalty ballads in his scanty leisure. As it is, he has composed *King Olaf.*'[11] Yet, despite his anxieties about London, he recognised that it was the place where his art was validated – notwithstanding his comment that 'the living centre of music in Great Britain is not London, but somewhere further North',[12] – and that he and his music had to achieve recognition there. First performances of his works in London took on an importance of their own and had to be achieved if he was not simply to remain a 'provincial' composer. He needed the London-based music publishers to add him to their list of composers and then to foster and market his work. Conducting and later recording his music in London became a necessary part of his life, as did mixing with and meeting metropolitan conductors, executants, orchestral and theatrical managers and the giants of the musical world. In London he forged many important, creative friendships and enjoyed London's artistic, social and cultural life; he was to find the company of actors, painters, writers, poets, singers and musicians congenial, particularly when living in Hampstead, and he could invite writers such as Henry James and Shaw and musicians of the calibre of Nikisch and Chaliapin to his appropriately impressive home. Much of his early adult musical education was refined in London and one of his most effective tone poems was to be an affectionate portrait of the city. He maintained his links with London for some fifty-six years, making his last visit in the autumn of 1933, less than six months before his death. Thus London was significant and of value to him for a multiplicity of reasons – it could not be ignored however much he might have protested about it.

It is sometimes thought, so far as his greater works are concerned, that they were written only when he found solace in the countryside of Worcester and Hereford – and latterly Sussex, where he retreated during the final stages of the First World War. This is largely true; but London was not inimical to successful composition. Several major works were composed there. The Concert Overture *Froissart*, his first recognisably Elgarian extended orchestral work, was written entirely in London, during the heady days of early married bliss when he and his wife Alice lived in Kensington and Upper Norwood, in 1890.

By 1910 Elgar was increasingly drawn to London, so that much of the Violin Concerto was written there. He and Alice began the year by attending Sir George and Lady Lewis's lavish New Year's Eve party, an annual event considered to be one of the highlights of the London season. They visited theatres, attended a private view at the Royal Academy, met friends; but the prime purpose of the visit was to seek out a flat to rent and by mid-January Elgar was working on the Concerto, alone, in a service flat in Queen Anne's Mansions near St James's Park. By 20 January he was trying out music that he envisaged for the *Andante,* with the violinist Leonora von Stosch (wife of Sir Edgar Speyer) who had been a pupil of Ysaÿe.

After the Jaeger memorial concert on 24 January the Elgars had supper with the Speyers and the *Andante* music was played and repeated; Elgar played it for Marie Joshua (sister-in-law of Sir George Lewis) a few days later and on 6 February he and Lady Speyer did the same for Frank

Schuster and the Stuart Wortleys. On 7 February he wrote to his confidante, Alice Stuart Wortley, that his London visit had not been a success and considered 'a decent obscurity in the country is all' he could attain to for 'there is really no 'place' for me here as … I am made to feel in many ways I am not wanted.' [13] There is an element of exaggeration in this, as the London visit had produced important new music but he added: 'I am not sure about that Andante & shall put it away for a long time before I decide its fate. I am glad you liked it.' [14] Yet that very evening he wrote a new theme 'in dejection' which was ultimately to be placed between the first movement's first and second subjects. He recorded 'Feb 7 1910 6 30 p.m.' against it and opposite a climax evolved from this theme wrote: 'This is going to be good!/ "When Love and Faith meet/There will be Light"/ Feby 1910. Queen Anne's Mansions.' [15] He left the service flat on 9 February, sent the 'dejected' theme to Alice Stuart Wortley on 10 February stating: 'I … like it myself very much' [16] and on 21 February returned to London, lodging with Frank Schuster while Alice followed from Hereford. On 28 February she found a suitable flat, 58 New Cavendish Street, and took it for three months. After a motor tour of Cornwall, Elgar returned to this flat on 11 April; resuming work on the Concerto he reported to Alice Stuart Wortley on 20 April that he was '… now ablaze with work & *writing hard*; you *should* come & see (& hear it!)' [17] It seems he was working both on the Concerto and on ideas for a second symphony, but by 23 April it was the Concerto which had him in thrall for, on the following day, Alice noted '… E. very thrilled with his Concerto & working at it.' On 26 April she recorded: 'E. very intent writing.' To Alice Stuart Wortley he reported: 'I have been working hard … but all stands still until you come & approve! [18] By 1 May the first movement was complete in short score.

Frank Schuster was advised on 8 May that '… the Concerto was well in hand … Ist movement finished & the IIIrd well on – these *are* times for composition.' [19] He went through the first movement with Lady Speyer on 12 May; and on meeting W.H. Reed (a violinist in the London Symphony Orchestra) in Regent's Street, sought his assistance. Reed came to the New Cavendish flat on 28 May 'to settle … some question[s] of bowing and certain intricacies in the passage-work.' [20] Elgar wrote to thank Reed for his 'kind help & most beautiful playing; I am anxious to send the first movement to the printers … any wisdom you may have to spare will be thankfully received …' [21] Reed returned to the flat on 31 May and the first movement was sent to the publishers on 1 June. Elgar wished to remain in London and find another flat when the lease ended but nothing suitable could be found. He was 'very sad' to leave the New Cavendish Street address and he 'really *hate[d]* going away.' [22] However he soon returned to London, staying at Schuster's riverside house, The Hut, at Bray near Maidenhead where he hoped to finish the Concerto. The Concerto's 'stepmother', Alice Stuart Wortley, was summoned, as was Reed, who played over parts of the slow movement and there, in Schuster's studio, Elgar worked on the Finale. On returning to Hereford, he completed the Concerto and, writing to Schuster, found that 'The world has changed a little since I saw you – it is difficult to say how but it's either larger or smaller or something.' [23] Perhaps to Elgar's surprise, much of the work had been composed in London, which was due in no small part to the presence there of his then muse, Alice Stuart Wortley, whose friendship with and importance to Elgar had intensified in the early months of 1910.

On 1 January 1912, the Elgars moved into their grand Hampstead home, Severn House, which they were to share until Alice's death in 1920, and where Elgar wrote music *inter alia* for the masque *The Crown of India* and the choral work *The Music Makers.* He had long thought of writing a work on Shakespeare's Falstaff and the Symphonic Study was written primarily at Severn House between April and August 1913.[24] The presence of Alice Stuart Wortley was, once more, vital to Elgar as he grappled with this intricate, coruscating orchestral score. He gave her some sketches on 17 April and Alice Elgar noted in her diary on 25 May: ' ... E. beginning to turn to Falstaff'. On 16 June at The Hut he was 'Alone all day & worked hard at Falstaff ...' and on returning to Hampstead was ' ... immersed in his music' Work continued throughout June and July and by 18 July he was 'very absorbed in Falstaff – Very happy over it ... E. & A.S.W. for drive ...' On 26 July he and Alice motored to The Hut; he remained there for a few days, with Alice Stuart Wortley in regular attendance. He was 'working at high pressure' on 31 July and with daily visits by Alice Stuart Wortley from 2 to 4 August, he 'finished his great work' early on the morning of 5 August 1913. This concentrated effort at Hampstead and Maidenhead had produced a masterpiece.

Most of Elgar's war-time works were composed at Severn House, save for the Violin Sonata, String Quartet and part of the Piano Quintet, which were written in the autumn of 1918 at Brinkwells, the isolated woodland cottage near Fittleworth, West Sussex – found by Alice the previous year as a refuge from London. Yet on returning to Hampstead in January 1919, Elgar worked on the *Adagio* of the Piano Quintet and the last movement was written entirely at Severn House in readiness for a private performance at Schuster's central London home, 22 Old Queen Street, on 26 April, and the first public performance, at the Wigmore Hall on 21

May. Admittedly, working away from Sussex was hard: 'Oh! It IS so difficult to keep up with London. No music & interruptions by the thousand – I think of the holy peace at Brinkwells in the early morn.' [25] In December he had complained to Schuster that if he had 'to live at Hampstead again composition is 'off'– not the house or the place but London – telephones etc *all* day and night drive me mad!' [26] Yet in spite of this, and even though Elgar stated Severn House was 'no home for me',[27] another key Elgar work had been completed there. It seems that his jaundiced comments on London primarily emanate from this period and may have been due to a combination of worry over his wife's illness, the burglary of Severn House in mid-December (when they were at Brinkwells) and a coal shortage which resulted in him 'sitting in [an] ice cold studio with no food'.[28]

London's prime role, especially in his early years, was to expand Elgar's musical education both technically and in a broader sense. It appears that his first visit to the capital was in August 1877, when at the age of twenty he travelled there on meagre resources, to have five violin lessons with Herr Pollitzer. Adolphe Pollitzer had played Mendelssohn's Violin Concerto at the age of thirteen, in the presence of the composer, and in 1846 gained the first prize for violin playing at the Vienna Conservatorium. He came to London in 1851 and for many years was leader at the Opera and of the New Philharmonic Orchestra and the Royal Choral Society; he was appointed violin professor at the London Academy of Music in 1861, becoming its principal in 1890. Pollitzer trained a large number of professional and amateur violinists and suggested that Elgar stay in London and concentrate on his violin playing. Elgar, however, 'had become enamoured of a country life, and would not give up the prospect of a certain living by playing and teaching in Worcester on the chance of only a possible success which ... [he] might make as a soloist in London.' [29] Yet by the following year, 1878, Elgar put an advertisement in the Catholic magazine *The Tablet* in an attempt to obtain partial employment as an organist or teacher: 'Neighbourhood of London preferred'. This yielded no response. He returned to Pollitzer, who on learning of Elgar's ambitions to compose, gave him an introduction to August Manns, conductor of the Crystal Palace Concerts. Elgar took full advantage of this, and over the next twelve years heard much music at these concerts and elsewhere in London, considerably widening his musical education. Years later, he recalled the circumstances in which he heard music in London:

> I rose at six – walked a mile to the railway station; – the train left at seven;
> – arrived at Paddington about eleven; – underground to Victoria; – on to
> the Palace, arriving in time for the last three quarters of an hour of the

rehearsal; if fortune smiled, this piece of rehearsal included the work desired to be heard; but fortune rarely smiled and more often than not the principal item was over. Lunch,– Concert at three; – at five a rush for the train to Victoria; – then to Paddington; – on to Worcester arriving at ten-thirty. A strenuous day indeed; but the new work had been heard and another treasure added to a life's experience.[30]

Here he heard works by Mendelssohn and Berlioz, including the first English performance of *Lélio*, in October 1881. He attended a Wagner memorial concert in March 1883, hearing music from *Die Meistersinger, Tannhäuser*, *Lohengrin*, *Götterdämmerung*, the Prelude and 'Liebestod' from *Tristan und Isolde* and the *Siegfried Idyll*, which he noted was 'beautiful'. Two months later he went to the first performance in England of Berlioz's *Requiem* at Crystal Palace and in August heard three movements from the *Symphonie fantastique* – a work he loved throughout his life. In April 1886 he went to a concert celebrating Liszt's seventy-fifth birthday – the composer was present. He heard concerts also at St James's Hall where in November 1878, he heard Hans von Bülow play Schumann's piano *Fantasy,* and where in October 1881 the *Meistersinger* prelude was the first work in a season of orchestral concerts conducted by the esteemed Wagnerian, Hans Richter, who also included Berlioz' s *Nuits d'été* in the programme. Later Richter concerts included Schumann's Symphony in E flat, The Rhenish (5 May 1884) and the first English performance of Brahms's Third Symphony (12 May 1884) – another work high in Elgar's estimation. On 25 May 1887 he heard Richter conduct the *Academic festival overture*, two extracts from *Die Walküre* and the first performance in England of Bruckner's Seventh Symphony: Elgar noted 'Fine intro.' in his programme.

Elgar married Caroline Alice Roberts at Brompton Oratory on 8 May 1889. Both were keen to break free of Worcestershire ties; taking a house in Kensington enabled Elgar to explore fully the capital's musical life. They went to the Richter Concerts at St James's Hall to hear the great conductor once more in Brahms's Third Symphony, Schubert's 'Great' C major Symphony, Dvořák's *Symphonic Variations*, music by Wagner, and the first performance of Parry's Fourth Symphony. They heard much opera: at Covent Garden they saw *William Tell, Carmen, Don Giovanni* and went to three much-cut performances of *Die Meistersinger* – in Italian! At the Lyceum they saw two acts of *Othello,* which was given for the first time in London. When they moved to Upper Norwood the Elgars were able to hear a large repertoire at the Crystal Palace concerts including selections from *Die Meistersinger*, Brahms's Second Symphony

and Mendelssohn's *Calm Sea and Prosperous Voyage* Overture. Wagner was a particular enthusiasm and Elgar later heard two further performances of *Die Meistersinger* and Meyerbeer's *Le prophète.*

After returning to Malvern, in June 1891, there were fewer opportunities to hear music in London due to the demands of Elgar's teaching commitments and the need to organise his time for composition. He hired scores, nominally for music to be played by an ensemble class at The Mount School, Malvern; and later, when he became conductor of the Worcestershire Philharmonic Society, he also had further opportunity to learn new music, hence there was not such a requirement to travel to and from London for this. Opera Malvern could not provide, so for several summers in the 1890s holidays in Germany, particularly Bavaria, were used to hear familiar and new music, especially opera in Munich and Bayreuth, and there were still occasional visits to London; he sporadically attended the St James's Hall Popular Concerts of chamber music. On 28 June 1893 he and Alice saw *Tristan* at Covent Garden. In June 1900 he saw *Götterdämmerung* and attended a Richter Concert. While he continued to attend London concerts – Compton McKenzie left a fascinating account of accompanying Elgar to the *Symphonie fantastique* in 1929 – the necessity to seek out new music lessened, as his 'musical apprenticeship can be said to have virtually concluded by 1899 … Nevertheless his style remained susceptible to major external influences until about the end of 1902.'[31] Perhaps a final influence on his style was that of Richard Strauss; in London on 4 June 1902 Elgar heard him conduct three symphonic poems and in December, the English première of *Ein Heldenleben* in Queen's Hall.

By then Elgar had experienced two important London premières of his own: that of the *Variations,* under Richter on 19 June 1899, and that of the concert overture *Cockaigne (In London Town)* on 20 June 1901. *Cockaigne* ' … was first suggested to me one dark day in the Guildhall: looking at the memorials of the city's great past & knowing well the history of its unending charity, I seemed to hear far away in the dim roof a theme, an echo of some noble melody'.[32] The overture is in effect a love letter to the capital city with its *nobilmente* citizens, Cockney urchins, military and Salvation Army bands, lovers, London parks and churches. To Jaeger he described it as 'cheerful and Londony – "stout and steaky".'[33] It was the precursor of later 'London' works by other composers, Vaughan Williams's *A London Symphony*[34] being the first.[35]

Elgar engineered the London première of the *Variations* in that he sent the score to Hans Richter's concert manager, Narciso Vertigliano, who forwarded it to Richter in Vienna. To have a major orchestral work performed in London by the conductor who had known and worked with Wagner, had played the trumpet in the *Siegfried Idyll* on Christmas Day 1870 at Wagner's home on Lake Lucerne, had conducted the first complete performance of *The Ring* at Bayreuth in 1876, championed Dvořák and who had conducted premières of symphonies by Brahms and Bruckner, was a significant achievement and marked a turning point in Elgar's British and European reputation.

Other important London premières included that of *In the South* at the prestigious three-day Elgar Festival at Covent Garden in March 1904 – in itself another significant milestone in Elgar's career – and the *Introduction and Allegro* in 1905. The First Symphony was premièred in Manchester in December 1908 but the London première on 7 December, conducted by Richter, was a huge success – certainly his most prestigious up to that time. This was followed by the successful London first performance of the Violin Concerto in 1910 and a less successful one of the Second Symphony in 1911. Most of Elgar's wartime works were first performed in London, as was the chamber music (in Wigmore Hall) in 1919 and that of the Cello Concerto, in the Queen's Hall. The *Severn Suite* was first performed at Crystal Palace in September 1930 and the *Nursery Suite* was first heard in a London recording studio in 1931. The BBC Symphony Orchestra would have performed the Third Symphony in London in May 1934, if Elgar had lived to complete it. London premières and performances all helped advance his burgeoning career and seal his reputation.

The major oratorios were first heard outside London, but the first London performance of *The Dream of Gerontius* in the newly completed Westminster Cathedral in June 1903 was a major event, long in the planning, and this had a significant effect in promulgating the work's future standing.[36]

Elgar often undertook conducting engagements in London but his most enduring connection with a London orchestra was that with the London Symphony Orchestra, which had been created in 1904, when players broke away from Henry Wood's orchestra on account of Wood's intolerance of the notorious deputy system. The LSO's first concert, on 9 June 1904, included the *Variations,* and Elgar was asked to conduct a concert in their first season as well as write a new work. A.J. Jaeger of Novello suggested ' … a *brilliant* quick *String* Scherzo, or something for those fine strings *only?*' The virtuoso *Introduction and Allegro* was the result. However, the early performances did not reveal the work's stature, which only became apparent, after repeated playing, when Elgar took the orchestra on tour in the autumn of 1905. His programmes included his own music and the Brahms Third and Schumann Second symphonies. The LSO gave two greatly acclaimed London performances of the First Symphony in December 1908, but were unsuccessful in their bid to give the first performance of the Violin Concerto. They were engaged for the 1913 Leeds Festival and so gave the première of *Falstaff,* together with that of the Cello Concerto in the Queen's Hall in October 1919 and that of the *Nursery Suite* when it was recorded in Kingsway Hall in May 1931.

Following Richter's retirement, Elgar was appointed the orchestra's principal conductor in 1911. This was a significant honour from the self-governing orchestra. Elgar happily accepted the post. But his first two concerts, in June, pointed the way for the future as they were very poorly attended and Elgar waived his fee. His further concerts included Beethoven's Seventh Symphony, Brahms's B flat Piano Concerto, Tchaikovsky's *Romeo and Juliet,* Mozart's Symphony No. 40, Franck's Symphony in D minor, Saint-Saëns' A minor Cello Concerto (with Pablo Casals) and Dvořák's Cello Concerto. His last appearance as principal conductor was on 9 June 1913, when he gave the first London performance of *The Music Makers.* Within a few days came a letter from the orchestra abruptly terminating his appointment, due to falling box office receipts; while harsh, it was ' ... probably necessary in commercial terms ... Undoubtedly, the composer was wounded by this treatment ...' [37] Despite this, he took the orchestra on a number of wartime tours, shared the conducting of their twenty-first anniversary concert in Queen's Hall on 9 June 1925 and conducted them when they attended Three Choirs Festivals in the 1920s and 1930s. His last link with the orchestra was in January 1934: as he lay ill in Worcester, a land-line connected him with the Abbey Road recording studio. where the LSO were to record two orchestral sections from *Caractacus.* Elgar could hear the orchestra and they his comments and suggestions to improve the interpretation, which was then recorded. It was a wonderful, moving last musical experience for the composer. A month later the LSO played at his memorial service in Worcester Cathedral.

The London Symphony Orchestra took part also in recording Elgar's major works under the composer's direction, after they signed a contract with HMV in 1927. All Elgar's recordings – save for those made in Hereford Cathedral in September 1927 – were set down in London and Elgar's twenty-year odyssey to record a large part of his *oeuvre* was a unique and substantial achievement which could not have taken place anywhere else than in the capital; it was there that the British recording industry had been spawned with the formation of the Gramophone Company in 1898. Its first recording studio was in a basement in Maiden Lane off the Strand and recording started in earnest when the young Fred Gaisberg, a protégé of Emile Berliner, inventor of the 'flat-disc talking machine', arrived from Washington DC in July 1898. By 1902 the company had acquired grander premises at 21 City Road, EC, and it was here that Elgar made his first exploratory recording on 20 January 1914. Following the signing of a contract, all Elgar's subsequent recordings, up to April 1925, took place at the specially constructed recording studios at Hayes, opened by Chaliapin in 1913. Thereafter with the advent of electrical recording, engineers were able to record in London's concert halls and thus Elgar's later recordings were made in Kingsway Hall, the Queen's Hall, and the Royal Albert Hall. However as competition to record in London's concert halls increased, the Gramophone Company found premises in St John's Wood and the famous Abbey Road recording studios were formally opened by Elgar with the LSO on 12 November 1931 – a short newsreel recorded part of the event. Thereafter Elgar made most of his last recordings there. He enjoyed recording and working with the Gramophone Company staff, together with favourite orchestral players, all under the gentle guidance of Fred Gaisberg, made it a highly congenial experience. Elgar was thus more than prepared to travel to London on a regular basis to set down his own interpretations of his music – he was the first major composer to do so. Gaisberg travelled with him to London for what was to be his last recording session in August 1933. He recorded that ' Sir E. pointed out all the beauty spots as the train rolled through Worcestershire … He said he had been travelling on the line for 60 yrs. and everyone knew him. He seemed to have a word & smile for everyone on the line and all responded happily to his sunshine.' [38]

His friendship with Gaisberg was a crucial factor in facilitating the recording sessions and if these included the LSO and its leader, Elgar's long time friend W.H. Reed, so much the better. Elgar had known Reed since 1902, when he was a young violinist in the Queen's Hall Orchestra but their friendship blossomed in 1910, when he assisted Elgar with the Violin Concerto.[39] A member of Reed's Croydon Orchestra, the violinist Vera Hockman, played in a performance of *The Dream of Gerontius* conducted by Elgar in November 1931. He was charmed by her, and a friendship quickly developed. Vera Hockman was to become his final 'muse' playing a role in the creation of the Third Symphony. Elgar often visited her at her newly built house, Robin Hill, Pine Coombe, Shirley when conducting in Croydon and in London.

Other London friends included the cellist Basil Nevinson; in the 1890s Elgar sometimes used his home in Tedworth Square, Chelsea as a London base. In May 1899 Elgar met the wealthy Frank Schuster; he was to become a lifelong friend and offered Elgar lavish hospitality at both his London house, 22 Old Queen Street, Westminster, and his riverside home The Hut, Bray near Maidenhead where Elgar often stayed for extended periods, using the studio for composition. Elgar was a frequent guest at the home of Sir Sidney and Frances Colvin in Kensington. Laurence Binyon, Colvin's younger colleague at the British Museum, became another London friend and collaborator, but his most cherished London friend was Alice Stuart Wortley and for many years he was a frequent visitor at her home, 7 Cheyne Walk, Chelsea. She was to become his intimate friend, muse and confidante who, as shown above, played a crucial role not only in the creation of the Violin Concerto but also in the Second Symphony, *Falstaff*, *The Music Makers* and other works. They shared a love of music and art – she was the daughter of Sir John Millais – and frequently went together to concerts, plays and exhibitions; her presence in London may have contributed to the decision to live there permanently. Furthermore she and Elgar visited Hampstead together in January 1911 and discovered Kelston, the Norman Shaw house that the Elgars were later to purchase, viewing it on their behalf when they had returned to Hereford. Elgar wistfully re-named it Severn House. All these friends provided a magnet to draw him to London.

There was one other vital London-based friend who played a major role in Elgar's life and who helped to forge another hugely important metropolitan connection. This was August Jaeger, a German employee and publishing manager of Novello and Co. from 1890 to 1907. His importance to Elgar cannot be overestimated; he became far more than just a publisher in that he was to be a friend, advisor, encourager and mid-wife to many of Elgar's finest works. His correspondence with Elgar began in 1897 and he soon realised that he was dealing with a composer who was in a different league from other contemporary composers published by Novello. While he understood Elgar's music Jaeger was not afraid to offer criticism, such as when he persuaded a reluctant Elgar to extend the finale of the *Variations*. Even more important, he followed very closely the creation of *The Dream of Gerontius* in the first half of 1900, stimulating, prodding and provoking Elgar where required, sharpening his creativity. With his acute musical knowledge and fine understanding of the technicalities of publishing, he was just the man Elgar needed to stretch his mind and push back the boundaries of his creative thinking, as well as undertaking the all-important job of seeing his music through the printing press. This often involved many face-to-face meetings in London at Novello's offices, first at 1 Berners Street and then at 160 Wardour Street after 1906. Elgar frequently visited Jaeger and his family at his London homes – 16 Margravine Gardens and later at 37 Curzon Road, Muswell Hill. Elgar's dealings with Novello were not always smooth. At times Jaeger had to be a tactful conciliator between Novello's directors and the composer, which could be a demanding role. Yet here was another London friend to whom Elgar owed much, for Jaeger expended his energies and even his health in promoting Elgar to the firm. To achieve publication of his music was Elgar's *raison d'être*, and that so many works were published by Novello is in no small measure due to Jaeger's belief in his genius.

Elgar needed his music to be promoted and disseminated and thus looked to London and its publishing houses for that essential role. Some early works were published by Schott, which had a branch in London. During the abortive London residence between 1889 and 1891 he trailed from publisher to publisher achieving a few modest successes, but in 1890 Novello accepted his part-song *My Love Dwelt in a Northern Land* thus commencing 'the richest publishing association of his life.' [40] Novello were eventually to publish the majority of his major works, but in 1899 there was a breach in relations and Elgar moved to Boosey & Co. 295 Regent Street, which published *Sea Pictures, Cockaigne,* the *Coronation Ode* and the lucrative *Pomp and Circumstance* marches. Relations with Novello were repaired and they remained his publishers until 1912, when Elgar terminated the near-exclusive contract with them, although they did continue to publish the major works written thereafter. In the 1920s, however, Elgar's connection with Novello became more distant. In his last years, as the will to compose returned, he established a new publishing relationship with Keith Prowse of 42 & 43 Poland Street, London, W.1., which was sustained until his death. They would have published the Third Symphony if it had been completed.

In London he met, so far as he wanted to, his fellow composers – Parry, Stanford, Vaughan Williams, Edward German, Arnold Bax, John Ireland, Herbert Howells and Rutland Boughton. The young Arthur Bliss presented himself at Severn House in 1913, was welcomed back subsequently and corresponded with Elgar. Here he met Strauss and the great European conductors Arthur Nikisch and Bruno Walter as well as Paderewski and Chaliapin. In London he became friendly with the conductors Henry Wood and Landon Ronald and those of the younger generation who were to guard his reputation after his death – Boult,

Barbirolli and Sargent. London enabled him to meet writers and poets –
Henry James, Laurence Binyon, Arnold Bennett, Algernon Blackwood,
Siegfried Sassoon – and Bernard Shaw. He knew the plays before he knew
the man, for Elgar was an inveterate theatre-goer. If he had taken part in
the riches of London's musical life during his first stay in London he did
so to an even greater extent when he lived at Hampstead after 1912.

He delighted in membership of a number of London clubs. He was
elected to the Athenaeum in 1904 at the proposal of Parry and Stanford
and later enjoyed membership of Brooks's, the Garrick (the haunt of
actors and artists), the Royal Societies Club and the Savile. He was a long-
standing member of the London Library. Thus even though Elgar
moaned about London on occasion there were many aspects of life there
which he relished; his life would have been poorer without them.

Elgar sold Severn House in 1921 but remained a Londoner until 1923,
when he leased a house in Worcestershire. However, he kept on his
London flat, 37 St James's Place, as a *pied-à-terre* until at least 1929. If it
is true that he found London so uncongenial, it is perhaps surprising that
he did not immediately return to Worcester after Alice's death and that he
maintained some presence there for many years thereafter.

There was a willingness on both sides to venture to London on their
marriage in 1889. Elgar wanted to break free of the round of teaching and
local music-making so he could devote more time to composition and
launch an attack on the London publishers – at the age of thirty-two he
was, for the first time, to be a full-time composer. For Alice, a move to
London freed her from Worcestershire ties and from disapproving relatives
who were appalled at her marriage to a lower-class, Catholic music teacher
with little money or prospects. One suspects that such a move might have
been long in prospect, for in her novel *Marchcroft Manor* published in
1882 Alice writes of her hero, Julian de Tressanay, as holding

> an appointment in the Foreign office ... and ... it secured to him the
> advantage of living in London. This was a weighty consideration, for he
> had thrown his whole soul into the stirring questions of the day, the
> improvement of the lower classes, the progress of humanity, and in London
> he found friends who sympathised with his aims, and scope for
> expounding his ideas.[41]

Such views may still have been in mind in 1889.Thus the crushing
realisation, after the initial euphoria, that London did *not* welcome them,
together with the dwindling of their resources, the indifference of
publishers, the paucity of pupils and Elgar's periodic ill-health, must have

been a bitter blow to them both, but more particularly to Alice who probably found the retreat to Malvern injurious to her pride. Yet that was the grit in the oyster that spurred her on achieve what she had lost; the desire to have her husband – the head of the musical profession in England – rightfully installed in a grand metropolitan house was eventually realised twenty-one years later, when she broke her family trust to raise the capital to buy their Hampstead mansion. Severn House was the pearl she obtained.

To Canon Gorton he wrote: 'I ape royal state, under my wife's kindly direction' [42] but there were sound reasons for Elgar wishing to move to London in 1911, for as well as realising Alice's ambitions, he had in recent years wanted to spend more time there and, as England's senior composer, the demand to do so was an increasing one.[43] His appointment as principal conductor of the LSO alone warranted a move from Hereford. Maybe he felt he needed these distractions to fill the time which would not, as previously, be given over to composition, particularly if he sensed that his creativity was on the wane. Elgar ruefully commented, following the conferral of the Order of Merit, that there was 'nothing left for me to achieve'.[44] If so, it is sad if he equated artistic fulfilment with the acquisition of honours.

Elgar took Rosa Burley to see the house before the purchase was completed:

> It was a very impressive house ... and as we walked through the empty rooms I saw that he meant, if it were financially possible – which I rather doubted – to live there. This was one of the strangest afternoons we ever spent together and I have never known the duality of his character so strongly marked as it was that day. On the one hand he clearly took a natural pride in the importance of the house with its fine panelling, its long music room and its great staircase at the head of which Alice would stand to receive her guests. But on the other hand he wanted equally clearly to make me feel that his success meant nothing to him and that there was always some lovely thing in life which had completely eluded him.[45]

It was a gloomy house – on one side it had few windows – and, as Rosa Burley predicted, expensive to run; that it was beyond their means was evident after the First World War as the house was put on the market in September 1919. Elgar's earlier comment that 'this is no home for me' could be interpreted as a response to its expense rather than a comment on its aesthetic qualities or location. The house was finally disposed of in late 1921 after no acceptable bids were offered at auction. It was demolished in January 1937. That so much was invested in Severn House, his grandest home, its ultimate destruction can be seen as an ironic metaphor for the reception of his music in the years immediately following Elgar's death.

Notes and References

1   Nicolson, Nigel: *The World of Jane Austen* [London: Weidenfeld and Nicolson, 1991] 83.
2   Millgate, Michael (ed): *The Life and Work of Thomas Hardy, by Thomas Hardy* [London: Macmillan, 1984] 141.
3   *ibid.*, 154.
4   Millgate, *loc.cit.*
5   Holroyd, Michael: *Bernard Shaw, Vol.1, (1856-1898): The Search for Love* [London: Chatto & Windus, 1988] 69.
6   Vaughan Williams, Ralph: 'What have we learnt from Elgar' in *Music and Letters*, XVI, No.1 [1935] in Redwood, C. (ed): *An Elgar Companion* [Ashbourne: Sequoia Press, 1982] 266.
7   McVeagh, Diana: *Edward Elgar: his life and music* [London: J.M. Dent, 1955] 90-1.
8   Elgar to Jaeger, 11 July 1900 in Moore, J.N. (ed): *Elgar and his Publishers: letters of a creative life* [Oxford: OUP, 1987] Vol. 1, 212.
9   Reed, W.H.: *Elgar as I Knew Him* [London: Gollancz, 1936] 141.
10 Conrat, H.: 'Edward Elgar' in *Neuen-Zeitung*, 24 December 1903, translated in the *Elgar Society Newsletter* [May 1976] 21–26.
11 *The World*, April 1997 in Anderson, Robert: *Elgar* [London: J.M. Dent, 1993] 34-5.
12 Elgar to Canon Gorton, 26 May 1903 in Hodgkins, Geoffrey: *Somewhere Further North* [Rickmansworth: Poneke Press, 2004] 49-50.
13 Elgar to Alice Stuart Wortley, 7 February 1910 in Moore, J.N. (ed): *The Windflower Letters* [Oxford: OUP, 1989], 38.
14 Moore, *loc.cit.*
15 Written sometime between 7 and 9 February 1910 in Moore, J.N.: *Edward Elgar: a creative life* [Oxford: OUP, 1984] 569.
16 Elgar to Alice Stuart Wortley, 10 February 1910 in Moore *Windflower, op.cit.*, 39.
17 Elgar to Alice Stuart Wortley: 20 April 1910, *ibid.*, 45.
18 Elgar to Alice Stuart Wortley: 27 April 1910, *ibid.*, 46.
19 Elgar to Frank Schuster: 8 May 1910 in Moore, J.N. (ed): *Edward Elgar: letters of a lifetime* [Oxford: OUP, 1990] 220.
20 Reed, W.H., *op.cit.*, 22.
21 Elgar to W.H.Reed, 30 May 1910 in Moore: *Lifetime, op.cit.*, 220.
22 Elgar to Alice Stuart Wortley, 31 May 1910 in Moore: *Windflower, op.cit.*, 49.
23 Elgar to Frank Schuster 29 June 1910 in Moore: *Lifetime, op.cit.*, 221.
24 A chronology for the composition of *Falstaff* based on Alice Elgar's diary is contained in Kent, Christpher: *'Falstaff*: Elgar's Symphonic Study' in Monk, R., (ed): *Edward Elgar: Music and Literature* [Aldershot: Scolar, 1993] 102 –104.

25   Elgar to Alice Stuart Wortley, [26 January 1919] in Moore: *Windflower, op.cit.*, 221.

26   Elgar to Frank Schuster, [3 December 1918] in Moore: *A Creative Life, op.cit.*, 732.

27   Alice Elgar diary, 16 January 1919 in Moore, *ibid.*, 736.

28   Alice Elgar diary, 18 January 1919 in Anderson: *Elgar, op.cit.*, 137.

29   Letter to *The Daily Telegraph,* 24 December 1920 in Moore: *A Creative Life, op.cit.*, 75.

30   *ibid.*, 79.

31   Dennison. Peter: 'Elgar's musical apprenticeship' in Monk, R., (ed): *Elgar Studies* [Aldershot: Scolar Press, 1990] 1.

32   'The question of programme music', undated MS fragment at the Elgar Birthplace in Moore: *A Creative Life, op.cit.*, 342.

33   Elgar to Jaeger, 4 November 1900, in Moore: *Publishers, op.cit.*, 254.

34   For an analysis of the influence of *Cockaigne* on Vaughan Williams and *A London Symphony* see Adams, B.: ' " What Have We Learnt from Elgar": Vaughan Williams and the ambivalence of inheritance' in Norris, John and Neill, Andrew (eds): *A Special Flame: the music of Elgar and Vaughan Williams* [Rickmansworth: Elgar Editions, 2004] 74–7.

35   Later 'London' works include Holst's *Hammersmith,* Prelude and Scherzo (1930), Ireland's *London Overture* (1936) and Eric Coates's *London* and *London Again* suites (1932 and 1936).

36   See Bury, David: 'Ludwig Wüllner and the Westminster *Gerontius*' in Hodgkins, Geoffrey (ed): *The Best of Me: a Gerontius centenary companion* [Rickmansworth: Elgar Editions, 1999] 237-244.

37   Morrison, Richard: *Orchestra The LSO: A Century of Triumph and Turbulence* [London: Faber & Faber, 2004] 42.

38   Gaisberg, Fred: Diary in Moore, J.N. (ed): *Elgar on Record* [Oxford: OUP, 1974] 214.

39   Reed lived at 33 Chatsworth Road, Croydon.

40   Moore: *Publishers, op.cit.*, 3.

41   Roberts, Alice: *Marchcroft Manor* [Remington Ltd., 1882] in Anderson, Robert: *Elgar and Chivalry* [Rickmansworth: Elgar Editions, 2002] 50.

42   Elgar to Canon Gorton, 16 July 1911, in Hodgkins: *Somewhere Further North, op.cit.*, 238.

43   In 1904 Elgar spent 122 days in Hereford and 25 in London; in 1905, 215 in Hereford, 34 in London; in 1906, 232 in Hereford, 32 in London; in 1907, 119 in Hereford, 20 in London; in 1908, 154 in Hereford, 43 in London; in 1909, 186 in Hereford, 41 in London. But in 1910, he spent 129 days in Hereford and 151 days in London. In 1911, he spent 116 in Hereford and 133 in London. I am grateful to Geoffrey Hodgkins for this information.

44   Elgar to Winifred Norbury, June 1911 in McVeagh, Diana: *Edward Elgar: his life and music* [London: Dent, 1955] 55.

45   Burley, R.: *Edward Elgar: the record of a friendship* [London: Barrie & Jenkins, 1972] 191–2.

Notes on Contributors

Robert Anderson, M.A., F.S.A., D.Mus.(Hon), was born in India, and educated at Harrow School and Gonville and Caius College, Cambridge. At one time Director of Music at Gordonstoun School, he was also an assistant conductor for Gian-Carlo Menotti at the Spoleto Festival. For eighteen years he was an associate editor of *The Musical Times*, a position which in turn led in 1984 to his appointment as co-ordinating editor of the *Elgar Complete Edition*. He divides his time between Egyptology and music and has written numerous articles and three books on Elgar. His *Elgar in Manuscript* was published by the British Library in 1999, followed by Elgar in the *Master Musicians* series in 1993. His *Elgar and Chivalry* was published by Elgar Editions in 2002. He has conducted the St Bartholomew's Hospital Choral Society in a number of Elgar performances in the Royal Albert Hall and has conducted *The Dream of Gerontius* in Germany. He is a Vice-President of the Elgar Society and has edited the score of *The Crown of India* for the *Elgar Complete Edition*.

David Bury was educated at The King's School, Macclesfield and at Leeds and London Universities. He taught History at Grammar Schools in Leeds and Surrey. A member of the Elgar Society since 1979, he was London Branch Secretary from 1984-1995 and has served on the Council of the Elgar Society. He contributed the essay 'Ludwig Wullner and the Westminster Gerontius' to Elgar Editions' anthology *The Best of Me - A Gerontius Centenary Companion*. His monograph *Elgar and the Awful Female and other essays* was published by Elgar Editions in 2003.

Michael Holroyd was born in 1935 and is half-Swedish and partly Irish. He was educated at Eton College and the Maidenhead Public Library. In 1968 his *Lytton Strachey* was hailed as a landmark in contemporary biography and, six years later, his *Augustus John* confirmed his place as one of the most influential modern biographers. The three volumes of his 'Life of Shaw', *The Search for Love, The Pursuit of Power* and *The Lure of Fantasy*, appeared to critical acclaim between 1988 and 1991. His fine autobiography *Basil Street Blues* was published in 1999. He was awarded a CBE in 1989. A past Chairman of the Society of Authors and the Book Trust, past president of English PEN and a former member of the Arts Council, Michael Holroyd is currently president of the Royal Society of Literature and lectures round the world for the British Council and at literary festivals. He is married to the novelist Margaret Drabble and lives in London and Somerset.

John Kelly is a retired banker. He spent his early years in Manchester where he regularly heard Elgar's music at Hallé concerts conducted by Sir John Barbirolli. A member of the Elgar Society since 1981, he served as treasurer of London Branch for twelve years and acted as Secretary of the national Society in 1995-96. He has lectured to all branches of the Society and sings with Epsom Choral Society. John's special interest in the Violin Concerto was stimulated by a lecture to London Branch by Professor Brian Trowell some twenty years ago and he has spent much of his subsequent years puzzling about and researching Elgar's 'most secret work'.

Michael Kennedy was born in Manchester and educated at Berkhamsted. In 1941, at the age of fifteen he joined the staff of *The Daily Telegraph*, becoming its music critic in 1948. He was Northern Editor from 1960 until 1986, also writing music criticism, and from 1986 to 1989 was joint chief music critic. Since 1989 he has been the music critic for *The Sunday Telegraph*. He has written a history of Manchester, two histories of the Hallé Orchestra and is author of the *Oxford Dictionary of Music* and the *Concise Oxford Dictionary of Music*. For the *Master Musicians* series he has written three volumes - on Mahler, Britten and Strauss - as well as *The Works of Ralph Vaughan Williams*, *Portrait of Walton* and *Richard Strauss, Man, Musician, Enigma* together with biographies of Sir John Barbirolli and Sir Adrian Boult. His classic *Portrait of Elgar* is now in its third edition and his *The Life of Elgar* was completed in 2004. He is a Vice-President of both the Elgar Society and the Elgar Foundation and Patron of the Society's North-West Branch. He is a broadcaster and lecturer and a cricket enthusiast (a subject on which he also writes). He was appointed OBE in 1981, CBE in 1997 and was awarded an honorary doctorate of music by Manchester University in 2003.

Kevin Mitchell was educated in London and Guildford and is a solicitor specialising in Personal Injury and Clinical Negligence litigation. He joined the Elgar Society over thirty years ago and having served on the committee of the London Branch for a number of years, is currently Vice-Chairman of the Branch. He has served on the Society's Council, is a founder Director of Elgar Enterprises and has contributed articles and reviews for both the *Elgar Society Journal* and *Newsletter*.

Andrew Neill was persuaded by the curator, Alan Webb, during his first visit to Elgar's Birthplace in 1967, to join the Elgar Society. Later he was a founder member of the Society's London Branch and served on the Branch and Society committees under the Chairmanship of Douglas Guest. He became Secretary of the Society in 1979 and, after working in Australia for a few years, returned to Britain in 1988. He was elected Society Chairman in

1992. Andrew was appointed a trustee of the Birthplace in 1984. He is Chairman of the Elgar Society Edition and a member of the Council of the Royal Philharmonic Society. He runs his own business in London, is married and has two daughters.

Carl Newton has been a member of the Elgar Society since 1984, has served on its Council, and has contributed to the Society's *Journal* on numerous occasions. He was author of 'The Nightmare of Gerontius' in *The Best of Me*, published by Elgar Editions in 1999. A graduate in Modern History of Oxford, he had a long career as archivist and records manager in local government and industry, culminating in being acclaimed Records Manager of the Year in 1999. Officially now retired he has continued to maintain his archive and records management interests and is currently Visiting Professor of Archives at Northumbria University. He is researching Elgar's finances and social environment, the reception of his music, and the Roberts family history.

Michael Oliver was educated at St Clement Danes Grammar School, Isleworth Polytechnic and the London School of Printing. After a varied early career he started broadcasting for BBC Radio London in 1970, and subsequently presented both *Music Weekly* for Radio 3 and *Kaleidoscope* for Radio 4, for many years. He was a regular contributor to Radio 3's *Record Review*, its successor *CD Review* and *Gramophone* magazine. He launched the quarterly *International Opera Collector* in 1996. A man of wide cultural interests, he wrote two biographies in Phaidon's *Twentieth-Century Composer Series*, one on Igor Stravinsky, the other on Benjamin Britten and edited *Settling the Score: a journey through the music of the twentieth century* based on the Radio 3 series *Sounding the Century*. Michael Oliver died on 1 December 2002.

Arthur Reynolds is a trans-Atlantic American who lives and works in both London and New York. While growing up in a small town in America, his enthusiasm for Elgar was fired due to exposure to recordings of Elgar's music his father and other serving soldiers brought back from England, where they had been billeted during the Second World War. Arthur holds degrees in English from Columbia University and from Emmanuel College, Cambridge, as well as a degree in Finance from New York University's Graduate Business School. While at Cambridge during the 1960s, he began a lifelong quest to rescue Elgar memorabilia from undeserved oblivion. He presently serves on the Elgar Society's London Branch committee and occasionally writes for the *Elgar Society Journal*.

Chapter One

'It's The Only Wish I've Got'
A History of the Elgar Birthplace Museum

Andrew Neill

Prelude

William James once said of his brother, Henry: 'He is a native of the James family, and has no other country'. For a great American writer, who was to die a British subject, so for a composer such as Elgar whose art transcends county and country even though we recognise that his music is rooted in the soil of Worcestershire and the shadow of the Malvern Hills. This universality imposes on us all a great responsibility as we ponder the history and preservation of his chosen memorial for future generations.

Elgar's birthplace is a building that has become as important as the artefacts it contains. This is partly because it was chosen by Elgar himself to be his physical memorial and because the building and its location clearly came to mean a great deal to the composer. The architect and builders of the cottage remain anonymous but, as it turns out, it is one of the more attractive buildings on the south side of Broadheath Common and, through its simplicity, casts a benign spell, which is difficult to resist. In some locations, the cottage might look ordinary or even commonplace, but the red brick of its façade immediately attracts the eye as does the garden, both of which have changed little in 175 years. If Elgar had chosen another house to be his memorial would we feel the same? We might have admired Plas Gwyn or Marl Bank but it is difficult to imagine visitors developing affection for either building in the way many have come to love Elgar's first home.

I visited Elgar's Birthplace for the first time in September 1967 and was greeted by the curator, Alan Webb, who persuaded me to join the Elgar Society that day. Little did either of us realise that we would, in due course, become friends and that so much of my life would derive from that visit thirty-seven years ago. I have lost count of the times I have visited Broadheath since that warm early autumn day.[1]

1 – Notes and references for this chapter appear on pages 41–46.

Because Elgar's life is well documented, it is easy to become diverted by the minutiae of his daily existence and I acknowledge that this history is concerned with some aspects of Elgar's life, which are of marginal benefit to the researcher. I have therefore attempted to relate the narrative to facts concerning Elgar's early life in Worcester, his own relationship with the cottage in Broadheath and the development of the Birthplace as a museum.

I
A Home and a Dream

'Will you come homeward from the hills of Dreamland,
Home in the dusk, and speak to me again?
Tell me the stories that I am forgetting,
Quicken my hope, and recompense my pain?' [2]

In 1929 Edward Elgar returned to Worcester to live permanently in the city of his youth and which had nurtured his early development as a composer. During that year's Three Choirs Festival, he rented a large house, Marl Bank, on Rainbow Hill, that had been the site of the headquarters of the Parliamentarian staff after the Battle of Worcester in 1651. He was happy there and resolved to buy his temporary home, which provided a fine view of the Cathedral and parts of the city. Elgar managed to complete the purchase of Marl Bank in time for the Christmas season, and from there he explored his roots in his chauffeur-driven car which, with his new home, were the material signs of the success he had achieved since leaving Worcester more than forty years before.

Many years later, Herbert Howells recalled a visit he made in Elgar's company to the village of Broadheath, three and a half miles from Worcester.[3] There he was shown the cottage where the older composer was born. It was then a labourer's home, but for Elgar his birthplace meant much more than somewhere he passed in his car or occasionally visited with a friend:

> He took me round Worcester one day. The music shop that his father kept had gone, but he showed me where it was. Another day he came out of rehearsal, on the Monday, which was always a general rehearsal day at the Three Choirs Festival … and he said, 'Have you had enough music today?' and I said, 'Yes, more than enough.' 'So have I', he said. 'Well, let's go up and see where I was born.' Well that meant going over the river Severn, and out into the country for about five miles to the cottage, Broadheath, which in those days was not titivated at all, it was just as it was – almost, I should think, identical to what it was when he was there, when he was born.

And he went through to the cabbage patch, along the path, and up to the front door; and a woman carrying a baby-in-arms came and let him in, called him 'Master', I remember; he'd obviously been over and she'd met him, but she called him 'Master' each time she addressed him. And he was very nice to her, and flicked the chin of the little child and so on, and he said to me, 'Oh, do you mind first if – I want to go right up to the little room in which I was born – I want to go alone?' I said, 'of course not,' So I stayed and talked to the woman with the child, and I suppose he was there about a quarter of an hour; and then he came down and said, 'Come up with me now, come and see where I came into this wicked world' – this funny little sloping roof in a way awfully like the room I saw in Bonn, where Beethoven was born, except that it was probably much smaller. And coming a way from her, I remember he said, 'I don't expect much from the nation, but if ever they think it worthwhile, I wish they would buy this little cottage.' And he said, 'It's the only wish I've got, about the nation and me'.[4]

Despite its proximity to Worcester, some early visitors often found difficulty in locating the Birthplace. In 1947 William McNaught took a third of a column in an article published by *The Musical Times* to describe how to get there, and ended his description by writing: 'When you first see it you are looking over the hedge at the bottom of the garden; if you were ten feet higher you could survey it as in the Buckler drawing.'[5] Previously, in the October 1942 edition of *The Musical Times*, Patric Stevenson had written of a visit he had made on 4 July: ' "Get a bus at Angel Place and ask to be let off at Crown East. The Birthplace is about half a mile's walk up the road to your right" a charming voice was saying over the telephone. It was the voice of Elgar's daughter, Mrs Elgar Blake…'

Basil Maine remembered a more intimate experience:

I recall … a Sunday in early March … The country was covered with a light mist which was invisible until one looked towards a distant point. … We had come by way of Broadheath, for Sir Edward had wished to show me the cottage in which he was born. It stands back from the road, flanked by stables (which were later additions), and surrounded by a small garden. At an angle with the roadside, the cottage shows its modest front of windows and a slate roof. 'Slow down a little, Dick,' Sir Edward called to the driver as we were passing, and we looked at the little house in silence. I shall not easily forget that suspended moment in which thought and emotion were mingled in an indescribable experience.[6]

On 26 June 1920 Lady Alice Stuart of Wortley visited the village, and two months later she wrote to Elgar, mentioning the roses she had picked from the hedgerow. In an undated note written shortly afterwards, Elgar wrote the following:

> So you have been to B. – I fear you did not find the cottage – it is nearer the clump of Scotch firs – I can smell them now – in the hot sun. Oh! How cruel that I was not there – there's *nothing between* that infancy & *now* and I *want* to see it. The flowers are lovely – I knew you wd like the heath – I could have shewn you such lovely lanes.
>
> The church is new but it is more than a mile from the cott: so we must go again. Let me know when you return but please make the most of the lovely sights, sounds & scents.[7]

It is almost possible to join Elgar in the intensity of his feelings for the sense of place he clearly felt. Moreover, because he wrote this note whilst staying at Brinkwells in Sussex, a place where he was always happy, his longing for the Worcestershire country and the place of his birth is all the more remarkable. To understand this we have to travel back sixty-three years to 1857, when Edward was born, the second son of the itinerant piano tuner William Henry Elgar and his wife, Ann.

William Elgar was born in 1821 and moved from Kent to Worcester in 1841. He came to lodge in the Shades Inn at 16 Mealcheapen Street, which was run by Francis Simmonds with his wife, Elizabeth. Eventually William married Elizabeth's sister, Ann Greening in January 1848. Although he never converted or even considered converting to Catholicism, William Elgar had obtained the position of organist of St George's Catholic Church in the city. There are memories of his time there:

> Old E. always handed the round the snuff-box before commencing the mass, "damned" the blower, and began. Went out at sermon for drink at Hop Market.[8]

Ann Elgar, who was to become the centre of the Elgar family, came from Herefordshire farming stock. After their marriage William and Ann Elgar moved into the centre of Worcester and lodged at 2 College Yard East, near the Cathedral.[9] Harry, the first of the Elgars' seven children was born on 15 October 1848, his mother converting to Rome in the same year, before her eldest two daughters were born, Lucy Ann on 29 May 1852 and Susannah Mary 'Pollie' on 28 December 1854.

Worcester, a low-lying community, had suffered more than most cities from the two main plague epidemics in the fourteenth and seventeenth centuries and over time a number of the richer merchants and professionals had moved away to villages such as Claines, Hallow, Kempsey and Powick. By the early nineteenth century, matters of health had not improved greatly. In London where the clamour for change was loudest, it was not until 1875 that Sir Joseph Bazalgette's design of the drainage system for London was completed. It was the Public Health Act of 1848 that stimulated debate in cities like Worcester, where the stench of horse manure and human waste was exaggerated by the narrow mediæval streets. The unhealthy water meadows to the west combined to make the city less healthy than other cities of the time.

In October 1831 the first cholera epidemic in Britain began in Sunderland and reached Worcester the following year. There was then no understanding of the disease so that, by 1851, only one third of the city of a population of approximately 27,000 was supplied with fresh water. Those without access to fresh water had to rely on wells, which were frequently contaminated by adjacent cess pits. In 1847 a report on sanitary conditions stated that

> The City of Worcester may … be said to be practically almost without sewerage [in] the lower parts of the City, pools of liquid filth perpetually stagnate on the surface of the streets, or sink into the soil, there being no adequate drains for their removal.[10]

The tainting of fresh water was a constant problem:

> Many of the yards and privies are in a filthy condition, especially those belonging to the lodging houses. The leakage from one cesspool leaks through the wall and runs down the yard. The one partly covered cesspool with side openings is 3 feet from a pump.[11]

Cholera, although only introduced into Europe in 1817, haunted the lives of many who lived in the cities of mid-Victorian Britain and in the summer of 1849 over 33,000 died of the disease.

In 1854, the year that the cause of cholera was identified, a further epidemic in Worcester brought the problem into the open again. The City fathers debated ways in which they could implement improvements, not just for the disposal of sewage but also in the supply of fresh water. A quarrel developed between those in favour of extracting water from the river Teme and those supporting the Severn, the latter river winning the argument in 1855. The foundations of the City's waterworks were laid in the spring of 1857 and by the following April it was reported that the installation was functioning well, and within one month the sewage works was ready too.

The city to which the Elgar family returned to live in 1859 was therefore on the threshold of becoming a cleaner and healthier place in which to live. For a country woman like Ann Elgar life in the city before these changes were implemented, would have been a constant reminder that the country life had many attractions, particularly for a young and expanding family. Those who could afford to live away from the city seized the opportunity. So it was that

> my mother's wish always for a country life prompted Father to go to Broadheath. Broadheath itself is only a hamlet, with a handful of houses, a large clump of fir-trees by the entrance gate of 'Newbury House', and a wide stretch of heath known as the 'Common', dotted about with little pools and ponds for the cottager's ducks and geese, and ponies and donkeys grazing.[12]

In 1856, William Elgar rented the cottage known as 'The Firs' apparently after the trees that then grew at the foot of the garden. The Elgars' new home, although measuring only twenty by twenty-one feet, provided sufficient if cramped accommodation for the growing family, which could be accommodated on two floors, access to the first floor then being by ladder. Buildings like the Elgars' cottage could also be 'improved', which may have led to the double parallel ridged roof we know today, although the original construction probably dates from about the middle of the eighteenth century, when only the rear part of the cottage was built. The front elevation may have been added at some time in the 1830s as part of this improvement.[13] As such it was bigger than the homes of most artisans and may have been used, at one time, by an employee overseeing the land and properties of one of the small landowners whose manors overlooked the city.[14] Before the 1830s cottages of this type would have had casement windows and not the sash windows in place today. The ladder to the second floor would have been replaced early in the twentieth century.

The only Elgar child to be born at Broadheath was Ann and William's second son, Edward William, on 2 June 1857, in a small room to rear of the first floor of the cottage. Lucy recalled the day vividly: 'How well I remember the day he was born! The air was sweet with the perfume of flowers, bees were humming, and all the earth was lovely.'[15] So, into the small home, a fourth child was fitted to share space, which included at least one servant.[16] Edward's birth was not recorded until 11 July, William declaring his occupation as that of 'pianoforte tuner' their address given as 'Broadheath, St Johns, Worcester'. Whilst at 'The Firs', the Elgars made a lasting impression on the cottage when William Elgar's younger brother, Henry, built the coach house for William's pony, 'Jack'. William found time to adapt the garden for his children, for Lucy Elgar writes of 'my garden' flourishing and the 'ladies' avenue which her father made and covered in sand on which Lucy and Pollie could bowl their hoops. In the Buckler painting it is the path to the left.

A flourishing middle class in the county and the Three Choirs Festival, which took place in Worcester every three years, ensured that the services of a piano tuner and music retailer would always be in demand. William Elgar was often away for days at a time and, as he journeyed home, he would take a whistle from his pocket and announce his return:

> I so well remember the intense pleasure and true joy we all felt when we at last heard the long-waited-for whistle Father always blew on his return home, at one angle of the lane, which could be heard distinctly across the meadows between.[17]

Edward adopted this habit in later life, which he immortalised in the *Variations* of 1898–99.[18]

William Elgar was a good pianist and improviser. His skill was recalled by Elgar's childhood friend, Hubert Leicester who felt Elgar senior was '… rather notorious as a tuner … producing wonderful effects on piano – he had finest touch on a keyed instrument.' [19]

Visitors included the Roman Catholic solicitor William Allen, to whom Edward was later articled, and John Leicester, the 'best tenor' in the choir of Worcester's Roman Catholic Church, St George's.[20] Lucy remembered: ' … they were thoroughly happy in our cottage home, and sang and sang for the very joy of singing. And Mr. Allen *always* (yes, every time he came) would sing to Father's accompaniment, "Di Provenza il mar" – oh! I can hear it now!'[21]

Was that aria from *La Traviata* by Verdi the first music of a great composer Edward heard? The music is imbued with nostalgia; father Germont looking over his shoulder in the hope that his errant son would follow his gaze. It is a call to and from home as well as a father's longing for the place he loved.

The sea, the hills of Provence – who effaced
them from your heart?
What destiny took you away from the sunny
land of your birth?
Oh, remember in your sorrow what joy
warmed you there;
and that only there can your soul find peace again.

Verdi sets these words to music of great sensitivity. Later, in *The Black Knight*, an early choral setting of Longfellow, Elgar's growing nostalgia may have manifested itself in his remembered sadness for his two brothers. Harry died in 1864 aged sixteen and Jo, born on 28 August 1859 and young Edward's inseparable companion, died in 1866. Within a period of two years the young Elgar had twice experienced death.

Each the father's breast embraces,
Son and daughter; and their faces
Colourless grow utterly.
Whichever way
Looks the fear struck father grey,
He beholds his children die.[22]

When the family left Broadheath, probably in March 1859, the intensity of separation permeated Lucy's memory: 'Leaving the dear home – (that has even *now* kept as a nook the memory of those who had lived in it) – seemed at the parting inexpressibly beautiful and dear, and we had the longing desire to live on here for always.' [23] So, less than two years after Edward's birth, the family returned to the centre of Worcester, back close to the Cathedral at 1 Edgar Street. Later in the year Elgar's younger brother, Frederick Joseph ('Jo'), was baptised on 4 September at St George's Church in Worcester, a week after his birth.[24]

Jerrold Northrop Moore has pointed out that, despite the Roman Catholicism of the Elgar family, close contacts with the Cathedral were essential for William Elgar's music business. The young Elgar visited the Cathedral from an early age, an experience that was to prove invaluable:

I drew my first ideas of music from the Cathedral, from books borrowed from the music library, when I was eight, nine or ten. They were barbarously printed in eight different clefs, all of which I learnt before I was 12 ... I was allowed by Mr. Done [the Cathedral organist] to borrow them, and they were administered to me by my friends who were lay-clerks.[25]

We can therefore see that the move to Worcester was essential for the development of Elgar as a composer, for there he obtained the stimulus of local music-making during the time he developed from child to adult. It was important, too, in laying a foundation of ecumenism in Elgar's character and music-making which ensured his free passage, in later life, between the Churches of Rome and England.[26] Even when young he took this literally on occasions: 'The Services at the Cathedral were over later on Sunday than those at the Catholic Church, and as soon as the voluntary was finished at the church I used to rush over to the Cathedral to hear the concluding voluntary'.[27]

The result of this freedom and the move to Worcester was extraordinary. It was there that Elgar discovered how to play many orchestral instruments and, through listening to visiting orchestras (in particular during the Three Choirs Festival), laid the foundations for his development as one of the greatest orchestrators. As an orchestral violinist in the Festival orchestra from 1878, for many years, he played Wagner and French ballet music; he heard much English church music and played in a wide range of oratorios (good and bad). In 1884, under Dvořák's direction, Elgar performed in the visiting composer's Sixth Symphony and *Stabat Mater*. He wrote afterwards: 'I wish you could hear Dvořák's music. It is simply ravishing, so tuneful and clever and the orchestration is wonderful; no matter how few instruments he uses it never sounds thin. I cannot describe it; it must be heard.' [28]

All this was a heady and varied mix. By the time of his maturity, Elgar only had to think of an idea and he would understand intuitively how it should be orchestrated. There is the story of the young Edward attending his first rehearsal in the Cathedral and afterwards running along the High Street with the score tucked under his arm and meeting Hubert Leicester: 'Oh my. I had no idea what a band was like. ... If I had that orchestra under my control & given a free hand I could make it play whatever I liked!' [29]

Elgar's first music is hardly nostalgic. His 'tune from Broadheath' is a lumpy, jig-like melody, and if it suggests a sense of loss it is because Elgar returned to it in one form or another throughout his life. This *Humoreske* was written, it is believed, after or during a stay in Broadheath in 1867 or 1869, when the Elgar children were sent for a holiday. The widow of Elgar's younger brother, Frank, recalled one such visit in a letter to Carice Elgar Blake in 1940:

When Grandma was particularly busy in the shop in High St. she sent Frank & Dot[30] out to Broad Heath [sic] to stay with some old people – Mr & Mrs Doughty; of course there was a well there & Mrs. D. would periodically come to the door and say "Master Alfred (Frank) be you in the well?".[31]

Elgar's music was written as part of an entertainment involving his siblings:

By means of a stage-allegory – which was never completed –it was proposed to shew that children were not properly understood. The scene was a 'Woodland Glade', intersected by a brook; the hither side of this was our fairyland; beyond, small and distant, was the ordinary life which we forgot as often as possible. The characters, on crossing the stream, entered fairyland and were transfigured.

Our orchestral means were meagre: a pianoforte, two or three strings, a flute and some improvised percussion were all we could depend upon; the double-bass was of our own manufacture and three pounds of nails went into its making ... [32]

Humoreske
a tune from
Broadheath
1867

Elgar grew up in Worcester, separated from Broadheath, a sensitive creative artist in a world of commerce, a Roman Catholic in a city where the Protestant Cathedral dominated the horizon as well as the musical life of the community. Most biographers have stressed that these areas of separation affected all aspects of Elgar's life: his faith, his social position and the vision of the countryside just across the river. Moreover, 'Heaven lies about us in our infancy' as Michael Kennedy reminds us in that quotation from Wordsworth, something which was 'true for Elgar who idealised his childhood the older he grew.' [33]

The recollections of Herbert Howells and Basil Maine are echoed by Mrs T.V. Davis, the wife of the last tenant of 'The Firs', when she recorded the memories of her life there:

> Mrs Davis, who is 82, was born and brought up in Broadheath and has lived all her life in the village. After her marriage in the 1920's, she heard of the cottage 'The Firs' being for rent, and took it with her family, and lived there until it was purchased by the Corporation of Worcester.
>
> Inside the cottage has been altered upstairs. [Before the removal of the 'Birthroom' wall]. Originally (and in her time) there was a wall immediately on the right as you came up the stairs. That was a box room, and the wall of the 'Birthroom' was farther on. But there were the same number of usable rooms as now. Downstairs the room now known as the 'Study' was the Davis family's best drawing room, and several times during their tenancy (in the summer) Dick Mountford would bring furniture &c and arrange that room as a temporary museum.
>
> Sir Edward used to be driven by Dick past the cottage, and once he came with Dick and asked if he could see his Birthroom. He said he 'only came here to be born', and didn't stop long; and that it was really his Aunt's, Mrs Davis understands. [This could only be one of his Mother's sisters, as Father's family were in Dover]. On leaving Sir Edward gave Mr Davis half a crown.
>
> We talked of the garden & surrounding land when Mrs Davis lived at 'The Firs'. Mrs D said that the hedge at the eastern boundary was exactly as now (and as suggested in Buckler's drawing), and that the garden was the same size and of the same general arrangement. That there was a drain between the central path and the 'ladies avenue', and that there was in her time no gate at the end of the central path, but only the hedge as now.[34]

It is not surprising, therefore, that the cottage in Broadheath was chosen by Elgar as his memorial; it spoke of his roots and he would have heard, from his mother and sisters, how happy his family had been there. It was secure and unpolluted, and it was there he heard his first music. Nearby, whilst away from the city, he composed his first melody as part of a childhood fantasy, which only served to emphasise the joy of separation from the city. But, above all, he was the only Elgar child to be born in Broadheath, which set him apart and could only have encouraged his self-awareness. In the June 1931 Birthday Honours he was created a Baronet. He chose to take the title of his first home and became the first (and only) Baronet of Broadheath. Long before, early in his marriage, Elgar took his wife Alice to see the cottage where he was born and the farm where he had stayed as a young boy :

> E. & A. by 2.46 train to Henwick then walked to Broadheath & saw the house in wh. he was born & where he used to stay as a lissy boy. Walked to Bransford & home by 5.59 train.[35]

We can observe the pride and love in Elgar's gesture in escorting his wife to his birthplace. As he became older these emotions mingled with his nostalgia to produce an intensity of feeling, which he felt unable to resist:

> I don't expect much from the nation, but if ever they think it worthwhile, I wish they would buy this little cottage. ... It's the only wish I've got, about the nation and me.

II
Carice Elgar Blake's memorial to her Father

Nor is it always in the most distinguished achievements that men's virtues or vices may be best discerned; but very often an action of small note; a short saying, or a jest, shall distinguish a person's real character more than the greatest sieges, or the most important battles.[36]

On 20 May 1935, fifteen months after Elgar's death, the conveyance took place of 'The Firs' 'from Catherine Mary Marshall to the Mayor, Alderman and Citizens of the County of the City of Worcester'.[37] Thus, for the payment of £400, 'The Firs' became 'The Birthplace' and Carice Elgar Blake could take forward her father's idea by bringing together music, artefacts and family history in what must have seemed, even then, a very small place in which to house her father's legacy. She had to begin very much at the beginning, and the establishment of the Birthplace Trust was the next step.

1935–1936

Unfortunately, most of the early minutes of meetings of the trustees of what was also called 'The Elgar Birthplace Fund' are missing. Minutes from 20 October 1936 are available, with no others currently traceable until the meetings of 1955. Nevertheless, the minutes of 1936 are of great interest. Sir Landon Ronald chaired the meeting, which took place at the Guildhall School of Music in London.[38] Also present were Carice Elgar Blake, Mrs Sybil Buckle, Mr John Littleton of Novello and Mr C.D.Medley, the honorary solicitor. Sir Barry Jackson sent his apologies.[39] The meeting was advised that the trust deed of 4 August 1936 had been completed and that a campaign organised by the editor of the *Daily Telegraph* had raised nearly £2,600. Contributors included John Barbirolli, Adrian Boult, Malcolm Sargent and Ralph Vaughan Williams.

For a peppercorn rent, paid annually to the City of Worcester, the trustees now had the responsibility of maintaining and running the Birthplace. Mr Medley went on to advise 'that the cottage had been acquired by the City of Worcester and that the present tenant, [Mr] T.V. Davis, had been given notice to quit as he was not thought to be a suitable person to act as caretaker.' Carice then reported to the meeting that :

> she had received a letter from the Town Clerk of Worcester from which it appeared that the Corporation might probably be able to supply suitable alternative accommodation [for Mr Davis and his family] and Mr Medley was requested to inform the Town Clerk that the Trustees would be prepared to apply the income of the fund for the upkeep of the cottage and the payment of a caretaker as soon as the place had been vacated, repaired and a suitable tenant who would also act as caretaker found...

It is at this point that Carice's diaries become of use, although there are obvious and frustrating gaps. For example, there is no diary available for 1935 and her only mention of the Birthplace in 1936 is from a weekend she spent in London:

> 1 March. Went to 12 oc mass at the Oratory & on to lunch with Lan & Mollie – & talked over Birthplace Fund – Back to Vera, Dora there, in Evening & on to Billie & James after dinner.[40]

Nevertheless, the Birthplace received visitors during 1935, as the new Visitors Book of the time shows. At 11 a.m. on Tuesday, 3 September 1935, during the Worcester Three Choirs Festival, Viscount Cobham, the Lord Lieutenant of Worcestershire, unveiled the Elgar Memorial window in the north aisle of the cathedral. The event attracted to Worcester many distinguished musicians, a number of whom took the opportunity to travel out to Broadheath, signing the Visitors Book before they left. Over the days of the Festival, signatories included W.H. Reed, Mr and Mrs Gerald Finzi, Harold Brooke of Novello, Arnold Bax, Leslie Woodgate, Alan Kirby, Ralph Vaughan Williams (who was accompanied by Harriet Cohen), Alan Webb (a future curator) and Fred Gaisberg of The Gramophone Company (HMV).[41]

1937

For 1937 the only mention of the Birthplace in Carice's diary is on Wednesday 30 June. Unfortunately, although reasonably comprehensive for the years 1938 and 1939, we have no further diaries, which could give us a detailed record of how the museum developed during the war and post-war years.

> 30 June. Dora & Mr Powell to lunch and tea – very nice time. Went to the Birthplace.

It is now that Carice takes steps to secure rooms in Worcester's Guildhall, from which she could manage the Birthplace:

> 28 September. Went to see Town Clerk at 10.30 – could not see him till 12.30 – doing his best about Birthplace. S[amuel] & I to Homestead at 3. & help Philip arrange drawing room as bedroom for Nella – Tea there.[42]
>
> 9 November. S & I to see (?) & Novello's. He went to station & saw Lord Mayor's show. Went to R.C.M. to lunch – saw Sir Hugh [Allen] & Dr. Colles. & Billie & Billie's talk on Concerto – & me[–] nice West Australian girl having lesson.[43]

On 17 November Carice heard that she could have use of rooms in the Guildhall, and for the remainder of the year she was busy working with friends and others to move the Birthplace towards something resembling a museum. She sought advice from Sir Ivor Atkins[44] and joined Hubert Leicester to sort through music at St George's Roman Catholic Church.

At Broadheath Mr Davis and his family still lived in the cottage and Dick Mountford showed the occasional visitor around. Carice also now lived in Broadheath, having moved there in November 1936. With her husband, Samuel Blake, she had bought Woodend, down the lane from the Birthplace towards Crown East, where they had stayed on earlier visits from their farm in Surrey, which had now been sold. Eventually Mr Davis and his family moved to a home near the Birthplace and in 1938 work on the fabric of the cottage began, enabling it to open that summer.

During 1938 and 1939 Carice devoted much of her time to fitting out the Birthplace, and to finding and appointing a curator. Her diaries from this time show that the fatal illness of her husband, became a counterpoint to her work, as did the imminent war and its eventual declaration in September 1939. She was happy to arrange for the local vicar to visit Samuel during his last days at home. Moreover she maintained her own faith, and almost every Sunday would attend Mass in Worcester and frequently dine or take tea at The Homestead afterwards. Carice also maintained close relationships with her cousins, in particular Clare, Madge and May Grafton. It was to Clare and May Grafton that Elgar's spaniel Marco had gone after Elgar's death. They lived at Lydiate Ash near Bromsgrove, whilst Madge Grafton lived with her brother Gerald in Broadway.

1938

1 March. Went to Hereford Orchestral Concert. Very nice saw Percy, Brent Smith,[45] ... Back before 6. S[amuel] & I to Worcester Concert in pm. Carmen. Enjoyed it.

29 March. Festival Executive Committee at Guildhall. B. drove us around Broadheath to look to see if there was a likely house ...

15 April (Good Friday). Church at 10.30. took children home[46]... Gerontius broadcast in pm.

31 May. Expected Webbs all a.m. with boxes of MS etc from the bank. Met Betty at Guildhall & worked –

2 June. After Dinner Sir Ivor & Miss Armstrong came for him to see the MSS. Chose some.

9 June. Went to fetch Dr. Colles from Tenbury College at 12 – Gave him lunch – & went thro' all 3rd. part of Kingdom & Grove's list – Tea – & took him down to 6.10 –

11 June. To tea with Nella [Leicester]. Agnes [Elgar] & the 4 children for twins 3rd birthday tomorrow. Huge success – cake with 3 candles.[47]

27 June. Dora & Mr Powell to lunch – nice time. Mayor[,] Lady Atkins[,] Town Clerk[,] Town Surveyor & Mrs [Sybil] Buckle came up to see Birthplace & arrange what was to be done. Came in here for drinks.

30 June. Sent off the list to Dr. Colles.[48] Went to see Mr Buckle's garden at 3.30. & saw furniture for Birthplace. Caretaker if required. Fetched Aunt Pollie [Grafton] here to tea – took her back & came home & got supper & went to Lecture. Music Makers.

21 July. Lady Atkins[49] etc came up about Birthplace & went all over the inside to see what had to be done.

23 July. S & I to races in pm. Hot tip ... did us good. Highlander came in second.

The forthcoming Three Choirs Festival week and in particular the need to have the Birthplace manned each day of the festival was now causing Carice anxiety.

27 July. Settle about wallpapers etc for Birthplace. Tea at Nella's & saw Fanny & Dick [Richard Mountford] coming for the week to the Birthplace.

As Carice made arrangements for a casket to be made available to display the cast of Elgar's hand, at the Birthplace, she heard that there was the possibility that help would be available during the week of the festival.

9 August. Mr Haycox came up and undertook to take charge of the Birthplace for the week.

12 August. Chose chintz for Birthplace curtains.

14 August. Heard of Landon's death.

21 August. Saw ... Mr Haycox to explain things.

28 August. Mass at 11. Borrowed book from choir for the Exhibition & Aunt Agnes lent me the Freedom pen.

30 August. Finished labels.

31 August. To London at 8.55 – went to Royal College ... came in for Gerontius – Astra Desmond – Hullo.[50] To service for Landon at All Souls – nice singing & service. Many there.

1 September. Mr & Mrs Shaw[51] to tea and saw Birthplace – Mrs Shaw hung the first curtains...

2 September. Arranging Birthplace all day – Clare SW here ... [52]

3 September. Mr Cox to finish hanging pictures. S & I to finish arranging the MSS which had arrived from Novello's.[53]

So, just in time, the Cottage was ready to receive visitors during the Worcester Three Choirs Festival week (4–9 September). For the first time, Carice took advertising space for the Birthplace in the Festival programme, stating that it would be open daily from 10 a.m. to 6 p.m.[54] She attended most concerts including performances of Mendelssohn's *Elijah* and Bach's *St Matthew Passion*. The opening service included Elgar's orchestral setting of the *Te Deum,* Op.34 and on 6 September *The Music Makers* was performed in the evening. She attended also the concert in the Gaumont Theatre at which Benno Moiseiwitsch performed Rachmaninov's second Piano Concerto.

Carice went to the Birthplace every day. During the week many distinguished people visited, but if ever there was a formal opening of the museum, it took place on Thursday, 8 September, when a number of notable figures attended, fitting in their visits during a busy day.[55] The Visitors Book shows the signatures of Percy Hull, Marie Hall, Troyte Griffith and Clare Stuart Wortley. Whether they attended the tea to which Carice refers it is not possible to ascertain, but the photographs of W. H. Reed (dressed for the Festival), Dora Powell and Troyte Griffith can almost certainly be attributed to that day, when they posed in the garden of Woodend before the concert, which began in the Cathedral at 11.15.[56]

8 September. S & I to Cathedral concerts in am. Terrific crowd at tea. Dora & Troyte – Peter photographed them together – met Mr Gaisberg. Dinner

at Atkins[es'] – Gerontius marvellous. Huge attendance.

9 September. To Birthplace & Cathedral all day – lunched with Clare – fetched 2nd Symphony for Novello's to take back …

After the Festival, Carice and Samuel went on a trip to Yorkshire and East Anglia, during which they shared the general concern of the country over the possibility of war with Germany, but:

28 September. Announcement of meeting in Munich tomorrow news came that agreement had been found & that there would be no war.

On returning to Broadheath the routine began again, with Carice sorting papers at the Birthplace, which seems to have been open only at weekends at this time.

16 October. Busy day with Birthplace. Mr Haycox came at 2.30. Only 1 visitor. He left about 5. Supper at Homestead. Piano arrived for Birthplace.

17 October. Sir Barry [Jackson] came. Saw Birthplace – had tea.

23 October. Birthplace open. Mr Haycox came – but no visitors.

28 October. S & I to Moseley in the car – & had tea with Dr Ratcliffe & his sister – saw film of father at Lawnside & other film.

29 October. 3 Visitors!

During November 1938 Samuel Blake's health deteriorated. However, despite the small number of visitors to the Birthplace, Carice remained undeterred as she continued to collect items for the museum.

10 November. S. in bed all day. Nellie [the Blake's maid] stayed until I got back. To London at 8.55, travelled with Sybil [Buckle] & Betty – met Lalla [Vandervelde] at Nat. Gallery, saw new Rembrandt. Lunched with Colles of Novello at Athenæum annexe – to Novello's for Birthplace party. [D. C.] Medley there & left early – Sir Barry [Jackson] & John Littleton Mrs Buckle & me. Saw Jack after. Met Clare at Padd. Travelled back with Betty. S[amuel]. all right.

11 November. Waiting for Dr Rook all day who only came at 5.30 said S. might have normal life again.

Concerts followed in Cheltenham and at home Carice listened, with approval, to the broadcast of an all-Elgar concert in Henry Wood's Jubilee season on 7 December. Samuel continued to feel unwell, but on 27 December he felt able to accompany Carice to:

Stratford on Avon – saw Donald Wolfit's production of Alice in Wonderland – very good.

At last, the next part of Carice's plan for the Birthplace could be realised by the appointment of a curator:

> 29 December. Mrs Goodman at 11 to see Birthplace etc.
>
> 31 December. Snow on ground. Saw Agnes re pantomime. Mrs Goodman settled in Birthplace.

But it was not until 6 April 1939 that Helen Goodman and her husband moved to live in the Birthplace permanently. The following day Carice and Helen Goodman attended a performance of *The Dream of Gerontius* in Worcester and, in due course they became firm friends, frequently going to Mass together on Sundays.

1939

During the first months of the New Year Helen Goodman came to the Birthplace nearly every day, and early in the January members of the Nevinson family visited, as did Percy Hull, who gave Carice a photograph of G. R. Sinclair and his bulldog, Dan.[57]

> 14 January. Heard Billie's concert – Shockheaded Peter[58] – *Dream Children* – *Handel Overture*. [Presumably Elgar's arrangement of the D Minor Overture from the Second Chandos Anthem]
>
> 20 January. Mrs Goodman came. Mr Carey Walker came at 11.30 – to see what had to be done to finish Birthplace & prevent water coming in at window on stairs etc.
>
> 25 January. Woke up to find it snowing hard – snowed all day. Did Gramophone list for Dr Colles. Mrs G. did not come.

On 6 February a telephone was installed in the Birthplace, and on 2 March Carice visited May and Clare Grafton and 'met 'mr wang' and saw dear Marco. Very pleased with us but one leg useless – sad.' [59]

On 3 March a photographer from the *Birmingham Post* came to photograph the cottage, followed the next day by a photographer from the local Worcester newspaper.

> 9 April. May, Clare Marco & Wang came to lunch & stayed till 6. Sat out all pm. Dogs very good. May & I to Birthplace after tea. Clare made us loaf of bread.

Carice continually concerned herself with the detail of running the museum, as we can see from her examination of the leaking window. She spent much of April worrying about the manuscripts and the need to insure them. There was a visit from the BBC about a possible broadcast from the Birthplace, but she found time to record a piece of sporting news:

29 April. Final – Portsmouth won.

During the spring Carice worked constantly at the Birthplace. She designed a catalogue and arranged for the garden to be re-turfed on 10 May. However, Samuel Blake's medical needs now became more evident. He spent some time in London, where from 16 May he underwent daily treatment. Meanwhile Carice, who accompanied him, visited Novello's to discuss her catalogue, lunched with Dr Colles, went to London Zoo, attended Mass at Spanish Place and heard a concert of her father's light music. On 22 May Carice and Samuel lunched with W. H. Reed and Sir George Dyson at the Royal College of Music. They returned to Woodend two days later.

30 May. Dr Stanton[60] came at 11 to go though broadcast. Uncle Hubert[61] taken ill.

31 May. Dr Stanton Sir Ivor & Mr Fry in pm & in to tea – arranging broadcast.

2 June. To Birthplace at 5.30. Rehearsing etc. – lovely evening with birds singing everyone seemed to enjoy the broadcast. Home by 9.30.

Margaret Elgar recalled a broadcast from the Birthplace at this time: '... when the BBC Midlands Singers went out there and they did a performance which was broadcast'.[62] At the end of her diary for the week commencing Sunday, 4 June, Carice noted the following:

Uncle Hubert ill all this week. His Knighthood announced on June 9th.

11 June. Sam ill so no Mass.

Sadly, Hubert Leicester was not able to appreciate his knighthood for long:

17 June. Went to Requiem Mass for Uncle Hubert.

On 21 June, Samuel Blake was admitted to South Bank Nursing Home, Worcester, which allowed Carice to get away for a few days, and on her return, she altered the layout of Woodend to accommodate his return home. A night nurse would now come every evening and, towards the end of Samuel Blake's time at Woodend, a day nurse would also be in attendance.

9 July. Sat out on lawn of Nursing Home all afternoon. Took S. drive after tea.

Carice continued to participate in family activities:

> 13 July. Went to garden party at Convent – saw Margaret [&] Pat drama – & had tea with Agnes & Hilary & Anne.[63]

Margaret Elgar remembers her time at the Convent, particularly the significance of her surname.

> When Reverend Mother was showing visitors round you could hear the rosary a-jingle as she came up the corridor; and I thought 'oh no, I know what's going to happen'. So she comes into the form-room: 'We have in this form a great niece of Sir Edward Elgar – stand up Margaret!' [64]

> 14 July. Took S. & nurse to Birthplace in car pm.

> 28 July. Went to Birthplace to label trees & plants. Pathé film man came. Anthony Bernard[65] about 5. Took to Birthplace.

> 1 August. Film man, Peter & telephone man arrived all at the same moment. Went to Birthplace for filming –

The month of August was dominated by Samuel Blake's illness, and on 26 August he returned to South Bank Nursing Home by ambulance. That night Helen Goodman slept at Woodend but, before then, there was another death to record :

> 23 August. Marco had to be put to sleep, was sent here about 12.15.

However, the impending death of Samuel Blake became Carice's main preoccupation.

> 28 August. Quiet day waiting. Sent for after tea but he was better again. Evening of waiting.

> 29 August. Heard the end had come at 2.45am. Telephoned … Guildford went to South Bank at 11. Said masses etc.

Two days later, Carice travelled to Guildford where 'everybody [was] worried over prospects of war.'

Wartime

> 3 September. Outbreak of war announced at 11.

Carice had no intention of closing the museum, and on the day war was declared visitors included Walter Legge and his wife.[66]

> 4 September. Busy trying to [get] Blackout right & sorting papers.

> 6 September. Percy & Billie[67] came over in the evening & had tea.

The war encroached in other ways too:

> 27 September ... went to Cathedral ... Elgar window being taken out.
>
> 9 October. Saw Birthplace – trying to reconstruct the study at Plas Gwyn all the time.

Before the year's end an event took place which has attracted the attention of many visitors to the Birthplace since :

> 2 December. Went to Birthplace to put Mina's little remains next to Marco & put up headstone. Went to Goodmans in evening for bagatelle again – home very late.

At the Birthplace Helen Goodman and her husband lived in three rooms including a bedroom upstairs and the front room on the ground floor on to which the front door opened.[68] Even then, the small size of the cottage was an obvious problem; when Carice brought over a group from the Worcester Women's Institute in July 1939, they had to be divided into two groups, with one group waiting in the garden. Carice continued to work on much of the cataloguing for the collection when she could, typing labels on her typewriter.[69] The Birthplace remained open during the war years and, although visitors were few she received Vera Hockman in January 1941 and in February 1943 Ivor Newton, followed by Alan and Joan Webb in August.[70] At the end of Elgar's life, Fred Gaisberg of The Gramophone Company had been quietly concerned for the ailing composer's welfare and, at Elgar's request, had made arrangements to photograph him in his room at South Bank Nursing Home on 12 December 1933.[71] This letter shows the affection Carice had for Gaisberg as well as her sensitivity towards the photographs:

> Woodend. 27 November 1940
>
> My dear Mr. Gaisberg –
>
> So many thanks for you letter. It was delightful to hear from you & know you are well – & safe – I am very well – alone at the moment with my dogs & really I prefer it – I haven't refused to have evacuees but they haven't been offered me & I am too far out for civil servants etc –
>
> I am so interested to hear about your memoirs – they will make wonderfully interesting reading – & it's lovely to think of the chapter about Father – I give you permission gladly to use his letters – but will you please write to my Trustees for permission also? ...
>
> If you do not mind my asking, how are you working in the one about those photographs in the nursing home – because no one – except the 20 or so people you gave them to know anything about them?

It is good of you to say the originals will eventually come to the Birthplace – That is still open & we get a few visitors in spite of the absence of signposts –

My love – & it is so nice to hear of you –

Yours affectionately
Carice.

Post-War life

When Diana McVeagh began her biographical research, in the early 1950s, little had changed since the outbreak of hostilities in 1939. Although the Birthplace did not open every day she was allowed to work uninterrupted. She recalls Helen Goodman as an elderly, rather frail lady who knew little about Elgar, but on occasions provided 'boiled eggs and soldiers' for lunch. Visitors were few, amounting to no more than two or three a day. Diana McVeagh remembers, a wonderful romantic 'sleeping beauty' atmosphere. She had the feeling that Elgar might walk in at any moment.

Other visitors also recall the peace of sitting in the garden and the joy of being able to wander around the cottage at will whilst Martin Passande remembers Helen Goodman waving him to the first floor with the comment: 'I don't do stairs!' Sir Adrian Boult visited on 28 June 1947 and returned three weeks later on 15 July in the company of his wife and 'Dorabella'. At about this time it was Sir Adrian who agreed to open the tea-room erected at Woodend. Sybil Russell, who had become Carice's companion, described the background to the building of the tea-room which took place during the immediate post-war austerity.

> When I first joined Carice, after leaving the Air Force, we were both in total agreement that the Birthplace should become better known by the music public. This suggested to me that as the Birthplace was in such a remote spot, it should be publicised as having a place to rest – possibly a tea-room. Carice owned land opposite, so we searched for a portable building. Luckily we found one, and quite soon it was erected. Fittings were difficult to come by, and decorative curtains quite impossible. Luckily I was able to secure some plain material suitable for my fabric painting, and lastly, we secured a dozen small tables and suitable chairs. ... Later I secured a reasonably large board, and painted 'Birthplace tea-room' which also served light meals when required.[72]

Early in the next decade, the first visits took place of those who would also become Elgar's biographers. Michael Kennedy and Jerrold Northrop

Moore travelled to Broadheath and signed the Visitors Book for the first time in July 1952 and July 1954 respectively. Both would agree with Diana McVeagh, whose first visit took place in 1951, when she tells of a time less sophisticated than ours, with books on open shelves, little or no protection from sunlight and letters kept loose in drawers. Although this runs contrary to modern curatorial practice it was, as most of those who visited Broadheath before 1970 can attest, 'a privilege to have known [the birthplace] then'.[73] Mr Goodman died in 1959, but Helen Goodman stayed on at the cottage until her death in 1964.

The centenary of Elgar's birth, 2 June 1957, fell on a Sunday. The weather seems to have mirrored that day 100 years before and the BBC sent a cameraman to film inside and outside the Birthplace, although Carice was not happy with the subsequent broadcast.[74] In 1957 Diana McVeagh wrote a description of the Birthplace. Her words remind us what was and is the purpose of the museum.

> It is still a home, for the curators, Mr and Mrs Goodman, live there, and the front door opens straight into their sitting-room, cheerful with oak and brass. To the right is Elgar's study. At first one almost listens for his footstep, ready to straighten up quickly so as not to be caught snooping, so strong is the impression that he may come in at any minute. That is his furniture, and there is his desk, cluttered with all the writer's paraphernalia, with his pipes and tobacco, and its drawers stuffed with oddments and even with sheets of paper covered by his writing. His diary is there, his metronome, his green baize board, and to hand is a small reference library. ... After looking at the formal photographs of the Elgars in the albums on the table, turn to their private scrapbooks of sentimental and comic souvenirs. In one there are a couple of season tickets for the Crystal Palace concerts in 1890. Another has a letter to Elgar, Special Constable: 'I have observed that you were always one of the earliest arrivals here on receiving the Emergency Call', and a 1927 summons for driving a motor lorry in a manner dangerous to the public.[75]

By the time the minutes of the Birthplace Fund can be read again (22 April 1955), The Master of the Queen's Musick, Sir Arthur Bliss, was in the chair and most meetings were held at the offices of Novello and Company in Wardour Street. In addition to Carice, who never missed a meeting, other trustees now included Sir Adrian Boult, Sybil Russell, Herbert Howells, Gerald Finzi, Alan Kirby and John Littleton of Novello.[76] Mr R.G. Medley[77] attended as Treasurer and the curator's wages were confirmed at £2 per week. The July 1955 meeting reported an annual income of £170 and in the October Carice confirmed she was donating

£500 under a deed of covenant. During the following year the main concern for the trustees was the need to undertake repairs to the Birthplace but by 1957 their minds were turning again to the need for the construction of a cottage for the curator 'after the retirement of the Goodmans'. They believed they would be able to utilise a site 'lying immediately to the north of the Birthplace across the bridle-path', and hoped that the plot would 'be purchased by Worcester Council'.[78]

Sir Arthur Bliss maintained a dialogue with what is now called the 'media', most notably the new independent television companies. However, it was the BBC which would contribute most substantially to a resurgence of interest in Elgar and his music as well as the Birthplace when, in 1958, the seeds were sown for the making of the film 'Elgar' by Ken Russell. Carice agreed to write to Huw Weldon suggesting that the BBC 'Monitor' programme should make a film at the Birthplace. That year Dr Percy Young and Anthony Milner were invited to become additional trustees and Carice moved, with Sybil Russell, to live near Bristol.

In 1959 Alan Kirby died, and during the following year the trustees realised that they now needed to catalogue the contents of the museum and Douglas Guest (then organist of Worcester Cathedral) and the wife of the Bishop of Worcester were invited to become trustees. During the following year, as Sir Arthur Bliss gave up the chairmanship of the Birthplace Fund, the trustees became increasingly concerned at the lack of simple amenities in the cottage. Dr Jack Britton had offered to purchase adjacent land on which to build a cottage for the curator and on 14 April 1962 the trustees met to receive proposals from the Treasurer, who was joined by Dr Britton. They were advised that Worcester City Corporation had agreed to purchase the land, leaving the trustees with the responsibility of constructing a bungalow.

By the summer the trustees were becoming frustrated by the lack of progress towards the purchase of the land, but they discussed also the replacement of Helen Goodman, whom they did not consider would be able to continue much longer. By the autumn there was a feeling that an architect should be commissioned to design the bungalow, even though Helen Goodman seemed content to remain living in the Birthplace, but by February 1962 the trustees were advised that the owner of the land was not prepared to sell.

At the July meeting Carice reported that the BBC would be visiting the Birthplace with a view to filming during the following month.[79] Frustrated by their inability to purchase the adjacent land, the trustees now turned their minds to building an extension to the Birthplace to provide 'accommodation at the gate and adjoining coach-house'. The plans for developing the Birthplace occupied the trustees during 1963 and 1964, and on 20 October 1964 they heard of Helen Goodman's death. Later that year Douglas Guest moved to Westminster Abbey and, in the November, the plans for the extension were approved by the trustees. However, these were not liked by the City Council, and the Royal Fine Arts Commission objected to the proposed destruction of the stable block. Meanwhile, a Mrs Holden was employed as caretaker.

By 1966 Sir Malcolm Sargent had also become a trustee, and amended plans for the development of the stable-block had been accepted. The trustees now realised that an appeal for at least an additional £10,000 would be necessary, and they appointed Mr Bernard van Dieren as their first official fund-raiser. It is now that the name of Alan Webb (and his wife Joan) appears for the first time as a possible curator and secretary to the trust. The trustees were notified that the Webbs would attend a meeting on 2 March 1966 when it was proposed that the new curator should be paid an honorarium of £250 per annum. Alan Webb's credentials for the position were undoubted. He was a first-rate communicator and had an encyclopædic knowledge of Elgar's life and music. His father, Frank Webb, who had been given violin lessons by Elgar, was the dedicatee of *Virelai, Op.4, No.3*.

At the beginning of 1966, authority was given for the building work to commence and, during a meeting of the trustees held at the Birthplace later in July, satisfaction was expressed on the progress of the work. The Birthplace was closed to visitors, but the trustees hoped that it would be open in time for the 1967 Worcester Three Choirs Festival. In December 1966, the Webbs moved into the cottage. Michael Kennedy remembers

> … the enthusiasm, knowledge and helpfulness of Alan Webb. He was a model curator. I was the first Elgar writer ever to ask him for the Stuart Wortley letters and he brought them to me with a knowing look as if to say 'How did you get on to these'? He set me up a table near [the] staircase upstairs and let me work on for ages. I read and copied and experienced the most extraordinary feeling that someone was watching me disapprovingly.[80]

Life was by no means easy for the Webbs. It was felt that the floor of the cottage would not support the weight of a double bed, so Joan Webb slept alone upstairs in the cottage and Alan in the coach house annexe. For the Elgar Society he took on the role of 'secretary for recorded music' petitioning EMI for a recording of *The Kingdom* and playing 78 rpm records to visitors whilst they sat on the edge of his bed.[81] Joan Webb kept the cottage clean and worked in the garden. In January 1967 the trustees met at the Birthplace, the meeting being chaired by Dr Percy Young. It was agreed to deposit Elgar's letters at the Worcester City Library 'on permanent loan'. This was the first meeting attended by Bernard van Dieren, who later became secretary to the trust. He succeeded Sir Malcolm Sargent as a trustee in 1967, following the conductor's death, and was present when the Birthplace re-opened on 12 May. Carice invited seventy guests, including Yehudi Menuhin, whose association with the trustees and the building would grow over the years, particularly when he became President of the trust.

By now visitors to the Birthplace exceeded 3,500 annually, which Alan Webb reported was due in part to the BBC Television Film, 'whatever may be said about [it]'. Later it was hoped that the BBC might make some sort of financial contribution in view of the fact that they had, by then, broadcast 'their Elgar film' twice. Alan Webb reported fixing a sign 'Elgar's Birthplace 2½ miles' to the wall of the garden of St John's Vicarage on the Broadheath side of Worcester.[82] For the first time sales of scores, books and postcards were contributing substantially to the income of the Birthplace. Nevertheless, Yehudi Menuhin agreed to lead an appeal for an additional £25,000.

In March 1968, in formal recognition of her tireless work, Carice was declared President of the Trustees for life. This was in advance of a 1969 tour of USA, which she made with Sybil Russell and Bernard van Dieren. Once in America they fulfilled 'a series of Television/radio interviews, Press Conferences, and "Question and Answer" sessions, ranging from San Diego to Boston … the establishment of an Elgar Society in California … and potentially a similar society in Massachusetts …'

In February 1970, John Whittle of EMI and Raymond Monk were elected trustees just before they, together with the existing board, confronted the first of a number of serious difficulties. The first occurred on 16 July 1970, when Carice died, and on 5 October an extraordinary meeting of the trustees was convened, during which Dr Young paid her tribute. He spoke

> of the very deep sense of personal loss which he experienced. He had met the late Mrs Elgar Blake almost by accident when, after reading some of his previous works, she had asked him to undertake the writing of a biography of her father. From that time onwards they had become firm friends and in all his connections with her he had been conscious of her deep loyalty to her

parents. She had given him constant and enormous encouragement in their joint agreement and understanding as to how a biography should be written … The last occasion when they met at Birmingham, in company with Miss Russell, seemed to set the seal on their mutual understanding and complete and wholehearted realisation and understanding that Carice Irene Elgar Blake was the worthy daughter of a great father and a great mother.

The minutes recorded: 'The foregoing tribute was unanimously conjoined by those present as an expression of their individual and collective irretrievable loss.' At the same meeting, Sybil Russell succeeded Carice as President of the Trustees. Carice bequeathed the last of her father's artefacts to the museum, but lack of space meant that some items had to be sold, including Elgar's bookcase from his study in Plas Gwyn.

Modern visitors to Broadheath will have little idea of the determination with which Carice attempted to fulfil her father's wishes. She it was who had the vision of what the Birthplace should be and what it could become. She had to balance her vision, against the constant background of a shortage of funds, throughout the thirty-six years of her life following her father's death. If this short history does nothing else, it should draw attention to her work in creating a collection and establishing and preserving a museum. The least our generation can do is recognise her achievement and, by naming a room at the new Elgar Centre after Carice, the Birthplace Trustees have acknowledged this for posterity.[83]

Carice Elgar Blake laid out the north-facing rear of the first floor of the Birthplace as 'The Birthroom'. This is to the right of the staircase on the first floor. In a brochure published in the 1960s, Carice wrote: 'At the rear of the house is the small back room looking on to the fields which Ann Elgar is said to have preferred for its quietness as the time approached for the birth of her child.'

III
After Carice

…but the faith and love and self-sacrifice with which she carried through her task, congenial though it was, are things which call for admiration and should be set down for all to read.[84]

Over the next two years, meetings were chaired by Dr Percy Young. Sir Gerald Nabarro MP had now become a trustee, and Councillor Allington had replaced the representative of the Worcester Corporation, Alderman

Mrs Ratcliffe. Eventually Sir Gerald was appointed Chairman, and confronted what developed into the crisis of the 'Van Dieren affair'. Sir Adrian Boult's generous support as well as that of the other trustees averted the potential bankruptcy of the trust.[85] A.T. Shaw, in his report to the 1971 Annual General Meeting of the Elgar Society described the

> surprising appearance of a rival organisation emerging, it seemed, from the Elgar Birthplace Trustees, who have since disowned the 'United Kingdom Elgar Society' and have asked its sponsor, Mr Bernard van Dieren, to resign as secretary/treasurer and a trustee.
>
> This unwelcome episode was at first somewhat disturbing, but, in the event, its effect on our membership was negligible.[86]

For the twelve months ending 31 December 1971, Alan Webb recorded 4,000 visitors, and in 1972, the 96-year-old Lionel Tertis donated £360 from the proceeds of the sale of his violas. The trustees now began considering the replacement of Alan and Joan Webb, who had given notice of their wish to retire. Sir Adrian Boult became closely involved in the selection of the new curator through

> a series of interviews which Boult and I conducted over three mornings in his office above the Wigmore Hall. I seem to recall that we had to interview about 15 people and we did 5 each day to be followed by a memorable lunch when we talked about many aspects of his career. I saw a different ACB then with all his BBC admin experience on display. We ended up by choosing Jack McKenzie for our Curator, or I should say ACB did![87]

McKenzie, with his relaxed approach, brought dogs and a change of atmosphere to Broadheath. He took over in November 1972, the Webbs moving back to their home in Dorset.[88] Vivienne McKenzie has described their time at Broadheath as 'the happiest ten years of Jack's life'. It was a time of greater responsibilities for the curator with a steady increase in visitors,

> the workload of many visits by schools, in the mornings when we were closed to the public, the increase in letters and the extensive mail order service; the interests of radio, local and national, and TV, and the fall out from events like the Malvern Festival and Three Choirs Festival.[89]

As with the Webbs, the McKenzies operated as a team at the Birthplace and, when she had time, Vivienne McKenzie involved herself in research as well as improving the labelling and cataloguing of the artefacts in the Birthplace.

At the meeting of the trustees in February 1973 additional appointments were considered, Sir Adrian Boult putting forward the name of Wulstan Atkins with the trust's legal advisor suggesting Christopher Harmer. There were a number of meetings in the first months of 1973, during which Dr Young continued to chair meetings, Mrs Lilian Wright was appointed secretary and Wulstan Atkins, Christopher Harmer, Dr Watkins Shaw and Professor Ivor Keys were appointed trustees. In April, Sir Adrian Boult was appointed President of the trust and Sir Gerald Nabarro became the first Chairman since Sir Arthur Bliss to be elected annually rather than appointed at each meeting. Later in the year Dr Young and Sybil Russell (now Mrs Wohfeld) resigned.

Sir Gerald Nabarro, who died in 1973, was instrumental in the formation of the Elgar Foundation. It was now felt that the powers of the original Birthplace Trust were too restrictive and, as the Charity Commissioners were unable to extend these, the trustees established the Foundation, which had wider money-raising powers. The trust, as constituted, required that both bodies have the same trustees. Wulstan Atkins, with his unique Elgarian associations, became closely associated with the subsequent development of the Birthplace and the Elgar Centre. He had retired from business in 1969 and soon become involved in Elgar activities, firstly through the newly-formed London Branch of the Elgar Society and later, nationally, when he became Secretary and Treasurer between 1973 and 1976.[90] Early in his Chairmanship a fund-raiser, Major Peter Pope was appointed at the meeting of the trustees held at the Royal College of Music in September 1975. This enabled a new appeal for £100,000 to be launched, and by June 1976 some £20,000 had been raised. However, the Birthplace cottage needed constant attention, and this absorbed much of the money collected. By the beginning of 1977 more than £50,000 had been raised, but Major Pope stood down in the February to be replaced by Sheila Anderson, as Appeal Secretary.

In 1974, an earlier benefactor, Dr Jack Britton, and A.T. Shaw, then Chairman of the Elgar Society, were appointed trustees. During 1976 Howard Flight (the future Member of Parliament), Dr Donald Hunt, Michael Kennedy and Sam Driver White became trustees and two years later the appointment of Anne Soden, David Hawkins and Dr Jerrold Northrop Moore took place. Michael Pope, as Elgar Society Chairman, was appointed in 1979.[91]

By the end of 1976 the number of visitors had exceeded 6,000 during the year, but a sign of things to come occurred in 1977 with the first publicly voiced concern over the proposed development of a car park and visitor reception area near the Birthplace. On 23 May the Duke of Gloucester unveiled a bronze head sculpted by Sam Tonkiss. Afterwards Dr Donald Hunt conducted the Worcester Cathedral Choir, which sang a selection of Elgar part-songs. Mr Tonkiss made a gift of the bronze during the ceremony, which was also attended by the High Sheriff of the County and the Mayor of Worcester. In 1978, buoyed by a further increase in visitor numbers, to over 7,700 in 1977, the trustees doubled the appeal target to £200,000. They also felt there was an opportunity to purchase Plas Gwyn in Hereford and restore the house to the condition and decoration of Elgar's time. During the year television crews from The Netherlands and Japan filmed at the Birthplace and the McKenzies received the cellist Jacqueline du Pré in her wheel-chair and in 1979 the violinist Pinchas Zukerman.

It was during 1979 that the trustees considered taking a lease of the ground floor rooms of 8 College Gardens in Worcester 'to set up a mini-museum'. This idea seems to have been dropped quickly when, later in the year, the opportunity for a substantial change at the Birthplace arose with the potential purchase of Rose Cottage, a building separated from the Birthplace by the undistinguished bungalow, The Elms.[92] Rose Cottage dates from 1862, although renovated and altered after the Great War. Over the years it had been known variously as Rose Cottage, Ponda Rosa and Ryden, but was renamed Rose Cottage by the trustees after its purchase. The purchase of Rose Cottage at last enabled Jack McKenzie and his wife Vivienne to move out of the Birthplace, allowing it to come into its own as a museum. Despite visits by prominent musicians and the increase in publicity which the museum was attracting, visitor numbers fell over the years from the peak in 1977 to 5,800 in 1979. However, numbers were rising again when, in the spring of 1982, the ceiling collapsed over the old kitchen. Later that year, the summer house, which had once stood in the garden of Marl Bank, was erected at the southern end of the garden. It was re-thatched at the same time.

In March 1983, the McKenzies retired and Jim Bennett took over as curator, moving straight into Rose Cottage once the McKenzies were able to leave. A formal hand-over took place on 2 June. Ronald Taylor, the editor of the *Elgar Society Journal*, in his tribute to Jack McKenzie referred to his 'courtesy and discreet assistance [to visitors]' and how well he had coped with the increase in visitors to the Birthplace, which seemed to coincide with his arrival.[93] Jim Bennett was joined by his son Chris who, for the last twenty years, has provided invaluable support to all involved in running the Birthplace including the management of the garden, ensuring that it always looks in its prime whatever the season. Jim Bennett's reports on the Birthplace for the *Elgar Society Journal* were infused with his love of bird-life and the changing seasons.

Despite the lack of storage space, the new curator received an increasing amount of material including, in 1985, the manuscript scores of *Froissart* and *The Light of Life,* which were given to the Birthplace, on 'permanent loan' by the Dean and Chapter of Worcester Cathedral. In 1993, a collection of manuscripts was given by the daughter of a clarinet player from the Powick Asylum Band.[94] Later in the year Japanese and BBC television filmed at the Birthplace and the curator received the complete cast of the Royal Shakespeare Company production of David Pownall's play *Elgar's Rondo.* In February 1994 the Birthplace and the British Library exchanged facsimile copies of the manuscript scores of Elgar's Symphonies; the British Library presenting a copy of the A flat Symphony to Wulstan Atkins and the latter handing over a copy of the E flat Symphony to Hugh Cobbe of the British Library. In 1995 Jim Bennett welcomed a party from Chetham's School of Music, shortly after he had been presented with a gift to mark his retirement at the dedication ceremony of the new Elgar Centre in the May.[95]

IV
The Elgar Centre

… lying immediately to the north of the Birthplace across the bridle path.

There remained the constant need to raise additional funds for the Birthplace and in March 1990, the Birthplace Development Appeal was launched, under the direction of Diana Quinney, who had previously been Appeal Director for the Radcliffe Hospital in Oxford. By 1992 a further £200,000 had been raised, but the design of the proposed visitor centre became the subject of widespread controversy often played out in the pages of the local and national press. An early proposal for a two-storey building immediately behind the Birthplace cottage had been abandoned at the suggestion of the trust's patron, HRH The Prince of Wales. The subsequent plan for a single-storey structure of rustic appearance also found little public favour, because of its proximity to the Birthplace.

Tim Waterstone and Laurie Watt were now, respectively, Chairman and Vice-Chairman of the Birthplace Trust. However, it was Laurie Watt acting as Chairman, whilst Tim Waterstone was in America, who played a pivotal role in resolving much of the controversy by persuading the trustees that they should pull down The Elms bungalow. As The Elms stood between the Birthplace and Rose Cottage the demolition enabled the site of The Elgar Centre to be moved farther away from the Birthplace cottage, thus paving the way towards resolving a number of the concerns of many observers. There is little doubt that the public controversy over the scale and site of the Elgar Centre affected the ability of the trustees to raise sufficient funds to complete the visitor centre but, nevertheless, they took the decision to commence building in 1994. On 3 May 1995 the much re-designed shell of what would be called the Elgar Centre was completed and dedicated by Dame Janet Baker.

The way ahead was by no means clear; except that it was obvious that a large sum of money was required to complete the Centre. The trustees now speculated as to whether the new National Lottery could come to the rescue and the trustees eventually agreed to proceed in this direction under the leadership of Tim Llewellyn. Although the application was rejected, a number of lessons were learnt in the process not the least the need to improve the professionalism of the Birthplace management. So it was that Melanie Weatherley, the first professionally qualified curator, was appointed in the spring of 1996. Following an appraisal by the Heart of England Tourist Board later that year, the Heritage Lottery Fund was advised that a new application for funding would be made. The Trustees were further strengthened with the appointment of Michael Messenger to the Board in 1997.

Following further renovation of the cottage during the winter of 1996–1997 Melanie Weatherley was able to report that full registration under phase two of the Museums and Galleries Commission registration scheme had been approved. This was formalised by a presentation of the certificate at the Birthplace on 10 June 1997 by Lady Cobham, Commissioner to the MGC. This was an important and necessary step for the forthcoming lottery bid. In the event, because of changes to the operation of the lottery, the new application was not made until November 1998. This was led by Michael Messenger as Chairman of the Birthplace Management Committee.

By now, Wulstan Atkins and Dame Janet Baker had become joint Presidents of the Birthplace Trust and David Bowerman had been appointed Chairman. With the crucial support of the Elgar family, it was hoped that one final push would raise the funds necessary to enable the new Centre to open.[96] Inevitably, the financial viability of the Museum became a matter of scrutiny by the Lottery Case Officer, but an expression of interest by the Worcester County Council Education Department in renting space in the Centre enabled the Management Committee to strengthen their case for support. Eventually the Heritage Lottery Fund agreed an award, following additional financial support from the Elgar Will Trust, and, through Sam Driver White, the Elmley Foundation and, additionally, the Birthplace Trust's Chairman.

Welcome though the funds from the National Lottery were, the sum would only go about half way to achieving feasibility. Thus it was that the trustees were able to reach agreement with the County Education Department, which became tenants of a substantial part of the new building in November 1999, allowing the Department the use of one wing of the Centre and part of Rose Cottage. A thirty-five-year lease was agreed as well as a capital contribution of £250,000. This agreement was essential to the viability of the Centre, but it came at a high price, as much of the building is now out of bounds to matters Elgarian.

The doors of the Centre were opened in August 2000, and on 19 October Dame Janet Baker officiated at the formal opening. The building was at last able to make its contribution to Elgarian conservation, research and education, and the removal of the shop and counter from the Birthplace returned the cottage to something more akin to a home. During the first six weeks, following the opening of the Centre, Margaret Fotheringham (the newly appointed Marketing Officer) reported 1,800 visitors, a level of interest, which regrettably has not been sustained. However, in November 2001, Cathy Sloan and Margaret Fotheringham were able to report that 'Despite the deterrent effects of floods, fuel crises, Foot & Mouth disease, and the dreadful events in America, visitor numbers ... have increased.' [97]

At the beginning of 2002, Melanie Weatherley moved to a new position in Shropshire and Cathy Sloan, who had undertaken so much of the work to support the application for lottery funding, was appointed Museum Director. She is now assisted by Margaret Sanders, the Archivist, and Chris Bennett the Museum Supervisor, as well as by a dedicated team of part-time helpers.

V
Carice's Legacy

...the worthy daughter of a great father and a great mother.

Carice Elgar Blake's dream has been partially realised, even though there remains much to be done. The most important task is that of creating the wherewithal to enable the Birthplace to support itself, for 12,000 annual visitors (or fewer) do not enable the Museum to be self-financing. The Elgar Centre has had a dramatic impact on the land adjacent to the Birthplace, and physically it is important to allow the landscaping around the Centre to be completed and the new building to merge into its surroundings as far as this is possible. Only when time has taken its course, can the original idea behind the construction of the building be appreciated, for only recently the Centre was described as having a 'design and atmosphere at odds with the rustic simplicity of the house [cottage]'.[98]

In the long-term it is important to move towards opening the Centre fully to the public by utilising all its amenities, so that it becomes more of a cultural focus for the region. What is more the additional space created by the Elgar Centre creates opportunities for the cottage too. When funds permit, the trustees could well consider re-building the birth-room. This was surely the part of the cottage that attracted Elgar when he visited Broadheath in the company of Herbert Howells, seventy-five or more years ago.

Thus the modern trustee has to balance what is hoped are an increasing number of paying visitors (the life-blood of the Museum) with its peaceful rural atmosphere and the hope that something of the great artist who was born there remains. For it is Elgar's music that is the reason for our continued interest in this little house which bridges his roots in the countryside to the great Cathedral and country beyond as well as to the city that became his final home.

The future of the Birthplace has looked uncertain at times, but it has avoided the fate of a number of Elgar's other homes, the most shameful being that of Marl Bank which ' ... was destroyed, ostensibly to make room for a block of flats. For years afterwards the ruin was left with the façade gone and the staircase visible. Only in England could this have happened and lovers of Elgar will never forget it.' [99] However, although the little cottage remains, 'only in England' it seems, do we struggle for decades to keep a place like the Birthplace functioning; raising money through a variety of means but finding, seventy years later, that financial security remains elusive. Elgar's first home has survived thanks to the vision, determination and generosity of a few devoted individuals. It was Carice who set the standard and is their example. For her sake and for that of her father and his music they deserve a secure and lasting legacy in a building, which should be 'as dear to lovers of music as the national monuments at Stratford, Chalfont and Grasmere are to lovers of poetry.'

Acknowledgements

Margaret Elgar, the great-niece of Sir Edward, joined me for a presentation I gave to the Thames Valley Branch in 2002, and generously contributed to the event by allowing me to interview her about her memories of Carice Elgar Blake, her time as a young girl in Worcester and her recollections of her great-uncle. Margaret's cousin, Paul Grafton, has also been of great help in clarifying genealogical issues and in providing more general advice. Their assistance is a small example of the great contribution the Elgar family has made to the Birthplace over the years.

I am indebted to Cathy Sloan, the Birthplace Museum Director, Margaret Sanders the Archivist and Chris Bennett the Museum Supervisor for their patient assistance whilst I pieced together this history and the story of the management of the Birthplace. I am also grateful to the Birthplace trustees for allowing the reproduction of photographs and excerpts from material written by Carice Elgar Blake, Lucy Elgar Pipe, Mary Agnes Elgar and Jerrold Northrop Moore. Four of Elgar's biographers, Diana McVeagh, Michael Kennedy, Jerrold Northrop Moore and Percy Young shared their memories of visiting Broadheath over the years as well as giving me more general advice. Joyce and Michael Kennedy generously read this chapter at an early stage.

Vivienne McKenzie and Chris Bennett, the widow and son respectively, of the third and fourth curator were generous with their time in recalling their experiences whilst living and working at Broadheath. I appreciated the help David Hawkins gave me in providing information on the physical history of 'The Firs' and that of Michael Messenger for clarifying more recent developments at the Birthplace. Arthur Walker and Sam Driver White also gave me helpful advice. Raymond Monk, the longest-serving trustee of the Birthplace, provided invaluable help and advice as well as lending me some of the photographs in his collection. He provided me also with copies of Carice's diaries, excerpts from which have been reproduced here. Martin Bird helped to decipher Carice's hand-writing and Susan Campbell undertook essential research at the Worcester Record Office. Lastly, I am pleased to acknowledge the translation by William Mann of the verse from Verdi's *La Traviata*, which is reproduced by kind permission of EMI Classics.

Appendix 1: The ownership of 'The Firs'

I cannot trace any records relating to 'The Firs' prior to 1828 and therefore we have to rely on a certain amount of conjecture as to the history of the building. Despite the fact it may have been enlarged on or about the time these records begin we cannot be certain when enlargement actually took place. We cannot even be certain when the cottage was built. The following is a summary of what I have been able to establish from the records of the Worcester Record Office and, in the circumstances, it is perhaps best to allow the facts to speak for themselves:

'The Firs': Title & Deeds Ref r.926.11 BA557
(originals held by the Town Clerk, The Guildhall, Worcester).

There is an indenture dated 14 October 1828 granting a lease of one year between Thomas Hodges of Broadheath, in the parish of St John Bedwardine and Thomas Linton of Crows Nest in the same parish, yeoman.[100] In consideration for the sum of 5 shillings which Linton paid to Hodges the latter 'bargained and sold that orchard plot or piece of land situate at the lower end of Broadheath Common in the parish of St John containing a quarter of an acre which premises were formerly the inheritance of Joseph Hodges the grandfather of Thomas Hodges party hereto and since of Thomas Hodges the father of the said Thomas Hodges party hereto & now of the said Thomas Hodges as eldest son & heir of the said father. For the term of one year Thomas Hodges & Sarah his wife of the first part and Thomas Linton of the second part & Thomas Cromwell Gwinnell of the third part.

The following day an indenture dated 15 October 1828 conveyed a piece of land at Broadheath. Between Thomas Hodges of Broadheath, yeoman & his wife Sarah of the first part, Thomas Linton of Crows Nest, yeoman of the second part & Thomas Cromwell Gwinnell of St Michael Bedwardine, gent of the third part. Thomas Hodges is seized of an estate of inheritance in fee simple in possession of the orchard or piece or parcel of ground & other hereditaments intended to be granted & released with the appurtenances. Thomas Linton has agreed to purchase this for the sum of £46.

Also on 15 October 1828 an indenture of release between Thomas and Sarah Hodges, Thomas Linton and Thomas Cromwell Gwinnell was drawn up. Linton, at the time of his death, was the innkeeper of the Duke of York in Leech (Lich) Street, Worcester. He died on 20 July 1835 and, in his will, there is the clause To John Woodyatt of Cradley, Hfd, farmer & Thomas Kinnard of Lulsley, Worcs, farmer his cottage or dwelling house with garden & appurtenances belonging situate in Broadheath in parish of St John lately in the occupation of William Drew but then void & untenanted in trust to keep it in repair & to pay the residue to his wife for life. After her death to his daughter Dorcas Linton her heirs & assignees.[101]

Tithe Map & Apportionment, Worcester St John Bedwardine
(Apportionment made 9 January 1840).

On the 1841 Tithe Map Thomas Silvester, a 60 years old farmer, was named as the tenant of the property (plot 143), the landowner being Mary Linton (the widow of Thomas Linton). The house then seems to have been called either [New]bury or possibly [Old]bury Cottage.[102] Plot 142 (approximately where the Elgar Centre is today) shows the landowner to be Thomas Bowater Vernon, the guardian of George Vernon and the occupier Sarah Hodges who was, presumably, the widow of Thomas Hodges who sold plot 143 to the Linton family.

In the early 1850s Dorcas Linton married Henry J Marshall, a tailor and woollen draper with premises at 86 High Street, Worcester, where he employed 10 men. Their only child, Catherine Mary Marshall was born in April 1856. Dorcas Marshall died in July 1857 and Henry Marshall remarried, although he died in November 1871 aged 44.

We know little of Catherine Marshall, but in June 1928 there was an *Order of Masters of Lunacy in the matter of Catherine Mary Marshall spinster appointing Harry Victor Plum of Rivington, Broadstone, Dorset retired schoolmaster as receiver.*[103] The conveyance of 'The Firs' to the City of Worcester in 1935 records a *Messuage or dwelling house & land known as The Firs, Broadheath. Catherine Mary Marshall of The Villa Turro Stablimento Sanitario Rossi Milan Italy Spinster represented by Henry Victor Plum the receiver. Proceeds of sale £400. Plot containing .234 acres or thereabouts.*

Appendix 2: The ownership of 'The Firs': A Summary

Prior to 1828:   Only identified owner: Thomas Hodges.

October 1828:   Thomas Hodges sells the site to Thomas Linton.

July 1835:   On the death of Thomas Linton the property passed to his widow, Mary Ann Linton, who was therefore the owner of the property when the Elgars lived there.

December 1863:   The will of Mary Ann Linton is proved and the property passes to Catherine Mary Marshall; the latter's mother, Dorcas Marshall (née Linton), having pre-deceased her own mother, Mary Ann Linton.

May 1935:   Catherine Mary Marshall sells the House and land amounting to 0.234 acres to the Mayor, Aldermen and Citizens of the County of the City of Worcester.

Note: Exhaustive searches of Electoral Rolls may disclose the names of virtually every tenant of 'The Firs' over the years. Each Roll is held on film at the Worcester Record Office and each year is on a different film. I felt such information was of marginal interest only (if that), although future researchers may feel otherwise.

The Vivian Durrant photo ['Vivian of Hereford'], taken on the last day of Elgar's last Three Choirs Festival in 1933. Durrant arranged to meet Elgar on the steps of the cathedral for what was supposed to have been the first and only photograph of Elgar in colour. Unfortunately, the process required three distinct shots. Elgar grew impatient and walked off after two.

[Photo: Arthur Reynolds collection]

Above: Watercolour of 'The Firs' by Buckler circa 1856. It is believed that Buckler paints the following scene: Sometime, shortly before the birth of Edward, the Elgar family takes the air in their garden. In the foreground Ann and William walk down the path with their eldest daughter Lucy. To the right Harry, their eldest child, leans against a tree and in the porch of the cottage the nurse holds 'Pollie' in her arms. William Elgar's younger brother, Henry, stands in front of the stable block he has just built and 'Jack' the pony can be seen looking out into the garden. To the left of the main path is the 'ladies' avenue.

Facing page, above: An undated photograph of the Birthplace. It is possible that this dates from before the Great War. Note the ground-floor window shutters matching the style of the front door, the vegetable garden and well-developed trees to the left.

Facing page, below: An undated photograph of the Birthplace. This may show the cabbage patch through which Elgar negotiated a path on his visit with Herbert Howells in 1923. The fact that a garden chair is laid out on the lawn suggests an early spring day, and either Mr and Mrs Walford or Mr and Mrs Davis are in the garden.

[Photos: Elgar Birthplace Museum]

SIR E. ELGAR'S BIRTHPLACE, BROADHEATH, WORCESTER.

In the garden of Woodend, 8 September 1938:

Above: From left to right, Clare Stuart Wortley, W.H. Reed, Agnes Nicholls, Troyte Griffith, Carice Elgar Blake, Winifred Norbury, Samuel Blake, 'Dorabella' (Dora Powell).

Below: From left to right, W.H. Reed, Troyte, 'Dorabella' and Carice.

Facing page: 'Dorabella' and Troyte.

[Photos: Raymond Monk collection]

Troyte Griffith leaves the Birthplace after tea on 8 September 1938.

Facing page: Carice Elgar Blake at Woodend, 1937, (above) standing outside the front entrance and (below) in the study.

[Photos: Raymond Monk collection]

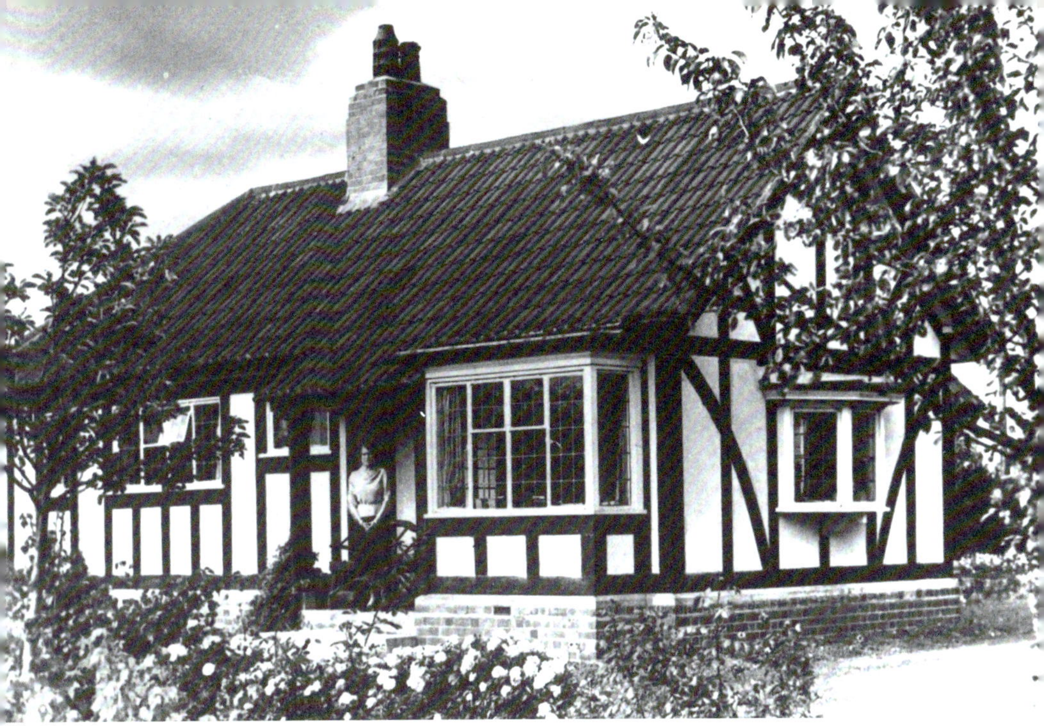

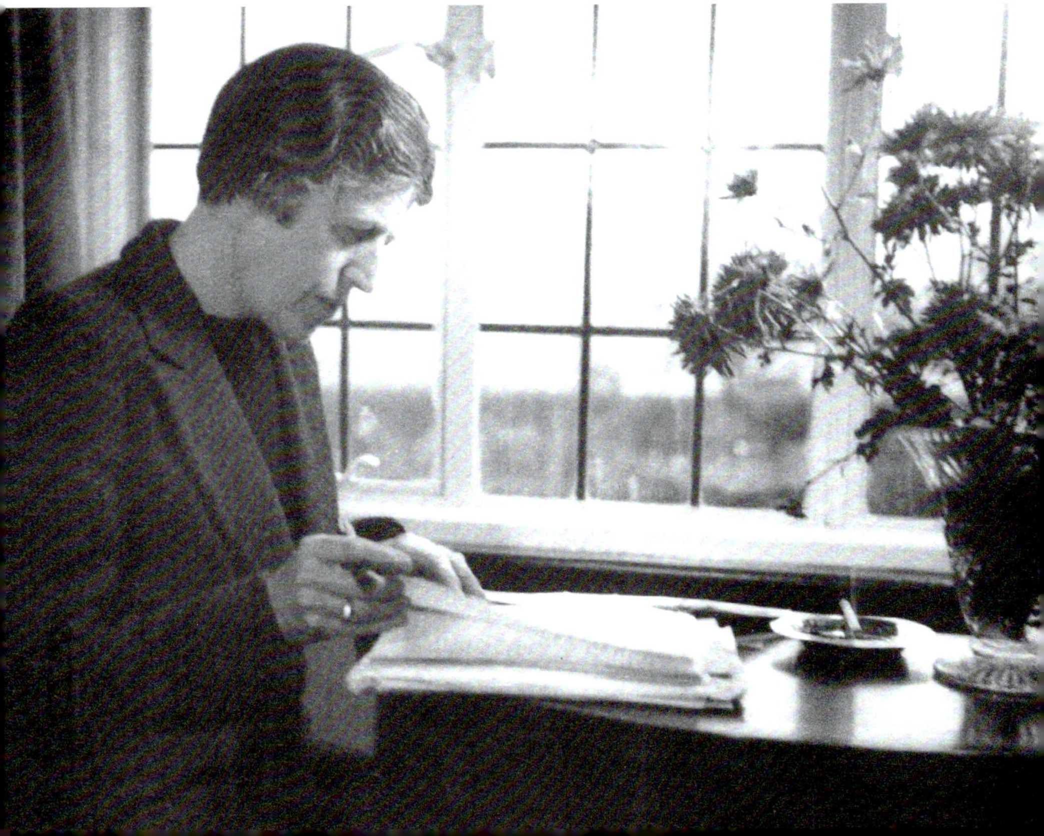

Left: The first curator: Helen Goodman talks to Raymond Monk in the porch of the Birthplace, c.1958.

Below: Dr Percy Young, Carice Elgar Blake and Yehudi Menuhin in the Birthplace garden, 12 May 1967.

Facing page: Herbert Howells and Yehudi Menuhin, 12 May 1967. In the background can be seen Winifred and Stanley Lambert, joint secretaries of the Elgar Society, and Society chairman A.T. ('Bertie') Shaw.

[Photos: Raymond Monk collection]

Richard Strauss: Photograph given 'to my revered friend E.Elgar'. Strauss conducted a concert of his works in Birmingham on 20 December 1904 that Elgar attended.

[Photo: Elgar Birthplace Museum]

Nancy Price as India in The Crown of India.

Joseph Mallord William Turner, *Dido Sitting ... of ... , l ... d ... C ... W ... R.T. ... (1832), ST ... G.B. ,*

William Dyce: Pegwell Bay-a Recollection of October 5th 1858 (1860). [Aberdeen Art Gallery]

William Bell Scott: Iron and Coal *(1861). [Wallington Hall, Tyneside]*

Appendix 3:
The Doughty Family & the 'Tune from Broadheath'

The Doughty family appear in the censuses of 1851 and 1861. In 1851 the Head of the family, George Doughty, was listed as a Spayer and Gelder aged 53 from St Johns. His wife, Sarah, came from Ashperton in Herefordshire and they had two unmarried children aged 28 and 18. The 1840 Tithe Apportionment shows George Doughty listed as a tenant of two plots (plecks) and as owner occupier of two further plots.

By 1861 Sarah Doughty, aged 68, was widowed and recorded as the 'Head' of the family. The only other resident at the time was a servant girl aged 16. Sarah Doughty had also become a shopkeeper. I believe it is fair to assume it was here that the Elgar children were sent to 'stay with some old people' and the possible location for the composition of 'the tune from Broadheath'. Doubts occur when we compare the note by Frank Elgar's wife, Mary Agnes, to the facts above. She refers to 'Mr & Mrs Doughty'. Frank Elgar was born in 1861 and would not have been old enough to have had his life threatened 'in the well' much before 1866 and, by then, George Doughty had then been dead at least 5 years. Mary Elgar was, however, writing from memory about a story, in turn, told to her.

But what of *The Wand of Youth* and its 'Woodland Glade intersected by a brook'? Was this something Elgar imagined or invented when explaining *The Wand of Youth* suites? Jerrold Northrop Moore in his interview with Mrs T.V. Davis from 1975 gets near the answer:

> On the question of water nearby; there were the deep drains (about 2 ft deep) everywhere; and it was part of Mr Davis's duties to keep these clear and deep. One went down on the other side of the eastern hedge from the cottage to the road. But there were also drains on either side of the road (not made up in those days). There was no water (except the little drain between the paths) in Mrs D's time <u>in</u> the garden. But in the place known as The Dingle (across the road, footpath leading in just north of Carice's bungalow 'Woodend' & over one field) there used to be quite a little brook, which in the Davis's time there was very thickly wooded and overgrown. (This in answer to my question about *The Wand of Youth* setting).

> Finally, one of 'Mrs D's' friends was Mrs Bowdin, who lived just north of the entrance to Broadheath Common. Here Sir Edward used to come as a boy in summer(?s), 'Mrs D' thinks not with family but alone.[104]

Appendix 4: Map of the vicinity of the Birthplace

It is unlikely that the ordnance survey map from 1884 would have shown much change to the area around the Birthplace in the 25 years since the Elgar family lived there. Although no fir trees are shown in or by the garden, the island of fir trees before the entrance to the driveway to Newbury House is clearly in evidence, as it is today.

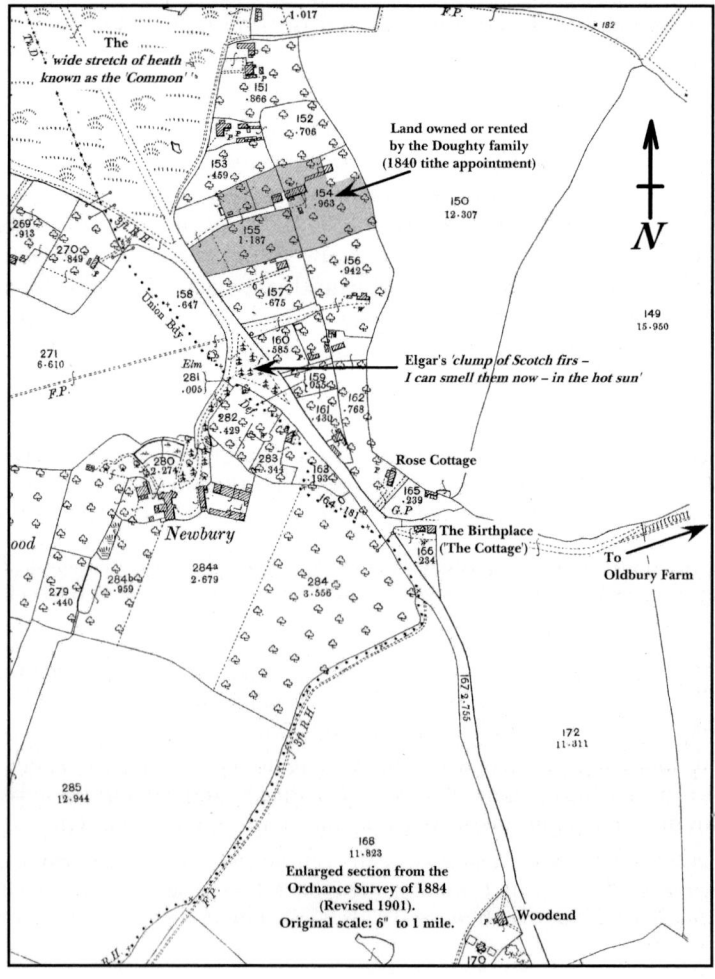

Notes and References

1   Thus I happily responded to a request from the Thames Valley Branch of the Elgar Society to talk about the Birthplace in February 2002. This short history is a much-expanded and altered version of that presentation, which was later repeated for the London Branch on 1 February 2003. Since making these presentations I realised further research was required to give a full history of the Birthplace – this has now been undertaken.

2   Arthur L. Salmon from his poem *Pleading* set by Elgar as Op.48.

3   The Birthplace, before the construction of the new road system around Worcester in the 1990's, was precisely 3½ miles by road from Worcester Cross.

4   Palmer, Christopher: *Herbert Howells – a centenary celebration* [London: Novello, 1978; repr.1992] 359–360. (From an interview Howells gave Richard Walker on 1 April 1971). It is probable that this visit occurred in 1932, for it was not until 1929 that the Elgar Brothers shop in Worcester closed following the death of Elgar's younger brother, Frank in 1928. Howells recalled the occasion when visiting the Birthplace in 1977, stating that he first visited the Birthplace in 1923 (*Elgar Society Newsletter* [January 1978] 5) when it is likely that the cottage was occupied by a George and Ruth Walford, both of whom appear on the electoral roll of 1920 when their residence is noted as Firs Cottage, Lower Broadheath. Herbert Howells (1891–1983), later became a trustee of the Birthplace Fund.

5   *The Musical Times* [June 1947].

6   Maine, Basil: *Elgar: his life and works* [London: Bell, 1933; repr. Bath: Cedric Chivers, 1973], Book 1, 'The Life', 1–2. 'Dick' was Richard Mountford, Elgar's valet and chauffeur.

7   Moore, J.N.: *Edward Elgar: the Windflower letters* [Oxford: OUP, 1989] 247. Lady Alice Stuart of Wortley (1862–1936), close friend and muse of Elgar.

8   Hubert or Philip Leicester quoted in McVeagh, Diana: *Edward Elgar* [London: Dent, 1955] 3.

9   Now College Precincts.

10 Report by Henry Austin, secretary of the Health of Town Society.

11 Harris, Joan: 'The Greatest of Blessings' in *A History of Worcester's Water Supply*, 1994, 8 (published on the internet).

12 Pipe, Lucy Elgar: 'Reflections' (MS at the Elgar Birthplace Museum).

13 Externally the rear elevation shows no evidence of chimneys having been constructed. However, there was a small corner chimney in the North West corner of the first floor. The Davis family recalled this being an extension from the kitchen below. (From a letter to the author from Vivienne McKenzie, 2004).

14 See appendix 1.

15 Pipe, Lucy Elgar: 'Reflections', *op.cit.* The birth-room wall has since been removed.

16   The Elgar servants included, at one time or another, an out-of-work actor, the children's nurse and a maid, Matilda Knott, who stayed with the family for thirty years or more.
17   Pipe, Lucy Elgar: 'Reflections', *op.cit.*
18   See Variation XIV.
19   Blake, Carice Elgar (1890–1970), MS notes of conversation with Hubert Leicester, c.1935 (MS held at the Elgar Birthplace).
20   It was John Leicester who obtained William Elgar's position as organist at St George's Church.
21   Pipe, Lucy Elgar: 'Reflections', *op.cit. La Traviata* was first performed at Teatro la Fenice, Venice, on 6 March 1853.
22   From *The Black Knight*, Op.25 from 1892, words from the poem by Henry Wadsworth Longfellow (1807–1882).
23   Pipe, Lucy Elgar: 'Reflections', *op.cit.*
24   See Simmons, K.E.L. and Marion: *The Elgars of Worcester* [The Elgar Society, 1984].
25   Moore, J.N.: 'Young Elgar at the Festival' in Redwood, C (ed): *An Elgar Companion* [Ashbourne: Sequoia Press, 1982] 26.
26   Readers will find a detailed re-telling of Elgar's early years in Moore, J.N.: *Edward Elgar: a creative life* [Oxford: OUP, 1984].
27   Extract of an Interview with Dr Edward Elgar by Cordova, Rupert de: *Strand Magazine* [May 1904] 538–9.
28   Moore, J.N.: 'Young Elgar at the Festival' in Redwood, *op.cit.,*30.
29   Blake, Carice Elgar, MS notes.
30   Helen Agnes 'Dot' Elgar (1864–1939), Elgar's youngest sister.
31   Letter dated 24 September 1940 by Mary Agnes Elgar (1859–1946). (MS at the Elgar Birthplace Museum). See also Appendix 3.
32   A note from the HMV Album 80, from 1929, quoted by Moore, J.N.: *Elgar: a life in photographs* [London: OUP, 1973] 12.
33   From a note for the *Hallé Magazine*.
34   Notes of an interview arranged by Jerrold Northrop Moore, 31 March 1975. (Manuscript held at the Birthplace). I have edited this slightly for the sake of clarity only.
35   Diary of Alice Elgar, 23 September 1895.
36   Plutarch: *Life of Alexander*, c.110.
37   Worcester Record Office 5557:926:11.
38   Sir Landon Ronald (1873–1938). Distinguished conductor and devoted interpreter of Elgar's music.
39   Sir Barry Jackson (1879–1961). Founder of the Birmingham Repertory Theatre and the Malvern Drama Festival, librettist of Elgar's unfinished opera, *The Spanish Lady*.
40   Sir Landon and Lady Ronald, Vera Hockman, Dora Powell and W.H. (Billy) Reed whom Carice always called 'Billie' and his wife who was known as 'James'.

41   Gaisberg signed himself 'F N Gaisberg of Washington DC'. Elgar's recordings were issued under the HMV label.

42   Samuel Henry Blake (1887–1939). Surrey farmer, husband of Elgar's daughter Carice. Philip Leicester (1887–1961) grand-son of John Leicester and eldest son of Hubert Leicester, Elgar's great friend from childhood. From 1926, Leicester lived with his wife, Nella, in 'The Homestead' on Lansdowne Crescent.

43   Sir Hugh Allen (1869–1946) Director of the RCM. H.C. Colles (1879–1943), critic and musicologist.

44   Sir Ivor Atkins (1869–1953) Organist and Master of the Choristers of Worcester Cathedral (1897–1950).

45   Percy Hull (1878–1968) Organist of Hereford Cathedral (1918–1949) and Alexander Brent Smith (1889–1950) composer and one-time director of music at Lancing College.

46   Margaret and Mary Elgar (see following note).

47   Agnes Elgar (née Walker) (1897–1978) the recently widowed wife of Elgar's nephew Francis Joseph Elgar (1894–1935). They had four daughters, Margaret Agnes Elgar, Mary Patricia Elgar and the twins Hilary Frances Elgar and Catherine Anne Elgar.

48   H.C. Colles.

49   Katharine Atkins, wife of Sir Ivor Atkins. She was Mayor of Worcester (1936–1937) and for a time a trustee of the Birthplace.

50   Astra Desmond (1898–1973) contralto and notable interpreter of 'The Angel' in *The Dream of Gerontius*.

51   A.T. Shaw and his wife Lydia. 'Bertie' Shaw was, among many other activities, Chairman of the Elgar Society (1952–1976).

52   Clare Stuart Wortley (1889–1945) only daughter of Charles (later Lord) and Alice Stuart Wortley.

53   The manuscripts were displayed in the Chappel Memorial Reading Room in College Green, alongside an exhibition of English watercolours and drawings.

54   In the first edition of the programme no advertisement was placed. The second edition was published one month before the festival.

55   During the week, visitors included Harold Darke, Basil Maine, Marjorie Ffrangçon Davies, W.H. Reed and his wife, H.C. Colles, Alan Webb, Walford Davies, Sir Hugh Allen, Ian Parrott and A.H. Fox Strangways. Bernard Shaw and his wife visited on 12 September.

56   This was a long day of substantial music-making. The morning concert began with Kodaly's *Te Deum* conducted by Sir Ivor Atkins, which was followed by Elgar's Violin Concerto with Albert Sammons the soloist and the orchestra conducted by Herbert Sumsion. Next came Vaughan Williams conducting his *Dona Nobis Pacem* and after the interval Lennox Berkeley conducted his *Domini est terra*, Atkins conducted Debussy's *The Blessed Damozel* and Sumsion Beethoven's Fifth Symphony. The evening performance of *The Dream of Gerontius* was conducted by Atkins, with soloists Heddle Nash,

Astra Desmond and Keith Falkner. It is fair to assume that the 'tea' at which
there was 'a terrific crowd' took place at the Birthplace. A photograph of
Troyte Griffith taken there towards evening adds credence to this assumption.

57   George Sinclair (Variation XI) and Basil Nevinson (Variation XII) were
      portrayed by Elgar in the *Variations* of 1899.
58   *Shockheaded Peter*, a suite for orchestra by W.H. Reed from August 1931.
59   Elgar's spaniel Marco. Mr Wang was a large handsome Chow owned by May
      Grafton.
60   Walter Kendall Stanton (1891–1978), Composer and Director of Music to the
      Midland Region of the BBC.
61   Hubert Leicester.
62   Interview with Margaret Elgar, 19 February 2002.
63   Margaret, Mary 'Pat', Hilary and Anne Elgar and their mother, Agnes.
64   Interview with Margaret Elgar, 19 February 2002.
65   Anthony Bernard (1891–1963) composer, conductor and pianist.
66   Walter Legge (1906–1979) of The Gramophone Company, then married to
      his first wife Nancy Evans, the mezzo-soprano.
67   Percy Hull and W.H. Reed. The 1939 Hereford Three Choirs Festival had
      been cancelled, at the last moment, prior to the outbreak of war. However,
      Reed had been conferred with the Lambeth degree of honorary Doctor of
      Music and this was presented on 5 September in the Hereford Deanery.
68   Margaret Elgar remembers the back room with its tin bath, which was filled
      from jugs of hot water. It was then the kitchen.
69   Margaret Elgar also remembers being sent out of Worcester to stay at
      Woodend during the Second World War and watching Carice busily typing
      labels. (Interview, 19 February 2002).
70   Vera Hockman (1896–1963), violinist and close friend of both Carice and her
      father. (Ivor Newton (1892–1981) pianist and accompanist. Taking one
      month at random, June 1943 saw 26 visitors to the Birthplace.
71   Moore, J.N.: *Elgar on Record* [London: OUP, 1974] 220–221.
72   *Elgar Society Journal*, Vol.VI, No.5 [May 1990] 8. Sybil Wohfeld (1903–1988).
73   From a note by Diana McVeagh, 2003.
74   Drew, John H.: 'Centenary Pilgrimage – A Memoir', *Elgar Society Journal*,
      Vol.III, No.4 [January 1984] 8.
75   *The Musical Times* [June 1957] 'Elgar Centenary Number'. Elgar's 1927
      summons is more than intriguing!
76   Sir Barry Jackson remained a trustee, but rarely attended meetings.
77   Mr R.G. Medley of Field Roscoe and Co. had replaced Mr C.D. Medley as
      Treasurer sometime during the 'missing years' 1936 to 1955.
78   Where the Elgar Centre is today.
79   Russell's film was first broadcast on 11 November 1962.
80   Michael Kennedy, letter to the author, 2003.
81   *The Kingdom* was recorded in 1968. Later Alan Webb organised a petition
      for the first recording of *The Apostles*.

82   The sign is still there – rusty, but just legible.

83   Raymond Monk, now the longest-serving trustee, proposed this tribute as the Elgar Centre was prepared for opening.

84   From a prologue to an uncompleted biography of Alice Elgar by Carice Elgar Blake, quoted in Young, Percy M.: *Alice Elgar, enigma of a Victorian lady* [London: Dobson, 1978] 13.

85   At the Birthplace Sir Adrian Boult is remembered in a small, but affectionate way. On the side gate into the Birthplace garden is affixed the sign: 'please Boult the gate'. This was first made for the five-barred gate at the end of the driveway, which joined the road below the stable block.

86   For an account of the formation of the United Kingdom Elgar Society and the problems associated with the finances of the Birthplace see Trott, M. (ed): *Half-Century* [Rickmansworth: Elgar Editions, 2001].

87   From a note by Raymond Monk, 2003.

88   Alan Webb, who taught Peter Pears at Lancing College and John Eliot Gardner at Bryanston School, died in December 1992

89   Vivienne Mckenzie, letter to the author, October 2003. Jack and Vivienne's marriage was blessed in Crown East Church on 13 July 1977, after which Nella Leicester hosted a party at The Homestead.

90   Wulstan Atkins MBE (1904–2003), only son of Sir Ivor and Lady Atkins. For most of this time Christopher Harmer was Vice-Chairman of the Foundation.

91   I have not identified all trustee appointments. It is now accepted practice that the Chairman of the Elgar Society will be invited to become a trustee. Christopher Robinson therefore succeeded Michael Pope. Both Michael Kennedy and Jerrold Northrop Moore resigned during the mid-1980s.

92   Almost simultaneously, Woodend and The Elms came on the market, but negotiations for the purchase of Rose Cottage were too advanced for any change of direction. It is not surprising the idea of the 'mini-museum' was quietly dropped, particularly when the Head Landlord (the Dean and Chapter of the Cathedral) expressed concern over the prospect of having a shop on the premises. The Elms, with its substantial garden, was subsequently purchased in 1987. The trustees hurriedly raised a bank loan when the property came on the market once more.

93   *Elgar Society Journal*, Vol.III, No.2 [May 1983] 11.

94   Elgar was musical director of the Powick Asylum Band from 1879 to 1884.

95   The death of Jim Bennett on 9 August 2003 reminds us of how much he contributed to the Birthplace at a time of great change and how tolerant he was of the disruption during his curatorship.

96   Mark Grafton for the Elgar family and Bob Montgomery for the Elgar Will Trust joined the Foundation Board in January 1999. However, the financial commitment of the Elgar Family came through the whole-hearted support of Elgar's eight, then surviving, great-nieces and nephews, sustaining a long and generous tradition. This generosity has also been matched by David Bowerman, currently Chairman of the Elgar Birthplace Trust.

97   *Elgar Society News*, No.15 [November 2001]29.
98   Jenkins, Simon: *England's Thousand Best Houses* [London, 2003] 853.
99   Webb, Alan: 'Elgar Houses' in *Elgar Society Newsletter* [September 1975] 29.
100 Nowadays the word 'yeoman' has largely fallen out of use which, for our purposes, fits the description from the 1933 edition of *The Oxford English Dictionary* of 'a man holding a small landed estate; a freeholder under the rank of gentleman; hence *vaguely* a commoner or countryman of respectable standing, *esp.* one who cultivates his own land'. Elgar, through his father, came from this stock, with many of his Kentish forebears happy to call themselves 'yeoman'.
101 This is the first written evidence that a building existed on the site.
102 The microfilmed copy of the Tithe Map shows the entry ' ... bury Cottage', the first letters being hidden. I believe it is fair to make the assumption that, in view of its proximity to Newbury House, that this is 'the cottage of Newbury House' and therefore called 'Newbury' Cottage. Presumably it was renamed 'The Firs' before the Elgar family moved there in 1856.There is also the possibility that it could have been named 'Oldbury' Cottage after Oldbury Farm, half a mile away, which would have been reached by the bridal track which runs along the north side of the Birthplace. However, I can trace no connection between the farm and what is now the Birthplace.
103 A receiver in the sense of a legally appointed receiver of monies.
104 Moore, Jerrold Northrop, 1975, MS notes.

Chapter Two

Elgar, Strauss and their Wives

Michael Kennedy

Seven years separated Elgar, born in 1857, and Strauss, born in 1864. A comparison of the two composers is illuminating because both achieved mastery of the post-Wagnerian symphony orchestra from startlingly different backgrounds. Neither had academic musical training, for although Strauss attended Munich University, he read philosophy, aesthetics and the history of art. Strauss was born into a fairly affluent family (his mother was from the Pschorr brewing family) and his father, principal horn in the Munich Court Orchestra under Hermann Levi, was acknowledged as Germany's leading virtuoso on the instrument. His father's colleagues gave music lessons in his childhood, and his early compositions were played either by the semi-professional orchestra his father conducted or, on occasions, by the court orchestra. His aunt, who was an excellent mezzo-soprano, sang his first songs. By the time he was sixteen, Levi had conducted Strauss's First Symphony. Some two years later, Hans von Bülow and the Meiningen Orchestra had taken up his wind Serenade, Op.7, and he was only twenty when his Second Symphony had its première, at a New York Philharmonic concert.

Whereas Munich was a centre of culture of all kinds, mid-nineteenth-century Worcester was not. Elgar, like Strauss, was born into a musical family, but it was not an affluent one. His father was an organist at St George's Roman Catholic Church and owned a music shop. Local musicians gave Elgar lessons, but there was no orchestra on which he could learn his craft, and his early compositions were religious choral pieces for the choir of St George's, wind quintets written for a group of friends, and some light orchestral pieces. He conducted the band at a lunatic asylum and arranged quadrilles for the staff dances there. Plans to become a solo violinist were abandoned and he had to make do with playing in small provincial orchestras or in the first desks of the orchestra at the Three Choirs Festival. He was twenty-seven when a modest orchestral piece, *Sevillana,* was performed at the Crystal Palace concerts. After his marriage to Caroline Alice Roberts, in 1889, he moved to London but this did not advance his career, although he heard a lot of music; so he returned to Malvern in 1891 to teach schoolgirls the violin, a job he hated, and to continue his life as a violinist, organist and conductor of *ad hoc* orchestras. In 1890 came a request from the Worcester Festival for an orchestral work; Elgar composed the concert-overture *Froissart*, Op.19, in which his self-taught mastery of the orchestra was first apparent.

This is a good point at which to match Elgar's career with that of Strauss. In 1889 Elgar sold, outright, his *Salut d'amour*, in versions for violin and piano and other combinations. On 1 October that year, Strauss was appointed third conductor at the Weimar Court Opera, and two months later he conducted the first performance of his tone-poem *Don Juan*. This work within a very short time was to make him the most talked-about young composer in Germany. During the 1890s Elgar achieved fame in the Midlands with the dramatic cantatas *The Black Knight* (1893) and *King Olaf* (1896). His oratorio *The Light of Life* was performed at the Worcester Festival of 1896. His name first came to the fore in London in 1897 with the *Imperial March*, Op.32, written for Queen Victoria's Diamond Jubilee; this was followed by the cantata *Caractacus*, at the Leeds Festival of 1898. But when he returned from the festivals at which the works were performed, it was to the chore of teaching schoolgirls and serving behind the counter in his father's shop. Not until June 1899, when Hans Richter conducted the first performance of the *Variations*, was Elgar recognised as an important composer and then chiefly by foreign conductors who took up the work Richter had praised.

The 1890s were productive years for Strauss. In 1890 he conducted the first performances of two more of his tone-poems, *Macbeth* and *Tod und Verklärung*. In 1894 he conducted the première of his first opera, *Guntram*, on which he had been working for several years. The role of heroine was sung by the soprano Pauline de Ahna, who had been his pupil and whom he married on 10 September, presenting her with a bridal gift of four great songs, including *Morgen!* They performed together at Bayreuth that year when he conducted *Tannhäuser* and she sang Elisabeth. He left Weimar that year to become an assistant to Levi at Munich, and was appointed conductor of the Berlin Philharmonic for the 1894–5 season. Although *Guntram* was a failure, *Till Eulenspiegel* in 1895 and *Also sprach Zarathustra* in 1896 continued the success of his tone-poems. He succeeded Levi as chief conductor of Munich Court Opera in 1896, but left there in 1898 to become conductor of the Royal Court Opera in Berlin. In 1898 *Don Quixote*, perhaps the greatest of his tone-poems, was first performed, and in March 1899 he conducted the première of its successor, *Ein Heldenleben*. Both new works caused controversy. Some regarded Strauss as the chief purveyor of cacophony. But he was world-famous and in constant demand.

The lives of Elgar and Strauss began to intertwine in 1897. Since 1893 the Elgars had spent summer holidays in Bavaria, often staying in Garmisch, which they loved. This was fifteen years before Strauss made his home there, and Elgar's memories of those holidays are enshrined in his part-songs *From the Bavarian Highlands* (1895). The Elgars stayed in Munich, and it was there in 1897 that they heard Strauss conduct *Don Giovanni* and *Tristan und Isolde,* and were introduced to him. Elgar could scarcely have guessed that less than five years later, in 1902, Strauss (at the suggestion of the financier Edward Speyer, who was a friend of both men) would conduct *Cockaigne* in Berlin. Elgar sent him some notes about tempi. In May of that year Julius Buths conducted *The Dream of Gerontius* in Düsseldorf at the Lower Rhine Festival. Strauss was there to conduct Liszt's *Faust Symphony* in the same programme (annoying Elgar by over-running rehearsal time allotted to Buths for *Gerontius*); but at a dinner after the concert Strauss unexpectedly rose to speak about English music. After some less than complimentary remarks about Arne ('somewhat less than Handel'), Sterndale Bennett ('less than Mendelssohn')[1] and some Englishmen of a later date, he declared that 'the gap has been closed' and raised his glass 'to the welfare and success of the first English progressivist, Meister Edward Elgar, and of the young progressive school of English composers'.[2]

Elgar was understandably proud of being called 'Meister' by Strauss. It was worth 'years of anguish',[3] he told his publisher. But Strauss's speech did not go down well in certain quarters in England. The names omitted from his brief history of English composition were noted, especially by Stanford, who hated Strauss's music and was cool about Elgar's. It is remarkable that *Gerontius* had made such an impression on Strauss, who did not like religious music. No doubt he recognised the high quality and imagination of Elgar's orchestration and perhaps noticed the similarity between the sickroom in the Prelude to *Gerontius* and that depicted in *Tod und Verklärung*! At any rate, in the 1930s he was still recommending the Prelude (and the *Variations*) to German conductors, and his praise of the work, together with Buths's championship of it, probably led to the several performances in Germany around 1903 and to the Vienna

1 – Notes and references for this chapter appear on page 57.

première on 16 November 1905, when Franz Schalk conducted. The bass role was sung by Richard Mayr – later to be an incomparable Baron Ochs in *Der Rosenkavalier*.

The two composers met again in London in June 1902, when they had supper together after a concert of Strauss's music which Elgar found 'absolutely great – wonderful and terrifying but somewhat cynical. *He* is a real clever good man'.[4] In December of that year Elgar attended the first London performance of *Ein Heldenleben*, which Strauss conducted. They had dinner together the evening before the concert and at a party afterwards at Edward Speyer's house, Strauss asked Elgar: 'Friend, did it satisfy you?' Elgar replied: 'Absolutely'.[5] His nickname for Strauss was 'Richard Coeur de Lion – the Lionheart'. At this time Elgar was writing *The Apostles*, far removed from the aggressive secularity of Strauss's autobiographical tone-poem. Can one imagine an English composer of that date writing music about his love-life with his wife? Granville Bantock, perhaps. Yet *Ein Heldenleben* left its mark on Elgar. During the next year he began to make sketches for a symphony in the same key as *Ein Heldenleben*, E flat major, and although it was to be eight years before the symphony was completed, it is possible to detect a connection between the impulsive start of *Heldenleben* and that of the Second Symphony and between the glowingly tranquil endings of both works. And in 1912, in *The Music Makers*, Elgar borrowed from the 'Works of Peace' section of *Ein Heldenleben* Strauss's use of self-quotation. Oddly, though, an English critic in 1908 had made a direct comparison between *Ein Heldenleben* and the First Symphony. 'In both', he wrote,

> we see a personality struggling against opposing elements, in both the central figure arouses sympathy by the union of indomitable purpose with purely human despondencies. But there the likeness ends. The symphony is more spiritual than the tone-poem. Both seem to speak of love, but in *Heldenleben* it is a human love, in the symphony it suggests the amor Intellectualis Dei.[6]

True enough. There is no eroticism to be found anywhere in Elgar and although we know that the Second Symphony is partly about his love for Alice Stuart Wortley, it is a chivalric love.

Strauss can be traced, too, as a potent influence on the next major orchestral work by Elgar after their meetings in 1902. This was the concert-overture, also in E flat – in effect a tone-poem – *In the South*. Its leaping opening calls to mind *Don Juan*. Elgar wrote the theme in 1899 as one of the 'moods of Dan' (G. R. Sinclair's bulldog) inscribed in

Sinclair's visitors' book. This was 'Dan triumphant after a fight'. But there is a similarity between Elgar's writing for strings in parts of *In the South* and Strauss's in a much earlier work, *Aus Italien* (1884). In their response to Italy, both men found a similar warmth, exhilaration and poetry. Elgar was rather wary about Strauss being mentioned in connection with his concert-overture. When A. J. Jaeger was proposing to begin his analysis of it with a comparison with Strauss's tone-poem, Elgar put him off. 'Not necessary', he wrote. 'Strauss puts music in a very low position when he suggests it must hang on some commonplace absurdity for its very life'.[7] When he had written *Falstaff*, in 1913, Elgar was at pains to point out that it did not provide a series of incidents with connecting links 'such as we have for example in Richard Strauss's *Heldenleben* and *Symphonia Domestica*. All I have striven to do is to paint a musical portrait'.[8] But there are more incidents in *Falstaff* than in either of the Strauss works he cites and, although careful not to mention it, Elgar may have taken *Don Quixote* as his model for *Falstaff*, Shakespeare doing duty for Cervantes.

Strauss and Elgar dined together in Birmingham in December 1904 after Strauss had conducted four of his own works in the Town Hall – *Don Juan*, *Tod und Verklärung*, the Violin Concerto and *Ein Heldenleben*. By this date Strauss had completed his *Symphonia Domestica*, which he conducted in London in February 1905. Strauss is mentioned several times in the lectures Elgar gave at Birmingham University in 1905 and 1906 – 'the greatest genius of our day'[9] was one reference – not by any means a generally held view at that date. When discussing imitation, Elgar mentioned those who transferred to their own works 'shrieks from the most livid pages of Richard Strauss. But they seem carefully to avoid all that is melodious, and I will add sublime, in Strauss and settle with considerable affection on what it is easiest to reproduce'.[10] There are plenty of shrieks and livid pages in the opera *Salome*. When Elgar went to America in 1907, he was met in New York by a group asking him to lead a prayer meeting to protest against this work being staged at the Metropolitan Opera House (where in fact it was taken off after one performance). Elgar vehemently refused what he described to Delius many years later as 'this staggering and screamingly absurd proposal'.[11] While in America, he again described Strauss as 'the greatest genius of the age', adding 'His later works I like best of all, much distinguished opinion to the contrary notwithstanding. His *Don Juan* is the greatest masterpiece of the present, and his *Heldenleben* and *Zarathustra* I find almost as inspiring'.[12]

After the First World War, Elgar was quick to mend fences. Hearing that Adrian Boult was leaving for a tour of Germany, he sent Strauss a message of goodwill, and before Strauss's return to London in January 1922, he wrote: 'I send you a word of warm welcome and an assurance that your return to our country gives the greatest pleasure to myself and to very many of my musical countrymen'.[13] Elgar and Bernard Shaw took him to lunch at the United Services Club where he met, at Elgar's instigation, a number of younger British composers. Elgar had at some time proposed that they should collaborate in an orchestration of Bach's Fantasia and Fugue in C minor (BWV 537) with Elgar transcribing the Fugue and Strauss the Fantasia. Elgar fulfilled his side of the bargain and later added the Fantasia when nothing was forthcoming from Strauss.

In the remaining years of Elgar's life, contacts between them grew fewer. Elgar was virtually silent where composition was concerned, whereas Strauss continued to write ambitious operas. Yet both were conscious that in the opinions of many, their stars had set and that they were out of favour and out of fashion – at least when compared with their pre-1918 heyday. When in 1933 Elgar began to return to creative life and to work on an opera, *The Spanish Lady*, based on Ben Jonson's play *The Devil is an Ass*, he ruefully commented 'Just my luck', when he was told that Strauss was at work on *The Silent Woman* (*Die schweigsame Frau*), based on Jonson's *Epicene*.

In their personal lives, Elgar and Strauss were blessed with wives who were almost obsessively devoted to their husbands' well-being and the furtherance of their careers. Both Alice Roberts and Pauline de Ahna were small, not particularly beautiful, and very forceful and with a determination to keep their man's nose to the grindstone. Both were older than their husbands, Alice by nine years (born 1848), Pauline by less than two (born 1863). Both were the daughters of generals. Alice's father was Major-General Sir Henry Roberts, whose military career was mainly in India, where she was born. He died in 1860. Pauline's father was Major-General Adolph de Ahna of the Bavarian army, who seems to have served most of his time behind a desk rather than in the field. He was a good amateur musician and had a pleasant baritone voice. He would give occasional recitals at which he would sing extracts from Wagner, including some of Sachs's arias from *Die Meistersinger*.

Her father having died when she was only twelve, Alice faced the fate of many an only daughter – looking after mother. They returned to England to live at Redmarley d'Abitot in Worcestershire; she had had piano lessons in Brussels and studied harmony. She wrote poetry and had had a two-volume novel published. In October 1886 she became Elgar's pupil for piano accompaniment and travelled to Malvern once a week. When her mother died, in 1887, she moved to Malvern. Elgar set one of her poems, and the song, *The Wind at Dawn*, was published in 1888. In September of that year they became engaged. Her relations were horrified. Not only was Elgar a penniless musician, he was Roman Catholic (she was not, at this time) and the son of a tradesman. One of her aunts cut her out of her will. Undeterred, she went ahead and they were married on 8 May 1889. Why, on the slightest evidence, she was convinced that her Edward was a musical genius we shall never know. But she was, and she was right. She devoted every waking hour to his welfare, even later almost ignoring the needs of their daughter. 'The care of a genius is enough of a lifework for any woman',[14] she said. Everything was arranged so that he could work without interruption. Those who knew him and knew he was lazy by nature believed that without Alice we would have had none of his music.

In 1887 Elgar was giving Alice piano-accompaniment lessons. Strauss spent his summer holiday that year at Feldafing with his uncle and aunt. Their neighbours were the de Ahnas. General de Ahna asked Strauss if he would give some singing lessons to his daughter Pauline, who had been studying at the Munich School of Music. It was not love at first sight. Strauss was already involved with a married woman, Dora Wihan. After 1889 he invited Pauline to sing as a guest artist with his opera company at Weimar. Her temperament was already unpredictable. In 1891, for instance, he wrote to her: 'You are now so set on going your own way that my presence and influence could only seem a burden to you'.[15] She sang many roles at Weimar with Strauss conducting, including Hänsel in Humperdinck's new opera and Isolde, but it was not until 1893 that their relationship blossomed. Although Pauline later liked to pretend to others that she married 'beneath her', the truth is that she was hesitant about accepting Strauss's proposal of marriage and tried to extricate herself from the engagement for other reasons. 'Will I be capable of being what you want and what you deserve?' she wrote to him. 'I'm afraid it will fail … We don't need to marry so soon – let's find all the happiness we can in our careers'.[16] She knew he was an ambitious composer and conductor and she herself obviously had a promising career ahead of her, which perhaps she was loath to give up for marriage. But her father and sister were furious with her. 'He'll get fed up', they told her – she would never find anyone better.

Strauss cast Pauline as the heroine Freihild (and another of his pupils, the tenor Heinrich Zeller, in the title-role) of his opera *Guntram* for the work's première, in May 1894. He wrote later of an amusing incident: 'In . . . one of the last rehearsals, when I had to interrupt Zeller time and time again, we at last came to Pauline's scene in Act 3, which she obviously knew. In spite of this she did not feel sure of herself and apparently envied Zeller because he had been given so many chances of 'repeating'. Suddenly she stopped singing and asked me "Why don't you interrupt me?" I replied, "Because you know your part". With the words "I want to be interrupted", she threw the piano score ... at my head but, to the delight of the orchestra, it landed on the desk of the second violinist'.[17]

Legend says that she stormed off to her dressing-room followed by an angry Strauss. They emerged engaged to be married. There are many stories of the quarrels between them and of Pauline's disparaging remarks about him and his music, some of them true, no doubt, others exaggerated. Much of it, as Lotte Lehmann perceived, was a kind of act or game put on for their benefit as well as for that of outsiders. Music was a strong bond between them. They gave many recitals together and he regarded her as the best interpreter of his songs. Her retirement from the concert platform, in 1906, was the chief of several reasons why he wrote no more songs until 1918. Thereafter she must have been of incalculable assistance to him with advice on writing operatic roles. They were married for fifty-five years and there is no suggestion that Strauss ever looked at another woman, or she at another man. His parents and sister found her hard to get on with, but he understood her perfectly. He wrote in 1895 to his parents describing Pauline's 'unthinking, excited, over-boisterous but essentially good-hearted, childlike and naive manner. I cannot play forever the unhappily unsuccessful explainer of the various characteristics of my wife whom I chose after very mature deliberation, and love and honour in spite of her faults'.[18]

There was one mishap in the marriage and it occurred in the summer of 1903, when Strauss was having a few days' rest on the Isle of Wight (where the Elgars had spent their honeymoon) after a Strauss festival in London at which Willem Mengelberg and the Concertgebouw Orchestra of Amsterdam had performed several of his works. While he was away, Pauline had attended to his mail at their Berlin home and opened a letter from a woman called Mitzi Mücke, who mentioned meeting him in a Berlin bar, where he had promised her tickets for the opera. Pauline immediately assumed the worst and sent a telegram to Strauss on the Isle of Wight to say she had started divorce proceedings. Strauss was mystified and shocked but wrote her an amusing letter saying he had never been in the bar mentioned and did not know any Mitzi Mücke.[19] Ironically, he was just beginning to sketch the *Symphonia Domestica* on his holiday. He asked a lawyer friend to make inquiries and discovered that Fraulein Mücke had in fact met a conductor called Stransky. She confused the names and found Strauss's address in the telephone book. So peace was restored. Although Strauss made light of it, he was undoubtedly shaken, and nearly twenty years later he used the incident as the plot of his opera *Intermezzo*, for which he wrote his own libretto, much of it based on true-to-life remarks by both Pauline and himself. 'What a relief when you go, you get in the way', says the 'Pauline' character to her conductor-husband as he leaves for an engagement in Vienna. 'Have you let off enough steam to last two months?' he asks her. 'Be careful then', she says, 'sit in the middle of the carriage of the train and when you go out at night, turn your collar up high'. And when he has left she sings: 'My dearest husband, he is *so* good, *so* faithful. O these long, lonely, weary evenings here'.

Intermezzo is not the only work in which she appears. The hero's consort in *Ein Heldenleben* is Pauline, disguised as a solo violin. Strauss wrote to a friend: 'It's my wife I wanted to portray. She's very complex, very much a woman, a little depraved, something of a flirt, never twice alike'.[20] Their home-life, including their bedroom-life, is illustrated in the *Symphonia Domestica* and there are elements of her in many of the operas besides *Intermezzo* – in *Elektra*, as the Prima Donna in *Ariadne auf Naxos* (when she refers to the comedienne Zerbinetta: 'Me on the same stage with a person like that? What are you thinking of?'), the Dyer's Wife in *Die Frau ohne Schatten* (in this case Hofmannsthal's portrait of Pauline) and others. At the end of his life, in the *Four Last Songs*, he set a poem about an old couple, at the end of their life, walking into the sunset. After he died, in 1949, she went to pieces. 'I never knew anyone could weep so much',[21] her daughter-in-law said.

Elgar's only music portrait of Alice is the first of the *Variations*, 'C.A.E.', music of a tenderness and grace that suggests a tall, stately creature rather than the dumpy, busy little woman Alice was. But the music is a tribute, written after nearly ten years of marriage, to her faith in and loving care for him. She knew he liked to have young pretty women, such as 'Dorabella', around him and she must have known that his feelings for their friend Alice Stuart Wortley went far beyond companionship, but she was never jealous and never intervened. She knew that whatever these women gave him, she gave him security and the capacity for work. She wrote the words for the six poems he set in *From the Bavarian Highlands*, music that captures their close domesticity. He set other poems of hers, notably 'Love Alone Will Stay' that became 'In Haven' in *Sea Pictures*. She ruled the bar-lines on his manuscript paper and wrote in the names of the instruments, all to save him time and trouble. She helped him correct proofs, and when a work was completed it was she who posted it to the publisher. She resorted to her own savings when they were short of money. She organised everything when they moved house. She wanted him to live grandly in London, as befitted his position, and when this proved a mistake, she found an isolated cottage for them in Sussex where he could have peace and quiet, even though she was bored there. After she died, in 1920, he was bereft, and it is no coincidence that he wrote nothing of real consequence in the next decade, until a final spurt of energy produced an opera and a third symphony, both unfinished. All Elgarians should be grateful to her for the diary she kept and from which it is possible to re-construct Elgar's activities and opinions almost day-by-day. We may smile at its continual references to 'E's beautiful music' and at its intolerance of any criticism of him, but are moved, also, by its loyalty and courage.

We can leave these remarkable people with a rather touching picture of them in 1909, when the Elgars visited the Strausses at the Garmisch villa into which they had moved the previous year. Strauss wanted to show Elgar some treasures, and Pauline, with a bunch of keys under her skirt, unlocked the cabinet for them. Later in the afternoon the Elgars wandered in the Alpine scenery, as if they were preparing to be characters in *An Alpine Symphony*.

This essay is based on lectures given to the London Branch of the Elgar Society (on 3 March 1998) and to the Richard Strauss Society. Both lectures were illustrated with recorded examples of music but it would be impracticable to indicate these in the text. For those interested, the music was chosen from the following works:

ELGAR: *Sevillana, Froissart, Caractacus, The Dream of Gerontius, Variations,* Second Symphony, *In the South, From the Bavarian Highlands, Sea Pictures,* Fantasia and Fugue in C minor (Bach)

STRAUSS: *Don Juan, Tod und Verklärung, Ein Heldenleben, Aus Italien, Intermezzo, Die Frau ohne Schatten, Four Last Songs.*

Notes and References

1   Recorded by Elgar in his lecture 'A Future For English Music' given on 16 March 1905. See Young, Percy M. (ed): *A Future for English Music and Other Lectures by Edward Elgar* [London: Dobson, 1968] 43.

2   *The Times,* 23 May 1902.

3   Elgar to Alfred Littleton [23 May 1902] in Moore, Jerrold Northrop (ed): *Elgar and his Publishers: letters of a creative life* [Oxford: OUP, 1987] Vol.1, 357.

4   Elgar to Nicholas Kilburn, 7 June 1902 in Moore, J.N.: *Edward Elgar: a creative life* [Oxford: OUP, 1984] 369.

5   Elgar to A. Jaeger, 10 December 1902 in Moore: *Publishers, op.cit.,* Vol.1, 380.

6   *The Star,* 4 December 1908.

7   Elgar to A. Jaeger, 13 August 1904 in Moore: *Publishers, op.cit.,* Vol.2, 577.

8   Interview with 'Gerald Cumberland', *The Daily Citizen,* 18 July 1913.

9   Elgar's lecture 'Retrospect' given on 13 December 1905. See Young, *op.cit.,* 207.

10 Young, *op.cit.,* 51.

11 Elgar to Delius, 25 December 1933 in Moore, J.N. (ed): *Edward Elgar: letters of a lifetime* [Oxford: OUP, 1990] 478-9.

12 Interview *Chicago Inter-Ocean,* 7 April 1907.

13 Elgar to Strauss, 12 January 1922 in Moore: *Lifetime, op.cit.,* 361.

14 Alice Elgar diary, 24 January 1914.

15 Strauss to Pauline de Ahna, July 1891. See Kennedy, Michael: *Richard Strauss, Man, Musician, Enigma* [Cambridge: CUP, 1999] 66.

16 Pauline de Ahna to Strauss, 24 March 1894, *ibid.,* 81

17 Strauss, 'Reminiscences of the First Performance of My Operas' in Lawrence, L.J. (tr): *Recollections and Reflections* [London, 1953] 147.

18 Strauss, R.: letter to his parents in Schuh, W. (ed): *Briefe an die Eltern 1882–1906* [Zurich, 1954] 201–2.

19 Kennedy, *op.cit.,* 95–96.

20 Strauss to Romain Rolland, *ibid.,* 92.

21 Alice Strauss, *ibid.,* 395.

Chapter Three

'Now He Belongs to the Big World'
The Historical Elgar

Carl Newton

Introduction

At 7.45 a.m. on 23 February 1934, Edward Elgar's music was cut free from its creator to take its chance before the judgement seat of future opinion. Its creator himself, on the other hand, was from that moment entrapped for ever in his historical context. As the first home-grown composer since Purcell about whom the English could boast, he inevitably became, even before his death, an icon of Englishness and cultural chauvinism. In consequence he had to be well defended, and over time he acquired a breastwork of memoirs, surrounded by a glacis swept by the big guns of musicology. But history shows that even apparently impregnable fortresses can be taken – and it is important that this one should. The music will take care of itself; its creator as an historical personage needs a more positive approach. The issues are legion. What educational, cultural, and religious factors influenced him? What were his real motives in life, not to mention those of his wife, his daughter, Jaeger, Reed and Alice Stuart Wortley (who seems doomed for ever to be the silent ghost at the Elgar feast)? How did contemporaries, outside the musical Mafia and his own epigones, actually view him and his music? How do his career and opinions reflect contemporary mores? What do they tell us of the England in which he grew up and worked?

How can it be believed that Elgar was a shy man? No one in English history was more self-promoting, though, no doubt, few have been so subtle about it. He presents a major opportunity for the interpretation, in the context of the society, economics, and politics of the time, of a remarkably well-documented middle-class life. The late-nineteenth-century English bourgeoisie is typified in him. He is an extraordinary case of the 'Wiener Thesis' (that once they had achieved success the English middle class were content to rest on their laurels), as applied to creative art. Of late, music, sport and holiday-making have all been reinterpreted in terms of 'new' social history. If the work of David Russell, Derek Birley, and John Walton makes it impossible to write a good history of England without reference to the social significance of the music hall, W.G. Grace, and Blackpool, it should not be possible without a reference to Edward Elgar either.

The great English historian A.J.P. Taylor was wont to urge his students to 'write history not anecdote'. A serious problem in approaching Elgar as an historical figure is the massive encrustation of anecdote which has to be chipped off to reveal a once-living human being, someone who had a locale of time and place, paid taxes, had a vote, read newspapers, earned a living and had political views. We know the names he gave his dogs and his bicycle (even the make of tyres he used) and we know all about water butts and parrots. Needless to say we know a great deal about the music. But what do we know about the historical context in which the life was lived and the music created? To what extent is Elgar a paradigm of his age and nation? Was he really the devout Catholic, enthusiastic Imperialist, frightened conservative, inveterate gong-gatherer he has, at one time or another, been called?

There are three main types of original source for Elgar's life: memoirs of acquaintances; Elgar's own correspondence and writings; and the archives of organisations with which he had contact. The writers of memoirs range from the acerbic Rosa Burley, through the romantic Vera Hockman to the effervescent Dora Penny. All are tainted by the fact that they would have remained unheard of had they not chanced to meet Elgar. They were determined to make the most of the opportunity.

Are the original letters any more reliable? In some respects not, for Elgar's own words can be very misleading on major issues. He was quite capable of putting what we would today call 'positive spin' on events, even more perhaps, 'negative spin'. Another difficulty with the letters is that we know that someone tampered with them. (Dr Moore believes that this was Carice, on the rather curious ground that she was employed by MI5 during the War. Perhaps, but if so one can only say that the Germans cannot have been seriously inconvenienced by her activities.) Elgar may himself have destroyed letters he received. There is also the intriguing possibility that whoever did the censoring may have been clever enough to distract our attention from their real objective.

Research has concentrated so heavily on Elgar's own letters that the third type of source has hardly been tapped. This is mainly because no scholar has produced the kind of modern, wide-ranging and in-depth biography, which for example, Fiona McCarthy, Juliet Barker, and Roy Foster have produced on Morris, the Brontes, and Yeats respectively.

Again there are problems in tracking down material and in interpretation. Yet the indications are that this source could yield rich, and sometimes disconcerting, returns.

When we turn to the secondary sources we find another problem. There are a number of serviceable Elgars available. There is the Catholic composer reaching apogee in *The Dream of Gerontius* and never quite touching this level again. There is the disadvantaged boy struggling against the English class system. There is the noble creative artist and perfect English gentleman exhibiting all the lovable characteristics thereof. There is the shrewd money-obsessed provincial determined to beat the academic establishment at its own game by clever manipulation of the media. There is the out-and-out Conservative and jingo imperialist, writing music to celebrate British superiority. All these views have been expressed over the last fifty years, and all have some elements of truth, but they are representations of the Elgar the writers wish to see; most are flawed by a failure to set Elgar in any sort of meaningful historical context.

Another issue is that the biographies have a significant imbalance. The years from 1857 to 1889 were critical in Elgar's development and they constitute 41% of his life. The post-1945 biographies devote, on average, no more than 10% of their space to this period. Yet Maine's, published before Elgar's death and which is, in consequence, the nearest to an autobiography we have, actually has 18%. It may also be noted that this work devotes 21% to Elgar's life *after* 1920. Could it be that, having persuaded ourselves that Alice Elgar played a key role we are skewing the story to underpin the assumption? Elgar himself, if Maine's testimony is anything to go by, had a more balanced view than his later biographers did, and we have to remember that he was a single man for his first thirty-two years and a widower for the last thirteen.

Then there are references in general historical works. Not always accurate in detail, but as the authors are professional historians, applying skills and knowledge from a non-musical viewpoint, they can provide a different dimension. Many are listed in the bibliography and some are specifically mentioned below.

So much for the sources, what about the thesis? It is that Elgar, in everything but his genius, was a typical product of his class, nation and time; that he was strongly influenced in his attitudes by contemporary cultural, social, and economic conditions and that he was, despite his quite deliberate attempts to hide the fact, a very hard-nosed businessman. He was a paradigm of his England, but it is important to identify the nature of that England. I seek to demonstrate that setting Elgar in historical context provides adequate explanation for much of his behaviour, without recourse to deep psychological analysis. This is not to say that the psyche is unimportant, but, like electricity, it is only visible when it meets the resistance provided by environment and events. I believe also, like Occam, that the most rational and obvious explanation for something is most likely to be correct. I have read or been told that the Third Symphony is a riposte to Fascism; that Elgar turned to chamber music because he had his tonsils out; and that he wrote *The Starlight Express* because he had become interested in Jungian psychology. None of these is a believable explanation.

Elgar himself had a very clear idea of how he wanted his life to read and from the beginning of his fame set about creating a suitable mythical version. With the assistance of those biographers whose works he and his wife carefully 'tuned', and which have, too often, been followed subsequently, this version runs something like this:–

> A boy, born in disadvantaged circumstances in a country cottage, hears music in the air as he moons around on riverbanks and on the Malvern Hills. He is looked down on because his father is a shop-keeper and, his career blocked by poverty, he has to play in an asylum orchestra and take pupils. He has the good fortune to meet and marry a woman socially and financially superior to himself, who, realising his genius and sacrificing her own considerable literary talents, devotes the rest of her life to inspiring his work and supporting him. He suffers a crisis of faith preventing the completion of his series of oratorios, and despite the popularity of some of his works, adequate recognition eludes him. The Great War so devastates him that he retires to Sussex to console himself by writing chamber works. His wife dies and, grief-stricken by the event, he abandons composition and spends the rest of his life in creative near silence.

The ineffable Romantic charm of this version should not blind us to its obvious untruth. That some biographers have too easily accepted it can be put down to the fact that, apart from composition, Elgar had a fundamentally boring life. He did not go blind, like Handel, deaf like Beethoven, or mad like Schumann. He was not seared in war, like Vaughan Williams. He did not suffer racial prejudice like Coleridge Taylor, or political persecution like Shostakovitch. He lost no one close to him in South Africa, on the *Titanic*, or in the First World War. Indeed this essay could be entitled 'Edward Elgar: An Incredibly English Life'. In consequence, having tonsillitis and falling off a bicycle have been taken as life crises, and turning to symphonic music has been ascribed to loss of religious faith. In the absence of real traumas in their subject's life it is always tempting for biographers to make them up.

The first section of this essay is devoted to the economic, social and cultural environment and an examination of Elgar's own finances; the second to Elgar's politics and involvement in political events, with a brief examination of his relationship to imperialism and nationalism. In the fashion of the day for provocative titles I call the first part 'The Tradesman as Composer' and the second 'The Composer as Politician'.

Finally, this essay has nothing to do with music. Let it be clear that I believe Elgar to be, not only the greatest English composer, but also one of the half dozen greatest of all composers. But history is a remorseless science. If Elgar was representative of a people, class and nation at a moment in time, he was equally representative of both their good and bad characteristics. It is necessary to be clear about this – too much Romantic deification has gone on and, to offset it, it is sometimes necessary to appear unduly harsh. Outside his music I hold no special brief for Elgar, but seek only to establish the facts, free from any political or cultural agendas.

The Tradesman as Composer

[At this point in the original presentation the speaker discussed mid-nineteenth-century attitudes as illustrated by reference to four works of art. These were: –

James Archer, *Summertime in Gloucestershire* (1860), National Gallery of Scotland. A romanticised view of the English countryside, with the subtext that middle-class dominance is essential to preserve it.

Joseph Mallord William Turner, *Rain Steam and Speed – the Great Western Railway,* (1838), Tate Gallery. The promise (and menace) of technology.

William Dyce, *Pegwell Bay – a Recollection of October 5th 1858* (1860), Aberdeen Art Gallery. Disquiet about the future of the human race as science demonstrates the immensity of the universe and time.

William Bell Scott, *Iron and Coal* (1861), Wallington Hall, Tyneside in a celebration of the commercial and industrial might of England, but with some ambivalence.]

The population of England and Wales in 1857 was 19 million. By 1897, when Elgar was emerging as a major composer, it was 31 million. This is a

61% increase in forty years. The birth rate was actually falling; the increase was the result of greater life expectancy. The impact cannot be over-emphasised. Potential mass audiences for all kinds of activity were being created. Large-scale musical performances became much more feasible. Moreover audience and performance could be brought together. In 1857 there were 8,000 route miles of railway, in 1897 nearly 20,000. Elgar could travel to the Crystal Palace, audiences could be brought from greater distances and provincial isolation was virtually ended. During the 1850s concert halls were being built as part of increasing civic and economic pride – St George's Hall, Bradford (1853), St George's Hall, Liverpool (1854), Manchester Free Trade Hall (significant name) turned over to concert use in 1856, Leeds Town Hall (1858), and St James's Hall, London (1859).

This pride had sound industrial and commercial foundations. In 1857 Britain was, in economic terms, the most powerful nation in the world and its principal manufacturer. The Balance of Payments was +27. It was to remain positive continuously for the next fifty-eight years. 75% of world sea-borne trade was carried in British ships. Basic rate of tax (there was no other) was 2%. The nation, unbeknownst, celebrated the birth of its future composer by lowering the Bank Rate a few days later: another gift for his tradesman father. By 1897 the rate was down to 2% and it was still 2% when Elgar died in 1934. Cost of living fell 20% between 1880 and 1897. No wonder there was a 'Feel Good Factor' in Jubilee Year.

The years 1848 to 1867 have been described accurately, if inelegantly, as the 'Age of Equipoise'. In 1848 England stood momentarily on the edge of revolution. Only a last-minute failure of nerve on the part of the Chartist leaders seems to have averted the kind of upheaval then sweeping Europe. For twenty years thereafter there was a degree of social and political stability. Elgar was born in the precise middle of this period. It is important to remember that this, <u>not</u> the Edwardian age, was the apogee of British power. By the time Elgar was in his teens an increasing sense of unease had begun to percolate through English society. This owed something to the realisation, after the Paris Exhibition of 1867, of the rising commercial and industrial challenge presented by the Germans, soon to be a united nation, and the United States. There was also increased awareness of serious social problems threatening class unity, and the growing strength of Irish nationalism, threatening political unity. It is also worth noting that his youth was marked by increasing withdrawal from Europe and a realisation, publicly unacknowledged, that the British army was both miniscule and of decreasing competence. Faith in the navy was untarnished (although undeserved) but Elgar grew up with a succession of military disasters in Africa and Asia which must have been more relevant to his perception of England overseas than any factitious imperialism.

The Worcester Elgars were a quintessential nineteenth-century middle-class trading family. William Elgar ran a highly successful business – it supported at its maximum three adults and seven children in modest affluence. By 1900 it appears from valuations that the turnover was around £100,000 per annum in today's money, though we cannot assess the profit ratio. He was able to rent a country residence in addition to a city address (from 1863 an established High Street shop), and to give his children a good education at private schools at a time when 40% of English children received no formal education at all. Edward was to stay at school until he was fourteen – only a minority of those who did go to school achieved that. It is clear that he received the standard education and training of the day, fitting him to take over the music business from his father. No biographer has been able to discover precisely when or why this plan was abandoned.

All that we can glean of the family indicates shrewdness. The renting of a country residence, even though it was a short-lived experiment, is significant, not only for demonstrating financial resource, but prudence as well. A house in the city may have been strategically placed for business but it was not well-sited for health, especially in the summer. The Elgars lost only two of their children. In the year of Edward's birth the Dean of Carlisle lost five of his seven children. The chance that Edward was born at Broadheath gave him the opportunity to claim that he was a countryman, humbly born in a cottage – an invaluable attribute of which he was to make full use. Others have done so on his behalf, with equal enthusiasm, ever since his death.

The political influence of the lower middle class grew as the century progressed. One reason for this was that the Reform Act 1867 gave most male urban dwellers the vote. They began to challenge the hegemony of the manufacturers and bankers who were themselves replacing the landed aristocracy as the natural political leaders. But like all upwardly mobile groups they were insecure as well, and excessively class-conscious. Elgar's later snobbishness may have been reinforced by the fact that, although his family was in trade, it was not manufacturing trade; in other words it was non-polluting. In view of the recent concerns about maintaining the

Birthplace as it was in the composer's day, it is important to remember that in 1857 the most prominent feature of the view from the top of the Malvern Hills was the huge smoke pall over the Black Country. If the wind happened to be in the wrong direction, it would not only have been the sight one noticed.

How much was religion part of English life in Elgar's formative years? There is an argument for saying that the English have not been a truly religious people since the failure of Barebone's Parliament. Certainly by the 1850s the decline in traditional religious beliefs and observance was marked and remarked upon. In 1851 there was a Religious Census of church attendance. Though doubts about its total validity were expressed then and have been since, the findings were striking. They showed that only 35% of the population attended any sort of service at all. There was a convenient dead heat between Anglicans and Nonconformists, but only 1% of the population attended Catholic services. Moreover, at that time their membership consisted of two kinds of adherents – immigrants, mainly from Ireland (and no one wanted to be associated with them) and the Old Catholic families who had maintained the faith down centuries of persecution and civil disability, and who tended to be distinctly upper-class. When William Elgar arrived in Worcester to become organist at St George's, Catholics had enjoyed civil rights for little more than ten years. Certain offices were still barred to them – one, of course, still is. Why did William accept a post which involved making his family, though not himself, Catholics? The organ at St George's may have been particularly fine but there were plenty of parish churches with good instruments. Surely we cannot regard the proximity of the Hop Market Hotel as a crucial inducement. I suggest that it was simply a piece of good business. The West Midlands had a higher proportion of Old Catholic families than most other parts of Britain. By linking himself to that persuasion he was achieving market differentiation. He would be a larger fish in a more exclusive pond. It may be remarked that he rapidly acquired some very 'upmarket' customers. If my view is correct, the effect on the young Edward can be imagined. It would suggest to him that religious observance was a tradable commodity, valuable in terms of self-promotion, but not to be allowed to get in the way of business or social success. It was an approach he would share with many Englishmen of the day.

Yet the outward adherence to Catholicism did have important consequences. Elgar was to remain outside two major schools of English thought and culture. He was excluded from the Nonconformist Tradition, with its enthusiasm for individual accountability, self-help, and democratic organisation, on the one hand; and effectively outside the new Catholic School, with its enthusiasm for historic continuity, Ultramontane politics, and beauty of worship on the other. At least he was saved from the Anglican persuasion, not widely known for generating enthusiasm for anything at all.

Received religion was under major attack in Elgar's youth: witness Miller's *Testimony of the Rocks* (1857), Darwin's *Origin of Species* (1859), and Renan's *La Vie de Jesu* (1863). By the 1870s Thomas Hardy was attacking God because He was against His Creation. Elgar was to attack Him because he was against Edward Elgar. But social acceptability required at least a veneer of observance, which Elgar was usually careful to demonstrate. Why did he write *Gerontius*? The fundamental reason is not resolved, despite the large quantity of published research. The simple answer seems to be 'because Johnstone told him to'. Elgar wanted to write a work on the life of St Augustine, surely a thoroughly Anglican idea. For some reason this was thought too Catholic for Birmingham and, incredibly, *Gerontius* was substituted. Afterwards Elgar nonchalantly suggested that he had been able to produce a masterpiece in the time available because he had been thinking about it for twenty years. Biographers have accepted this claim ever since. Even more intriguing is the question: Why did Elgar plunge into the writing of religious works, having just established himself with *Caractacus, Sea Pictures*, and the *Variations* as a major and successful composer of secular works?

The cultural climate in which Elgar grew to manhood and developed as a composer is of major importance. The first significant factor is that the English had been forced to recognise that they were no longer a rural people living in a kind of Arcadia. The 1851 Census was the first to show that more people lived in urban areas than in the country. By the end of the century, 78% of the population were town dwellers, then the largest proportion of any nation in the world. The reaction to this was the creation of the great rural myth, which was so significant in the production of an idealised picture of the nation. The theory that England was all about villages and sturdy yeomen, ploughing immemorial fields, larks in the clear air, and sounds down by the river, was generated then and remained well into the twentieth century.

Elgar made skilful use of this myth while shrewdly not surrendering to the folk industry. His forthright assessment of the dubious nature of much

English so-called 'folk music' is borne out by Georgina Boyes in her amusing and astringent study *The Imagined Village*. Despite his clever advertising Elgar was always the essential 'townie'. His wife told Gerald Cumberland that 'although devoted to nature and the Country he keenly enjoys the Society and the higher Social recreations which await him in the great cities, and he is equally at home in the house of Princes as in the fields'.[1]

The great cities, with higher social recreations, did not include anywhere north of Watford. Edinburgh was 'grim', Leeds 'weary' and service at the Queen's Hotel bad. Liverpool was full of Americans, and he certainly hated Newcastle, as his letter to Alice Stuart Wortley of 7 November 1909, on his return to Hereford, makes clear: 'it is lovely here, the air so pure after the loathed North with all its mysteries of commerce – I saw locomotives building & torpedoes & other maleficious things'.[2]

This letter was addressed to the wife of an MP for Sheffield whose ancestors came from Barnsley. Moreover it was Northern businessmen – Rodewald, Kilburn and Embleton – who played major roles in promoting his work and Northern choirs and audiences which created the means of his success. Yet he could write (again to Alice Stuart Wortley) ' the North is never part of me'.[3] This is all the more astonishing in that in 1910, when the Elgars were house hunting, he says of one prospect that '(it) seems to be miles from any station & has *no* bathroom! I really cannot go back to savagery'.[4] So Broadheath, rural sanitation, and no trains was savagery! Back to that – certainly not. Three cheers, then, for the loathed North, which was making bathrooms, plumbing, railway locomotives, and other no doubt 'maleficious' things, and spending some of the wages and profits on performances of Elgar's works. This perception divorced Elgar from the everyday reality of English life as it was developing in his time, and strengthened his social and class isolation. It might also be noted that by 1917 he seems to have been happy enough with Brinkwells, a cottage in rural Sussex, probably equally bath-less though not quite so far from the nearest station as Broadheath.

A further factor of major significance is that Elgar was strongly influenced by the second stage of the Romantic Movement. This I suspect to have been mediated through his mother, who grew up at precisely the time when the influence of Byron and Wordsworth was at its height. Her role in introducing her son to the works of Longfellow is well documented. The concept of the Romantic artist as a lone figure battling against a

1 – Notes and references for this chapter appear on pages 90-93.

hostile and philistine society was almost obsessively acted out by Elgar
throughout his life, as was that other key notion, the primacy of the
creative artist's psyche and personal feelings over all social considerations.

A consequence of this approach was a change in the attitude towards
music. By the mid-century music had become a serious art as opposed to
being high-class wallpaper. 'Cometh the hour cometh the man' is a
recurring theme in Elgar's life. There is a story of Ralph Waldo Emerson
and a friend at a performance by the famous ballerina Fanny Elssler. The
friend whispered to him 'this is poetry'. To which he, the pragmatic, down-
to-earth Yankee, replied 'No, it's Religion'.[5] It was a perceptive comment,
when we reflect on the adulation being bestowed at the time on Liszt and
Mendelssohn. O'Shaughnessy in *The Music Makers* applied Shelley's view
that poets are the real legislators to musicians. Kant declared that genius
is always opposed to imitation, Schiller that freedom exists only in dreams.
These views held a relevance for Elgar.

Another factor arising out of the Romantic Movement was an
increasing obsession with the macabre and the enigmatic, especially in the
later nineteenth century. This ranged from the appearance of the mystery
writers, such as Wilkie Collins and Conan Doyle to the more
psychologically disturbing Kipling. It also affected painting. A most
popular work of art was Bocklin's *Die Toteninsel,* painted in 1879,
inspiring musical works by Rachmaninov and Reger. This was of
undoubted significance to Elgar; Alice told Jaeger in 1905 that Elgar was
himself doing paintings in the manner of Bocklin and Segantini.[6]

Then again, an important aspect of Romanticism as experienced in
nineteenth-century England was the remarkable obsession with chivalry.
There has never been any doubt about Elgar's own subscription to
chivalric ideology. It clearly influenced his music and choice of subject.
Already present in *Froissart*, it also permeates *Caractacus, King Olaf, King
Arthur,* and may well be the origin of his devotion to the 'nobilmente'
style. Even his language is coloured by the phrases of the chivalric. His
remark in the Birmingham lectures that English music should be 'broad,
noble, chivalrous, healthy and out-of-doors ...' is an unconscious (or
conscious) recollection of Kenelm Digby's *Broad Stone of Honour*.[7] This
obsession is also an explanation in part for his nostalgia, and his
objections to the trading classes, to which, unfortunately, he had to admit
he belonged himself. He read Ruskin and Morris, not for their social
radicalism, but for their interest in the chivalric ideal. If Elgar saw himself
as a sort of musical knight errant, rescuing traditions in distress from

menacing Socialists, it would explain a lot about his behaviour and his political opinions. Allied to formidable social snobbery (which it would reinforce) it could have provided him with an effective cultural agenda.

If music was becoming more 'high art', it was also becoming professional and institutional. Whereas in the 1851 Census only 12,000 persons claimed to be employed in musical activity, by 1897 this had risen to nearly 40,000 and musicians were classed as a separate category, although still treated as 'tradesmen'. Elgar was joining a growing and increasingly organised profession. The Incorporated Society of Musicians was founded in 1882 (Elgar was to be a member), The Royal College of Music in 1883, the Union of Graduates in Music (Elgar was to be President) and the Musicians' Union in 1893. Brown and Stratton published their *British Musical Biography* in 1897. Grove published the first edition of his famous Dictionary in 1889, devoting more space to British composers than to any others. There is no doubt that a conscious effort was being made to claim a place for Britain on the musical map, but as Theodore Hoppen points out in the *New Oxford History of England*, 'the Victorians could do anything with music except compose it'. That is, compose it memorably. The importance of this in creating the right climate for the emergence of a major British composer is obvious. Once again, 'cometh the hour cometh the man'.

Prof. Hoppen's work contains an important chapter entitled 'The Business of Culture'.[8] He points out the shrewd business sense of novelists such as Trollope, George Eliot, and especially Dickens. Victorian painters were even more successful. In the same year in which a Titian sold for just £90 Edwin Long received £7,300 for *The Babylonian Marriage Market*. (Elgar was subsequently to live in Long's Hampstead house.) Composers were not far behind the artists. Gounod received a £4,000 payment from Novello's for *Redemption* and is said to have made the equivalent of £168,000 from his British royalties.[9] By 1881 Sullivan was receiving £10,000 annually. No wonder Elgar was to say in 1899 'music is a trade'.[10] He went on to say 'I am no tradesman' but in fact the evidence is all to the contrary. He had already told Jaeger in March 1898 'you know that £.s.d. is a serious matter to me'.[11]

Elgar had a very clear view of the commercial aspects of his art and was as skilful a businessman as his contemporaries Lipton, Rowntree or Lever. In the middle of the first of those flebillously lachrymose letters of which he became such a master, he suddenly says 'you see I want so little: £300 a year'.[12]

Jaeger himself was on £4 per week then and must have swallowed hard on receiving this letter. This was when £100 per year would rent a five-bedroomed house in a fashionable London square. It is also rather tendentious, for Alice had an annuity of precisely that amount. Did he mean another £300 or is it, as I suspect, a revealing slip meaning that he wanted to avoid any suspicion of dependence on Alice? [13] In any case he admitted in the letter quoted above that his income for 1897 was £200, the equivalent in today's money of £11,000. How well did Elgar achieve his economic aims? In the years 1897 to 1903 he secured down payments of £2,219, an average of £369 per annum. This excludes any income from royalties or other sources. By 1903 he was able to ask and get £1,000, plus a 25% royalty for *The Apostles* (and then not deliver part of it). The Funeral March to *Grania and Diarmid* lasts seven minutes but Elgar demanded £100 for it from Novello's despite the fact that it was actually commissioned by someone else.[14] Given that, in modern terms, that equates to about £700 per minute, it must be amongst the most expensive music ever written. The First Symphony produced £800 in performing fees in the first 18 months. From the cancellation of his exclusive contract with Novello's in June 1911 to June 1914 Elgar received £500 per annum from down payments alone, this at a time when only 2% of the population had incomes above £200 a year. By 1909 his income was in excess of £2,000 per annum – the modern equivalent is £100,000.[15] Elgar was well aware of marketing techniques, product differentiation, discounted cash flow, and capital renewal.

For example he wrote to Jaeger, on 13 January 1902:

> My music does not arrange well for piano & consequently is of no commercial value. If I had a free mind I shd. like to write my chamber music & symphony … on all of which forms of art Providence has laid the curse of poverty.[16]

Then follows the famous statement that 'providence … is against all art', frequently quoted but rarely in context. Providence took some hard knocks from Elgar but the real significance of his words has not been grasped. If this is what he wanted to do why didn't he? If the creative artist does not have a free mind, who does? In effect he is setting out a blatantly commercial attitude – no divine afflatus here, but a keen calculation of the kind of music the market would bear. A perceptive Australian critic of 1903 said 'Dr Elgar is not only a musician of undoubted talent but also a smart businessman'.[17]

Precisely. *Gerontius* was just as much a British export as a Dorman Long rolled-steel joist, a Parsons turbine, or a ton of Welsh steam coal.

Like them it was a high-quality product, skilfully marketed, making a valuable contribution to the balance of payments. The real reason Elgar abandoned religious music was simply that it no longer paid. He plainly states as much in a letter to Ivor Atkins in 1913.

> I longed to complete *The Apostles*, but you see the fee ... would be the *only* return for a whole year's work.[18]

Which brings us to the intriguing question of Elgar's productivity. In a creative career effectively extending from 1885 to 1933 he produced 38.5 hours of performable music. Allowing 10% addition to cover lost and incomplete works this produces an average productivity of fifty-two minutes per year.[19] Elgar was no compulsive genius, pouring out music in uncontrollable streams. Before 1907, when he finally turned to serious work on a symphony, almost all his major products had been commissioned. The *Variations* are, perhaps significantly, the obvious exception. Until then his had been a manufacturer's approach to art. For comparison note that his beloved Schumann was four times more productive. But Elgar knew that over-production reduces price and he undoubtedly wrote a higher proportion of masterpieces than more fecund composers. The move into chamber music is significant. I suggest that it was to pre-empt what he saw as a potential growth market after the War. However, Alice's death removed the need to continue writing music at all, at least until he had got through his inheritance in the late 1920s. The actual pattern of production is fascinating. Diagram 1 (following page) shows how he peaked around 1900 then established a plateau of work. Most fascinating, however, is the clear fact that there was a consistent reduction from around 1915 to the late 1920s and the death of Alice made no difference to the 'secular trend'.

How much did Elgar make from writing music? 'More than he pretended' is the short answer. Diagram 2 (following page) is a model of his music-related income for the last twelve years of his life. This graph deliberately takes no account of the large infusions of capital which he received between 1920 and 1933, notably nearly £15,000 in 1920 from Alice's will and the sale of Severn House. This inheritance I suggest is the real reason why Elgar virtually gave up composition in the 1920s – he simply no longer needed to earn.

Elgar's attitude to money was a crucial factor in his life. I believe that his upbringing in a commercially orientated household, in a commercially orientated country, unduly influenced him. Not only did he make financial comparisons, he always chose the best possible. He wanted the same sort of income as Millais in art, or as Sullivan or Gounod in music. He saw

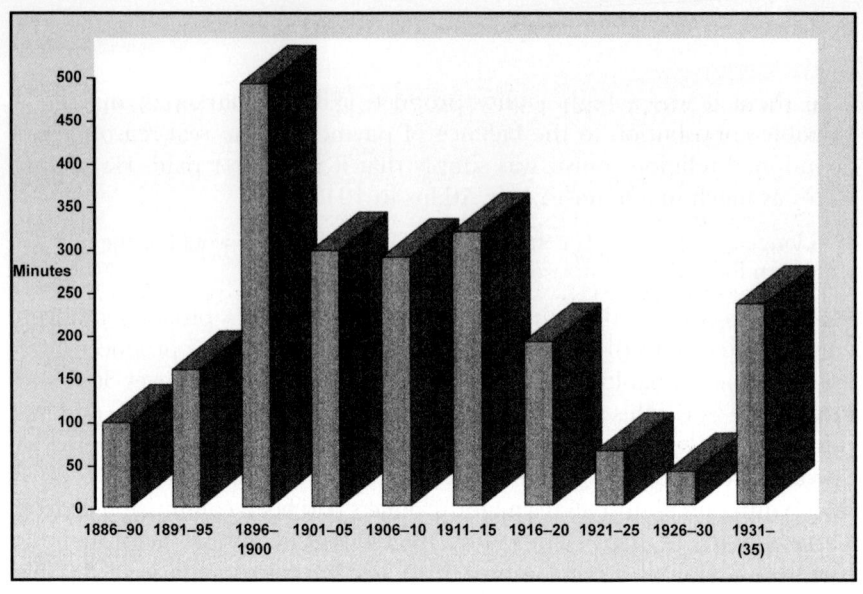

Diagram 1 (above): Elgar's productivity: 1886-1934

Diagram 2 (below):
Elgar's musical earnings 1922-1933 in the money of the day

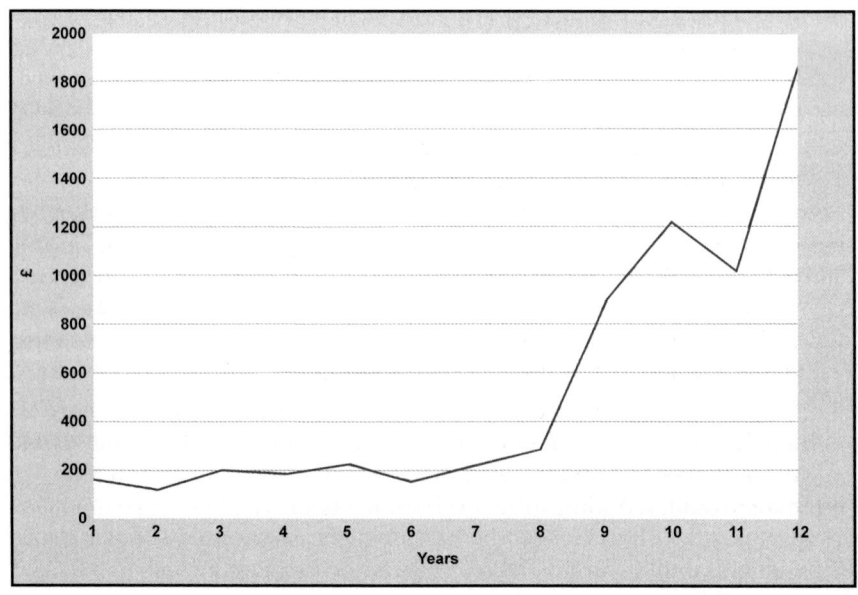

himself as a commercial enterprise, a sort of Elgar plc. His mission statement would have read: –

(1) to become a major world composer and to be recognised as such;

(2) to make as much money as possible in consequence;

(3) to attain the honours appropriate;

(4) to become a gentleman, having sufficiency without too much obvious effort.

The Composer as Politician

The later supporter of the Conservative cause was born under a Whig-Liberal Government, returned to power only a few weeks before.

The Tories, split in the 1840s over the repeal of the Corn Laws, only began to revive in 1874 after the widening of the franchise. William Elgar was enfranchised in 1868, but his son may not have had an exercisable vote until 1892, when he was 35.[20] Alice Elgar did not have an exercisable vote until the last few months of her life. On the face of it, William Elgar should have been Liberal but the urban middle class drifted into the Tory camp as the century progressed. Also, Catholics, despite the obvious conflict in joining the Anglican Church at politics, could not adhere to the party supported by Dissenters. However, the extremism of Edward's political views remains difficult to explain. Could it have been that William was in fact a Liberal and his son automatically took the opposite view? Since part of his programme was to move into high social circles and turn his back on his origins, he may also have believed ultra-Tory views a necessary corollary. Many contacts, friendly and otherwise, noticed his desire to appear lordly. Ivor Atkins says 'He went about the place like a Grand Seigneur'.[21] Elgar affected the Grand Seigneur approach so wholeheartedly that he even equipped himself with a 'maitresse en titre' in the person of Alice Stuart Wortley. Gerald Cumberland was inevitably more scathing than his intimates, and Sassoon called him the 'Duc d'Elgar'.[22] Yet, curiously, most of Elgar's friends and acquaintances were Liberal, if not Socialist, in their political loyalties.

It is hard to say whether support for the Tories plays any part in the Gordon factor. Elgar's apparent obsession with this plainly demented figure is hard to account. Gordon's death at Khartoum took place when Elgar was twenty-eight and too old for boyish hero-worship. Theories about Gordon being about to convert to Catholicism as result of reading Newman's poem *The Dream of Gerontius* can surely be discounted as a reason. However, it is true that the Tories seized on the Sudan fiasco as a useful stick with which to beat the Liberals – totally ignoring the fact that had Gordon survived he could, technically at least, have been court martialled and shot. Elgar's flirtation with a Gordon symphony in 1898 was surely prompted by the renewal of interest in the Sudan as a result of the belated final defeat of the Mahdi, widely regarded as revenge for Gordon's death.

When the South African War broke out, in 1899, Jaeger wrote to him: '...when the Boers are bottled up in this glorious campaign for Goldmines we shall require the Triumphal March for Grand Patriotic concerts'.[23]

After a series of stunning defeats, the British recovered sufficiently to annex the two Republics in the summer of 1900, but the War was to last another two years. Strong feelings were aroused, as many shared Jaeger's views. Apparent success turning sour by October 1900 increased tensions. These ran especially high in Birmingham, notorious for Nonconformist and anti-Boer sentiment. Suggestions have been made that the first performance of *Gerontius* was sabotaged for political reasons. This may be extreme, but it is worth noting that a year later there was a riot when Lloyd George was nearly lynched during a visit to the city. Birmingham was not the best place in 1900 to launch an ostensibly Catholic work by an upstart from a rival West Midlands city, and whose theme was, after all, death.

Elgar really emerged on the political stage in 1904. In March of that year he met the then Prime Minister, Arthur Balfour.

Balfour has been described as 'cynical, unprincipled and frivolous' [24] and it is a sustainable case. However, he did like music. By 1904 it was clear that the long reign of the Tories (twenty years of almost uninterrupted office) was drawing to a close. The honours lists of their last two years were marked by naked attempts to win support by handing out favours. Did Elgar hint to Balfour that a knighthood would not come amiss for such a keen Conservative? If he did, it would have been very attractive to Balfour, who needed to cloak the list with some well-deserved awards. It was the last year in which Elgar could expect any honours from the state for a long time. In January 1906 the Liberals won their famous 243-seat majority. Elgar had to wait twenty-seven years to receive another honour dependant on political recommendation, and then, by one of those ironies of which history and Elgar's life are full, it was a Labour Prime Minister who awarded it.

In 1905 Elgar was a guest with Schuster on a cruise with the Mediterranean Fleet, under its Admiral, Charles Beresford, and Vice-Admiral, George Warrender. As both these gentlemen were senior Masons it was odd company for a devout Catholic. The cruise was influenced by an historical factor, but all the biographers misinterpret it, partly as a result of an erroneous entry in Elgar's own journal. Anderson says that the fleet could not go to Constantinople because of a delicate situation in Turkey; Moore simply suggests that it was because of the general diplomatic situation. There is a suspicion that someone was pulling the composer's leg, perhaps a bright young naval lieutenant. Certainly bombs were going off in Constantinople – they always were; that would certainly not have been a consideration. The contortions of the various authors in their attempts to equate historical fact with Elgar's inaccurate reminiscences are both amusing and revealing. One has actually invented a European crisis called the 'Akaba Incident', an event known to no one else, in order to explain Elgar's comments. The fact is that, as a result of a clause in the Treaty of Berlin of 1878, no foreign warship could pass the Dardanelles in time of peace. The Treaty of Berlin was the result of a confrontation between Russia and Turkey in which Britain became embroiled and war with Russia was a distinct possibility. Given his supposed enthusiasm for the music hall Elgar would probably have heard then *MacDermotts Great War Song*, which put the word 'jingo' into the English language. The relationship with Beresford, then beginning to develop his notorious controversy with Fisher, and his wife Jeromina ('Mina'), raises some interesting questions in itself. The impression that Elgar was brought along as a sort of prize exhibit on this curious expedition is very strong.[25]

The Liberal victory of 1906 has been given as one of the reasons for Elgar's apparent deep dejection and abandonment of the religious trilogy at this time. Conservatives seem unable to anticipate electoral defeats which everyone else can see clearly, but I have already given my reason for Elgar's reaction. I suggest that this theory is simply another example of the attempt to make it appear that Elgar's motives were always derived from some major principle, or a high-minded response to public events.

Nevertheless he was undoubtedly displeased with the outcome. He wrote to Schuster on 22 January that year: 'Having turned out the respectable Hotel Cecil and having installed the Waiters in place of the gentlemen you will probably have to drop music & musicians to seem respectable among the artistic governing body'.[26]

While the sentiments are obviously silly, the letter is of interest because of its use of the in-phrase 'Hotel Cecil' to describe the former Government. This was because most of its members were related to the Marquis of Salisbury. Elgar does seem to have had more contact with party politics than has been recognised. The Conservatives actually held Worcester in 1906, but perhaps that was not too surprising given that shortly afterwards their man was unseated on a petition for bribery – the only occasion in the twentieth century when the <u>candidate</u> was so convicted. The accusations were so serious that there was even a possibility of the City being disfranchised, and, indeed, Worcester was without an MP for two years. Elgar made the preposterous suggestion that he should stand as the Conservative–Unionist candidate in the by-election. Later he was to sign nomination papers for Conservative candidates in Hereford and to give real consideration to becoming Mayor of Hereford. As late as 1922 he is said to have been writing texts for political pamphlets for, presumably, local elections.[27] Moreover, he was involved in political campaigns in connection with copyright legislation on three occasions (1904, 1911 and 1929) and he certainly had contact in consequence with another unlikely figure, that of T. P. O'Connor, left-wing Liberal and Irish Nationalist MP. Elgar's involvement with party politics deserves more study.

The Liberals commenced a cautious policy of mild reform (*not* Dr Moore's 'swingeing programme of social change', which would have frightened the life out of them).[28] But the House of Lords embarked on obscurantist obstruction and met their match in the new Prime Minister, Asquith, and his Chancellor, Lloyd George.

The 1909 Budget was deliberately provocative to the landed class in order to ensure its rejection in the Lords, thereby bringing on a constitutional crisis. It would also have been unpopular with Elgar as it introduced supertax on incomes over £2,000 per annum. Elgar complained about the new tax, which provides us with one important piece of evidence about his income. We also know that some of Elgar's friends hated Asquith, and he probably shared their views. Notable among them was Admiral Beresford, who associated later with the eccentric MP, Pemberton Billing, in an attempt to remove foreigners and Jews from public life. Indeed, another Elgar irony is that their only victim was Edgar Speyer, Elgar's financial adviser. Asquith had made Speyer a Privy Councillor. He is alleged to have been the prototype for the foreign villain in John Buchan's *The Thirty-Nine Steps*.[29]

The consequence of the crisis was an election in January 1910. The Liberals lost their overall control and came to rely on Irish Nationalist and Labour support. The Government introduced a Bill to curb the Lords. Edward VII died. The new king agreed to Asquith's request to create 500 Liberal peers after a second election in December. A list was drawn up. In view of his future anxiety for a peerage Elgar might have been piqued to know that Parry's name was on it. In the end, the Lords narrowly capitulated and passed the Parliament Act 1911.

The year 1912 was one of calamity. It began with the Scott Polar disaster followed in April, notoriously, by the loss of the *Titanic*, which Elgar told Alice Stuart Wortley he felt acutely.[30] Perhaps, but it was to present him with one of his major public appearances. He was conductor-in-chief at the *Titanic* Memorial Concert, an obviously emotionally-charged event, at which an orchestra of 500 players performed the *Variations* to an audience allegedly of 10,000.

The start of the First World War caused one of Elgar's more notorious outbursts, in a letter to Schuster:

> Concerning the War I say nothing – the only thing that wrings my heart & soul is the thought of the horses ... the men and women can go to hell.[31]

While the sentiments are indefensible, it has to be remembered that at the time most people believed the War would be short-lived. Moreover, the British tended to think that their only involvement would be at sea, where the Royal Navy would be victorious at minimal cost. Cannadine has pointed out that the upper classes regarded the War as a tiresome interruption to the Season. Elgar's attitude seems to be comparable – he seems to say 'damn, now you've spoilt my chances of being a European composer'. This is not to suggest that he did not dislike war, but it cannot be claimed that he was wholeheartedly against it. He enrolled as a Special Constable and a Volunteer Reservist and, within days of the above letter, was urging A.C.Benson to write anti-German words for *Land of Hope and Glory*. Benson's measured response is certainly in contrast to the jingoism of Elgar.[32]

In truth, as Jeremy Crump has shown, Elgar had a good war.[33] Both he and his music became popular. Royalty income increased and the letters to Alice Stuart Wortley indicate the high living in which he was now able to indulge. It has been suggested that *The Starlight Express* was the result of a personal desire to dissociate himself from the mood of the time. However, there is plenty of evidence to show that this kind of work was extremely popular. After all it was precisely at the same time that *Chu Chin Chow* was running up the highest number of performances before *The Mousetrap*. I suspect that he saw it as fitting in very well with public demand and expected a long and profitable run. However, Elgar's 'nose' for dramatic success was always distinctly faulty and *The Starlight Express* was no different.

Nor did the events of the War have much impact on the Elgars. However, when German warships emerged from the mists of the North Sea and bombarded middle-class resorts, Alice Elgar had hysterics – in her diary. By the standards of later atrocities, it was small beer indeed, and perhaps had the Germans shifted their target to say, Seaham Harbour, where the only casualties would have been miners, outrage might have been less. There is another irony in this story. The officer commanding the sector, whose laxity allowed the Germans to get away with a risky venture, was none other than the Elgars' old friend Sir George Warrender. He was forcibly retired as a result and died soon afterwards.

After the Great War Elgar became increasingly obsessed with status. Alice has been made into a kind of 'bomb shelter' for her husband on this question, it being implied that her social snobbery was the real reason for what Cannadine has called his 'gong grabbing'. True, she wanted a Nobel Prize for him – for what? – Chemistry? But the nineteenth-century English trading class had a strong upwardly mobile urge, which clearly affected Elgar. Alice's death did not curtail the desire for recognition. Indeed it became, if anything, more frenetic.[34] The death of Walter Parratt gave Elgar his chance. He not only urged the retention of the post of Master of the King's Musick but put himself forward for the appointment. His assertion that abolition would have a bad effect abroad is nonsense.[35]

In 1923 Elgar began his campaign for a peerage. In a letter to Alice Stuart Wortley of 12 September that year he makes a claim based, intriguingly, only on his choral works.[36] The date may be significant. The previous year the sale of honours had become a national scandal, as a result of the activities of Lloyd George and Maundy Gregory. Was Elgar hinting that the Wortleys might buy him a peerage? It should be noted that he finally gave up the attempt when the Honours (Prevention of Abuses) Act was passed, effectively blocking for him that route to the House of Lords.

But Elgar was not without political contacts of his own. He knew three Prime Ministers personally, and refused to know a fourth. In 1924 he resigned from the Athenaeum on the grounds, he says, that: 'they had admitted a person whom I think unfitted for membership'.[37] This was Ramsay MacDonald, the recently elected Labour premier.

Elgar was always vitriolic about left-wing politicians. In 1929 he was to write to Boosey about *Land of Hope and Glory*: 'don't let any blasted labour rogue or liberals use the tune'.[38]

On 12 January 1931 in a letter to the Dean of Worcester about revision of the National Anthem, he surpassed himself:

> ...' Confound their politics' in this National address to the Almighty would have the effect – if the Almighty ever took notice of anything ... of putting the whole Government in Hell with MacDonald in the lowest place ... [39]

But even he could scarcely have believed that Ramsay MacDonald, avid frequenter of Marchionesses' drawing rooms, was a dangerous Red. Could it be that the real reason was that Elgar did not want to have to meet, as a social equal, a man who had unquestionably risen from the very humblest of beginnings to a high position in public life? MacDonald's attitude was more generous than Elgar's for it was he who granted the baronetcy, only a few weeks after the outburst I have just quoted. It may possibly have been at his Chancellor's suggestion. Phillip Snowden was a keen music lover. It was he who began the annual grant to Covent Garden, which now distresses the Labour Party so much.

The other Prime Ministers he knew were: Arthur Balfour, mentioned above; Stanley Baldwin, who was associated with him as one of the original Friends of Worcester Cathedral and, a fellow son of Worcestershire; and Neville Chamberlain, who was a guest at the dinner to mark Elgar's honorary degree at Birmingham in 1907.

Elgar's objections to MacDonald are all the more remarkable when we remember the former's connection to Emile Vandervelde. When Elgar visited Vandervelde, did his host play him the *Internationale* in welcome? For Vandervelde was no ordinary Socialist. He was chairman of the Permanent Bureau of the Second International. A colleague of August Bebel, Jean Jaurès and Rosa Luxembourg, he was surely a curious figure for the ultra-right-wing Elgar. Nevertheless, Vandervelde was the son of wealthy parents who were 'models of bourgeois virtue'. This I think indicates that Elgar's objections <u>were</u> social rather than political. Vandervelde was acceptable in class terms, MacDonald was not.[40]

How much of an Imperialist was Elgar? The theory that he was a rampant believer in British Manifest Destiny to Rule Lesser Breeds stems in part from the association of his music with Imperialist propaganda. This began in the First World War and survived into the 1940s. How many remember watching Stanley tramp over Africa to the strains of the fourth *Pomp and Circumstance* March? It has become fashionable in some circles to suggest that he was a dyed-in-the-wool Colonel Blimp, revelling in the Empire on which the Sun Never Set. Much of this seems to come from

James Morris in *Pax Britannica,* published in 1968: 'Elgar reached middle age in the heyday of the new Imperialism … and succumbed to the glory of it all. In Elgar's Worcester the manifestations of … imperial pride must have been inescapable.' [41]

They would have been eminently escapable there and in any case by the time Elgar was middle-aged he was safely ensconced in Hampstead. The heyday of Imperialism was the early twentieth century and indeed the Empire did not reach its greatest extent until 1920. In 1857 it barely existed in a form we would recognise. Canada and Australia were largely empty, New Zealand was in a state of savage civil war, there were two small colonies in southern Africa, and a few trading posts. India, the future Jewel in the Crown and birthplace of Alice Roberts, was not yet officially part of the Empire, being a private fiefdom of the East India Co. It, too, was convulsed by rebellion. Despite Disraeli's fantasy of making the essentially domesticated and bourgeois Queen Victoria Empress of India in 1877, imperialism only began as a creed with the scramble for African colonies at the century end. Middle-class businessmen were unconvinced of the benefits, especially those who, like William Elgar, could not sell overseas and had no need of cheap raw materials. The Empire was always a Grand Illusion, depending on absence of serious challenge. Had the United States invaded Canada or Russia India it is difficult to see how Britain could have defended them. When, seven years after Elgar's death, such a challenge was made the Empire duly collapsed.

I can find no solid evidence of Elgar's enthusiasm for Empire. His ostensible imperial works (*The Crown of India, Pageant of Empire,* and *Empire March*) are, for the most part, the weakest music he ever wrote. Apart from a short trip to Canada, which he described as 'awful', he never visited any part of the empire (unless one counts Belfast). The only colonial he ever knew was the New Zealander 'Anzy' Wylde, and he hated him. His letters tend to indicate Little Englander sentiments. This would not be surprising given his origins. Lacking an interest in cricket, he did not even have the excuse of seeing the colonies as providing teams for the Mother Country to beat.

Mackenzie in *Imperialism and Popular Culture* draws attention to Elgar's involvement in Empire Day celebrations. It is these which seem to have given credence to the idea that he was himself an Imperial enthusiast. Official recognition of the Day was not achieved until 1916, and serious celebration did not begin until 1920. Elgar certainly appeared frequently on these occasions, and indeed wrote *Pageant of Empire* for them. Mackenzie goes on to say:

the music played constituted an aural equivalent of an iconography ... Elgar's naturally figured most prominently ... although the jingoistic chorus from *Caractacus*, much used in Empire Day concerts before the First World War, in the inter-war years seems to have been banished.[42]

Of course he was always pleased when his music was taken up, and he would not have complained about the association. But the argument *post hoc, propter hoc* is always dangerous and never so much as when dealing with Elgar. Indeed, he claimed that he found the Wembley Exhibition vulgar and disgusting and was moved to tears by the sight of flowers.[43]

It is salutary to recall that the United Kingdom only existed for little more than a century. From 1922 what is now the Irish Republic was in effect an independent nation. Elgar's involvement with the Irish is a strange story. It began in 1901, when George Moore asked Elgar to write a horn call for the play *Diarmid and Grania* he had co-authored with Yeats. That England's leading composer should have been asked to write six notes for an Irish play seems astonishing. That he accepted even more so. Once Moore had him on the hook he proceeded to increase the demands. A request for a funeral march and then a song quickly followed – all to be done for nothing. What was behind it?

The disclosure of the Parnell–Kitty O'Shea relationship, followed by Parnell's death in 1891, had split the Irish Nationalist Party and, despairing of political progress, militants, led by the Gaelic League, turned to a revival of indigenous language and culture. The promotion of Irish literature thus became a political act. The play was part of a double bill with *The Twisting of the Rope* by Douglas Hyde, prominent member of the League and future President of the Irish Republic. It was the first play in Irish for several centuries. But it was to be performed by Benson's totally Anglo-Saxon company.

The production was a shambles. A critic wrote: 'at the end of the first act the actors go to sleep, at the end of the second the audience do'.[44]

They would have needed to be good sleepers because the line 'the fools are laughing at us' brought the house down. The League demonstrated against Elgar's music by singing Irish songs. Elgar clearly knew of the debacle since he wrote to Littleton at Novello's on 25 March 1902:

I don't think the play will ever be heard again.[45]

He had astutely offered his music to Novello's as an incidental suite (to a play never to be performed) within a month of the production. Edward Martyn, a wealthy eccentric, had originally backed the play. The text was sent to Edward Gordon Craig as potential producer, but having read it (which incidentally Elgar failed to do), he wisely refused to have anything to do with it. Elgar was seen as a cheaper option. 'The more music we can get from Elgar the better', Yeats declared (especially if it came free). Martyn thus saved his money to invest in a new political party, campaigning for Irish independence without involvement at Westminster – hence its name – Sinn Fein. How the Unionist Elgar would have regarded that is a matter of conjecture. Despite his concerns over the title, expressed in the letter quoted above, Elgar still managed to get it wrong. It should be 'Diarmid and Grania.' The whole question of Elgar's involvement with this work is intriguing and would repay closer research. George Moore's account in *Hail and Farewell* indicates that it had some aspects of a conspiracy, and the received theory that he (Moore) had been at the première of *Caractacus* seems to stretch his, admittedly unreliable, memoirs a long way.

The Moore–Yeats–Elgar triangle was long-standing. Clearly Moore had some scheme in mind – it would appear for an opera, presumably with Moore–Yeats as librettists. Possibly the fact that their association ended because of the *Grania* debacle may have resulted in the scheme being abortive. Moore made several later attempts to get Elgar to collaborate in the writing of an opera. The latter's well-known comment that he had only been offered blood and lust as librettos is often assumed to refer to Hardy, but surely it was really aimed at Moore, whose penchant for the sexually liberated was well known. Nevertheless Elgar was signatory to the public testimonial to Moore on his eightieth birthday in 1932, in company with Gide, Joyce and the hated Ramsay MacDonald.

Yeats met Elgar more than once and in particular visited him in 1916, when he is said to have been very taciturn to Alice. Well he might have been, for no one seems to have noticed the significance of the date of this meeting. The events in Dublin that year which were to turn Yeats, a good poet, into a great one, had inspired his famous poem *Easter*, published only a few days before the meeting with the Elgars. It is incredible that he could have borne to be harangued by Lady Elgar, quintessential representative of the Anglo-Saxon regime, which had just been shooting his countrymen with minimal legality. Roy Foster has suggested that Yeats was hoping to enlist Elgar in his campaign for the return of the Lane pictures to Ireland.[46] Perhaps he had a memory of his host's previous lurch into Irish politics.

Following the Parliament Act of 1911 the Liberals introduced an Irish Home Rule Bill which the Lords could no longer reject. Ulster Unionists, wearing bowler hats, met at Belfast City Hall and pledged to resist Home

Rule, many signing a Solemn League and Covenant to that effect. To gain respectability, the Unionists sought signatures from prominent figures this side the Irish Sea. Incredibly Elgar signed. In so doing he was pledging himself to resist constitutional authority ' by any means found necessary'. Not only that but he was proclaiming to the world at large his abandonment of his co-religionists. Hughes calls it ' the last utterance in Petrine denial'.[47] Remembering *The Apostles* Elgar should have realised the significance. The Unionists claimed that the break-up of empire would follow Home Rule, but for reasons already given I do not believe this influenced him. I suspect it was simply a way of keeping his name in the papers at a time when he was beginning to fear that interest in him was declining.

Elgar's final Irish relationship was with George Bernard Shaw. He had seen *John Bull's Other Island* in 1912. Even Alice approved: 'most delightful, the noble and ideal left in instead of the poison'.[48]

It seems to be out of fashion these days but it is one of Shaw's more intriguing works. In it he ponders the limitations of reason, but also the dangerous power of dreams. Like most Irishmen, he knew how to manipulate an Englishman, and he did so quite shamelessly with Elgar. He acutely spotted the conflict between Elgar's essentially commercial (rational) drive and his emotional (dreaming) nature. He recognised also his vanity and used it to gain influence over him. Shaw was another interested in getting Elgar to write an opera. He claimed he would have written the libretto but had a prior commitment to Richard Strauss. This he asserted came to nothing because Strauss wanted to write the words and Shaw the music. The relationship with Elgar was less surprising than some have supposed. Both were in flight from their origins, Shaw because his had been awful, Elgar because his had not been awful enough.

Was Elgar a Nationalist Composer?

To be an effective nationalist composer, three things are needed. First, the political circumstance must be such as to give significance to the work produced. Second, it must have some point of reference to the history and culture of the nation represented. Third, there must be an innate understanding of the nature of that nation.

Concerning the first of these attributes the music of Dvořák, Sibelius and Grieg, for example, is undoubtedly nationalist in its concept. It should be remembered that Grieg was a citizen of an independent state for only the last few months of his life; that Dvořák was always an Austrian citizen; that even Sibelius spent his first fifty-four years as a subject of a foreign power. Elgar belonged to a nation with a thousand years of independent sovereignty. Moreover, as the short-lived UK was a purely political construct, no <u>British</u> nationalism has ever existed and Elgar was not interested in limiting his appeal to a tribe.

Second, his music bears no dependency on any previous English music. It is largely *sui generis*. Any dependencies are to Europe rather than England. Quotation is limited and hard to spot when it does take place.

Third, and most important of all, his view of England was particular and partial. It certainly did not include the urban and industrial society that was in fact the majority of it, and it never extended to any kind of imaginative understanding of the qualities and failings, hopes and fears, of the mass of his fellow citizens. Despite his interest in racing and football, he had no real point of contact with the working class, not even with many of the middle class. He famously once said that he was giving a tune to the 'People' but no one has attempted to tell us precisely what Elgar meant by the term.[49] Nothing demonstrates better Elgar's remoteness from 'grassroots' politics and perceptiveness about world events than the letter he wrote to Adela Schuster on 17 March 1933: –

> I am in a maze regarding events in Germany – what are they doing? ... The Jews have always been my best & kindest friends – the pain of these news is unbearable & I do not know what it really means.[50]

It was typical of Elgar to personalise a major world calamity in these terms, and intriguing that by this time he was classing his former German friends as Jews. I am more concerned with his lack of awareness of the realities of European politics. Had he not heard, for example, Gerhard Husch, distinguished lieder singer, performing 'Deutschland Erwache!' or 'Das Hakenreuz'? That other, but very different, West Midlands composer, Havergal Brian, knew exactly what was happening and knew also what a composer's response should be – to compose. So he wrote his Fourth Symphony, deliberately giving it a German title – *Das Siegeslied,* and most significant of all beginning it with a setting of the great seventeenth-century Roundhead battle hymn 'Let the Lord Arise and His Enemies be Scattered'. It is the sort of musico/political statement the patricianly Elgar could not have made. He could be, indeed was, a popular composer; he could never have been a populist composer.

Conclusion

It is vital to remember that in the last 200 years of English history everything, even culture (perhaps especially culture), has been mediated through class. Class is therefore of prime importance in understanding Elgar.

I have presented, however briefly, an alternative to the romantic life outlined at the beginning. Elgar was born into an aggressive, upwardly-mobile, social class and was a typical member of that class. He experienced few real barriers to the pursuit of the profession in which he was unusually gifted. He was able to marry a woman both matrimonially and financially desperate, who, so he believed, could open the door to the upper-class world he desired to enter. He rapidly established himself in the ranks of the comfortably-off, although he would never admit it. Realising that the market for religious works was declining, he switched first to major symphonic productions, and then later, believing that the Great War would cause a flight from such works, he started to write chamber music. The War was instrumental in reviving flagging interest in his music and he entered with enthusiasm into the moods of the time. However, the death of his wife enabled him to cease composing and to indulge his taste for high living, but he underestimated his stamina and, surviving long enough to start to run out of the means to support himself, had to return to composition late in life.

His origins made him a shrewd and highly capable businessman with a strong sense of the market. His right-wing politics were never allowed to get in the way of business or self-promotion. His marketing was superb and helped his music to survive a century of political and social change. A master of orchestration and a great Romantic he orchestrated and romanticised his life with the same panache he gave to his works, even orchestrating his deathbed. An obsession with the chivalrous aspects of Romanticism reinforced his social and political exclusivity.

A number of chance factors in British (especially English) society assisted him. Increased nostalgia for the rural, the creation of mass audiences, an infrastructure network encouraging and making possible large-scale works and forces, a declining political power resulting in the need for national icons and a desire to assert superiority over European rivals. Yet Elgar himself was neither Imperialist nor Nationalist, since either would have locked him into an insular culture he wanted to escape. His role as the only English composer to be made into a national icon created for him a conflict whose significance, I suggest, is seriously underestimated. I believe that the life of Edward Elgar tells us a great deal about our nation and people at a crucial period of our history. Like the career of his nation in these years, his own life was a compound of success and failure, self-doubt, 'safety first', arrogance, nostalgia, and class-consciousness. I suggest that the music is both deeply influenced by these attributes and remarkably representative of them. He is thus too important to be left solely to the musicologists. When he is finally recognised and seriously studied as a key English historical figure then, paradoxically, he will at last fulfil his mother's words, and belong to 'The Big World'.

Explanatory Note

This essay was originally written in 1998 as a presentation to the London Branch of the Elgar Society given at Imperial College, London on 7 December 1998. It was repeated in a slightly amended form for the Southern Branch in 2001. For this publication the temptation to re-write, or seriously expand, has been resisted, eg the endnote on Alice Elgar's finances could have been expanded considerably but this would have changed the nature of the essay. In consequence almost all references are to sources available in 1998 and, as the original text was to be read, not every statement has been carefully referenced to an original source. The style has been made more literary, but some statements are deliberately retained in a provocative manner, the purpose of such a presentation being to challenge and stimulate. Slides, overheads and tapes were used. The two most important 'overheads' have been incorporated as diagrams, but the rest are omitted, except where they are essential to the text and have been therefore 'written-in'. Otherwise textual amendments are limited to clarification, but the endnotes have been used to indicate further issues, and incorporate some subsequent research results.

Appendix – Elgar's Honours
(Excluding organisations, etc., joined on his own initiative)

1899	Royal Academy of Music
1900	Cambridge Doctorate
1904	Knighthood
	Peyton Professorship, Birmingham
	Leeds Doctorate
	Durham Doctorate
	Athenaeum Membership
1905	Oxford Doctorate
	Yale Doctorate
	Freedom of Worcester
1906	Aberdeen Doctorate
	Royal Academy
	Royal Swedish Academy
	Société des Compositeurs de Musique
1907	Carnegie Institute, Western University of Pennsylvania
	Birmingham MA
1907	President of the Music Teachers' Association
	Dutch Society for Promotion of Musical Art
1911	Order of Merit
	Royal Societies Club
	Worshipful Society of Musicians
1912	President of the Union of Graduates in Music
	Académie Royale de Belgique
1914	Regia Accademia di Santa Cecilia
1919	Accademia del Regia Institutio di Firenze
	Académie des Beaux Arts
	Savile Club
	Council of the Royal Academy of Music
1920	Literary Society
	Commander of the Order of the Crown of Belgium
	Membre de l'Institute de France
1922	Executive Committee of the Savile Club
	Brooks
1924	Master of the King's Music
1925	Gold Medal of the Philharmonic Society
1928	KCVO
1930	American Academy of Arts and Letters
1931	Baronetcy
	Vice President of the Council for the Preservation of Rural England
	Grand Council of the English Baronetage
	London Doctorate
	Hon Freeman of the Worshipful Company of Musicians
1933	GCVO

Bibliography

(The works listed exclude works specifically devoted to Elgar. General historical works are included if considered to be of particular relevance or have been quoted in the text).

Best: *Mid-Victorian Britain 1851–1875* [1971]. A classic history of the key period in Elgar's life, concentrating on social and economic factors.

Boyes: *The Imagined Village: Cultural Ideology and the English Folk Revival* [1993]. Some references to Elgar also valuable on the 'business' of folk music.

Cannadine: 'The British Monarchy and the Invention of Tradition' in *The Invention of Tradition* [1983]. Elgar's music in the Coronation Service.

Cannadine: 'Sir Edward Elgar' in *The Pleasures of the Past* [1988]. A highly critical review of Moore's 'A Creative Life'.

Cannadine: *The Decline and Fall of the British Aristocracy* [1992]. Mentions Elgar, with photo, as a symbol of class change.

Chase: 'This is No Claptrap This is our Heritage' in *The Imagined Past: History and Nostalgia* [1989]. A discussion of the persistence of the rural myth.

Crump: 'The Identity of English Music and the Reception of Elgar' in *Englishness: Politics and Culture* [1986].

Ehrlich: *The Music Profession in Britain Since the 18th Century* [1988].

Ehrlich: *Harmonious Alliance: A History of the Performing Rights Society* [1989]. The politics and finance of the music business. Elgar references inc. Novellos' use of Elgar as a political stalking horse.

Foster: *W.B.Yeats: A Life* Vol.1[1998] for *Grania and Diarmid*.

Gay: *The Naked Heart: The Bourgeois Experience, Victoria to Freud* [1995]. Pages 11–35 on nineteenth-century middle class approach to music.

Gilmour: *The Victorian Period: The Intellectual and Cultural Context* [1993].

Holroyd: *Bernard Shaw* [1997] esp. 577–9.

Hoppen: *The Mid Victorian Generation 1846–1886* [1998] esp. 372–416.

Hughes: 'The Duc d'Elgar; making a composer a gentleman' in *Music and the Politics of Culture* [1989].

Hurd: *Vincent Novello and Company* [1981] esp. 108. A relatively short account of the company which played a key role in Elgar's career.

Mackenzie: 'In Touch with the Infinite' in *Imperialism and Popular Culture* [1986] several references to Elgar.

Mackerness: *A Social History of English Music* [1964].

Morris: *Pax Britannica; The Climax of an Empire* [1968]. Several references to Elgar esp. 341–2 but largely nonsense.

Newsome: *The Victorian World Picture* [1997]. No references to Elgar but valuable on late nineteenth-century 'neurasthenia'.

Peacock and Weir: *The Composer in the Market Place* [1975]. Valuable on the business issues, copyright etc.

Read: *The Age of Urban Democracy 1868–1914* [1994].

Royle: *Modern Britain: A Social History 1750–1985* [1987].

Russell: *Popular music in England 1840–1914: a social history* [1987]. References to Elgar.

Sassoon: *Diaries 1920–1925* ed., Hart-Davies [1981,1985]. Frequent revealing cameos of Elgar and his music, with appendix on Schuster.

Seymour Smith: *Rudyard Kipling* [1990]. Several references to Elgar, esp. the relevance of the enigma obsession to RK and EE

Shonfield: *Precariously Privileged: A Professional Family in Victorian London* [1986]. A family similar to the Elgars, much about music.

Stradling and Hughes: *English Musical Renaissance 1860–1940* [1993]. Much important comment on Elgar, overstrained in places but of major significance.

Taylor: *English History 1914–1945* [1965] esp. 178–9. References to Elgar (laudatory), Delius (sarcastic) and others.

Tuchmann: *The Proud Tower* (various editions) esp. the account of Elgar's relationship with Strauss, with important insight into its political context.

Wheeler: *Death and the Future Life in Victorian Literature and Theology* [1990]. Despite the title this contains (325–339) an account of Elgar's treatment of Newman's poem, in the context of the Victorian obsession with theology and eschatology.

Young: *Music's Great Days at the Spas and Watering Places* [1968]. Many references to Elgar.

(The above list excludes the *Elgar Society Journal* but reference must be made to the important article by Hague Holmes, 'Elgar and the Class Society' in Vol. IIX, No.3 [September 1993], 114–8, 152–7.

Notes and References

NB Conversion of money values is based on the table in D Hobson *The National Wealth* (Harper Collins) 1999, 1185–6, where 1998 £ = 1.

1   Anderson, R.: *Elgar* [London: Dent, 1993] 74. The capitalisation should be noted.
2   Moore, Jerrold Northrop (ed): *Edward Elgar: the Windflower letters* [Oxford: OUP, 1989] 32..
3   *ibid.*, 194.
4   *ibid.*, 66.
5   Gay, P.: *The Naked Heart; The Bourgeois Experience Victoria to Freud* [Harper Collins, 1995] 4, 24.
6   Moore, J.N. (ed): *Elgar and his Publishers* [Oxford: OUP, 1987] Vol.1, 613. Gay points out (*op.cit.*, 297) that Arnold Böcklin (1827–1901) created a market for himself by appearing enigmatic, thus appealing to the middle-class urge to find 'deep' meanings in art. The parallel with Elgar is striking to say the least, especially in view of his interest in the artist. Giovanni Segantini (1858–1899) was an Italian-Swiss artist whose work tends to the weirdly symbolic, e.g, 'The Punishment of Lust' in the Walker at Liverpool, probably Elgar's favourite gallery. For Elgar and Kipling's obsessions with enigma see Seymour-Smith, M.: *Rudyard Kipling* [London: Papermac, 1990] 335.
7   Girouard, M.: *The Return to Camelot* [New Haven: Yale University Press, 1981] 56–66. An analysis of Elgar's vocabulary would provide some interesting clues to his thinking. It is noticeable that in the Birmingham lectures for example the most frequently occurring words are 'noble' and 'imitation'. In other contexts 'picture' or words derived therefrom are prominent.
8   Hoppen, T.: *The Mid-Victorian Generation, 1846–1886* [Oxford: OUP, 1998] 372–426.
9   Hurd, M.: *Vincent Novello and Company* [London: Granada, 1981] 86.
10   Moore: *Publishers, op.cit.*, Vol.1, 105.
11   *ibid.*, 69.
12   *ibid.*, 100.
13   The precise nature of Alice Elgar's finances remains something of a mystery. The received version is that she was well provided for and therefore made a great sacrifice in marrying Edward and being his helpmate in straitened circumstance. There are problems with this view, not least the fact that by 1888 Hazeldine was a considerable financial burden for a single woman with a fixed income, and at a time of agricultural depression. Moreover, her father had, probably ill-advisedly, sold off most of the productive parts of the estate in the 1850s. Its annual valuation for tax purposes in the 1880s was a mere

£80. Far from the romantic version it may well be that she saw marriage to Edward as an effective meal ticket.

14   Moore: *Publishers, op.cit.,* Vol.1, 340.

15   Since this lecture was prepared I have considerably extended my analysis of Elgar's finances, but the figures stated here remain valid. In the thirty-seven years from 1897 to 1934 Elgar's total income from all sources must have been around £3 million in today's money, giving an average of at least £80,000 per annum. This was at a time when the tax regime was very benign by modern standards (except during the First World War) and includes two periods of falling prices when the purchasing power of Elgar's income was actually rising. Whatever problems Elgar faced in his later career, lack of money was certainly not among them.

16   Moore: *Publishers, op.cit.,* Vol.1, 326.

17   Foreman, L.: 'Elgar and Gerontius: the Early Performances' in *Elgar Society Journal,* Vol.X, No.6 [November 1998] 279. The quoted critic also acutely noted Jaeger's role in 'puffing' Elgar's work by effective pre-performance publicity.

18   Atkins, E. Wulstan: *The Elgar–Atkins Friendship* [Newton Abbot: David & Charles, 1984] 250.

19   See diagram 1. One activity which has not been highlighted in the standard accounts and which must have absorbed much of his time is the making of transcriptions and arrangements for the popular market. Nothing demonstrates Elgar preternatural tradesman's approach more than this. There is even an arrangement of *Speak Music* for quartet. (I am grateful to Mr A.D. Walker for this information).

20   Subsequent research has essentially confirmed these dates, with one curious variation. William Elgar appears as a voter in the 1863 list, but not again until 1868. As 1863 was the year the Elgars moved to 10 High Street this may be significant, but as a leaseholder William would not be expected to have a vote before 1868. It is worth noting that Edward actually qualified as a lodger with his brother-in-law Charles Pipe in 1885, but as the next election was only a month later he may not have voted before 1892. This fact indicates relative affluence – the whole city then contained only about a dozen lodger voters.

21   Anderson, *op.cit.,* 143.

22   Hart-Davies, R. (ed): *Siegfried Sassoon Diaries 1920–1922* [London: Faber & Faber, 1981] 124. Cumberland, G.: *Set Down in Malice* [London: Grant Richards, 1919] 79–87, 246. Sassoon also gives a wickedly revealing sketch of Elgar and the painter Sickert at dinner together, acutely noting Elgar's desire to talk about music only with those who had no knowledge of it. Elgar's provincial middle-class attributes are coming out very strongly here.

23   Moore: *Publishers, op.cit.,* Vol.1, 149.

24   Taylor, A.J.P.: *From the Boer War to the Cold War* [London Penguin, 1996] 55.

25   Although apparently guests of Admiral Beresford on this trip, it should be noted that Schuster and Elgar were accommodated in a despatch boat – not the most comfortable of berths! Perhaps unsurprisingly Maud Warrender's memoirs, *My First Sixty Years* [London: Cassell, 1933] provide a cameo of a very seasick Elgar disembarking at Brindisi at the end of the trip.

26   Moore, J.N. (ed): *Letters of a Lifetime* [Oxford: OUP, 1990] 170.

27   An issue of particular interest is to what extent Elgar's political opinions were simply derivative. It is noticeable that his great early friend Hubert Leicester was a prominent Conservative Unionist and actually wrote political pamphlets under a 'nom de guerre'. Intriguingly this was 'Eusebius'. Did he borrow the name from Schumann via Elgar in gratitude for Elgar agreeing with his political views?

28   Moore: *Lifetime, loc.cit.*

29   Speyer, Edward: *My Life and Friends* [London: Cobden-Sanderson, 1937] is curiously reticent about his cousin Edgar – in fact he does not mention him at all – and almost equally so about Elgar. He devotes less space to the latter than to the totally insignificant Wimbledon composer, Clement Harris (1871–1897).

30   Moore: *Windflower, op.cit.*, 99.

31   Moore: *Lifetime, op.cit.*, 277.

32   Moore: *Lifetime, op.cit.*, 279. See also Chapter 4: Bury, D: *Elgar, the Eton Housemaster and the* Coronation Ode, 122-126.

33   Crump, J.: 'The Identity of English Music: The Reception of Elgar 1898–1935' in *Englishness – Politics and Culture 1880–1920* [Colls & Dodd, 1986] 164–190.

34   See the list of Honours in the Appendix. It is worth noting that one third of these came after Alice's death, more or less a *pro rata* scale of 'honorification' for his whole career.

35   Moore: *Windflower, op.cit.*, 289.

36   Moore: *Windflower, op.cit.*, 284.

37   Atkins, *op.cit.*, 383. Elgar is referring in the quoted letter to the custom of automatically offering membership to the Prime Minister of the day. As he was clearly aware of this custom, his resignation must seem an even more quixotic and class-conscious act. There are unpublished letters in the Worcestershire Record Office (BA 5184 (ii) 139) that indicate that Elgar was positively obsessive about MacDonald's politics.

38   Moore: *Publishers, op.cit.*, Vol.2, 860.

39   Moore: *Lifetime, op.cit.*, 434.

40   Tuchmann, B.: *The Proud Tower* [London: Penguin, 1966] 418. This book also contains a lengthy chapter on Richard Strauss, including comments on his relationship with Elgar, which Tuchmann hints may have had as much a political as an artistic base. The connection with Vandervelde came about through his wife, the glamorous Lalla, a daughter of Edward Speyer. (See Vandervelde, L.: *Monarchs and Millionaires*. [London, 1925). Just before his

death, in 1937, a young lecturer from Manchester University interviewed Vandervelde. Unfortunately A.J.P.Taylor, later a keen Elgarian himself, did not know his interviewee's connection with the composer.

41   Morris, J.: *Pax Britannica: The Climax of an Empire* [London, 1968] 341.

42   Mackenzie, J.M.: 'In Touch with the Infinite' in *Imperialism and Popular Culture* [Manchester: Manchester University Press, 1986] 179. There are several Elgar references in this chapter. It is perhaps worth noting that the Indian High Commissioner, Khrishna Menon, lodged a formal complaint with the British Government about the use of Elgar's music in India. Was this a late revenge for the activities of Sir Henry Gee Roberts?

43   Moore: *Windflower, op.cit.,* 290. Elgar's comment in this letter has been much used to demonstrate his refined sensibilities but some might be more impressed by the revelation that flowers were allowed to grow on the Cup Final pitch!

44   Foster, R.: *W.B. Yeats: a Life* [Oxford: OUP, 1998] 251–2.

45   Moore: *Publishers, op.cit.,* Vol.1, 342. See also the letter to Jaeger in Moore: *Publishers, op.cit,* Vol.1, 306.

46   Letter to the author.

47   Hughes, M.: 'The Duc d'Elgar: Making a Composer a Gentleman' in *Music and the Politics of Culture* [London, 1989] 51–52.

48   Anderson, *op.cit.,* 109.

49   Since this lecture was prepared I have come across a remarkable similarity between parts of this paragraph and comments in Cannadine, D.: *Aspects of Aristocracy* [London: Penguin, 1994] 130 *et seq.,* relating to Winston Churchill. The author suggests that Churchill's characteristics were a result of his déclassé aristocratic origins. Elgar was a déclassé bourgeois, with strong aristocratic aspirations. Both men were wayward, autocratic, and self-indulgent. Both suffered periods of deep depression and loss of confidence. The comparison is certainly intriguing.

50   Moore: *Lifetime, op.cit.,* 466–7.

Chapter Four

Elgar, the Eton Housemaster and the *Coronation Ode*

David Bury

Elgar's *Ode,* which was composed to mark, and first performed in the year of the Coronation of Edward VII, is a setting of words by Arthur Christopher Benson. On the face of it, this collaboration between the son of a Worcester shopkeeper whose formal education ended when he was fifteen and the son of an Archbishop of Canterbury, educated at Eton and King's College, Cambridge and now teaching at his old school was, perhaps, unlikely. The two had never met; nor were they to do so until after the work had been both finished and performed.

Arthur Benson was born in 1862 and died in 1925. He was the second of the six children of Edward White Benson and Mary 'Minnie' Benson, née Sidgwick. Arthur's younger brothers, Fred and Hugh, achieved fame of their own – his elder, and brilliant, brother Martin died while a schoolboy at Winchester. The entire family might be described as 'literary', and Arthur certainly played his full part in ensuring that, as has been observed, it is possible that 'no family in history has written so prolifically about itself.'[1]

Edward White Benson (1829–96) came from a Yorkshire background, but his father sold the family property in the Dales and became a factory owner in Birmingham specialising in the production of white lead. The failure of the business in 1843 coincided with his death, and Edward at the age of fourteen found himself, in effect, head of a family comprising a widowed mother and six children. He was not, however, to be put off an academic career and entered Trinity College, Cambridge in 1848 via King Edward's School, Birmingham. Edward owed much to the generous support at Trinity of the Bursar, Francis Martin, and emerged with a First in Classics in 1852. He became a Master at Rugby and was ordained in 1854. By 1858 he was the first Headmaster of Wellington College, where he remained for fifteen years before moving to the ecclesiastical phase of his career. In 1877, after a brief spell as Chancellor of Lincoln Cathedral,

1 – Notes and references for this chapter appear on pages 133-137.

he became the first Bishop of the new Cornish diocese centred in Truro. In 1882 he was appointed to Canterbury at the age of fifty-three and remained there until his death. Archbishops of Canterbury were in Victorian times more central figures in the affairs of the nation than their contemporary successors. Benson was the '1st Peer of England', commanded a stipend of £15,000 a year and had the run of the Palaces of Lambeth and Addington. He died after collapsing in Hawarden Church during a visit to Gladstone.

The Sidgwicks were cousins of the Bensons, and Mary was the fourth and youngest child of a widowed mother and living in Clifton, Bristol, in 1852 when Benson visited. He was twenty-three and recently a graduate; she was eleven. Notwithstanding this discrepancy in age Benson was determined to marry her and this seems to have become a general assumption, the event duly taking place in 1859. She was totally inexperienced and the honeymoon disastrous. In any case it seems reasonably certain that her sexual preferences were for women. However, aged eighteen she found herself the Master's wife at Wellington. Children rapidly ensued – five by 1867 and another in 1871. The marriage, however, was never a love match.

But 'Minnie' was very intelligent and became increasingly self-reliant. Gradually it became clear to her husband that she could not be taken for granted and, indeed, she was the stronger of the two. He needed her more than she needed him, and to his horror there was one point when he felt he might – notwithstanding Victorian propriety – lose her. In fact she established a right to lead her own life, which fortunately included great devotion to her children. Of his parents it was 'Minnie' whom Arthur (and the others) loved. Father was admired and respected, but also feared. He was headmasterly as both churchman and parent. He set high standards for and had high expectations of his children. Arthur rarely felt that he lived up to expectations. Edward White Benson was unable to communicate love. Moreover, he was haunted by a sense of terrible loss at the death of the brilliant eldest son, Martin, aged seventeen. Arthur always felt himself to be in Martin's shadow and occupied in projects which his father would have thought 'trivial'. It was made clear, for example, that the Archbishop disapproved of any notion of Arthur seeing, let alone meeting, the actor Irving; and also that reading a good (i.e., useful or improving) book was preferable to listening to music.

So it was that 'Minnie' set up a semi-detached relationship with her husband. On his death she was still only just over fifty and was to live until

1918. His death having removed any last inhibitions, she further developed a relationship with Lucy Tait, daughter of Edward Benson's predecessor at Canterbury. They took to sleeping in the same double bed in what Fred Benson (the author E.F. Benson) had little hesitation in describing as a lesbian relationship. 'Minnie' now became more commonly known as 'Ben'.[2]

Arthur Benson obtained a First in the Classical Tripos at Cambridge and in 1885 was invited by Edmond Warre to return to Eton to teach. He did so and stayed for almost twenty years. He was a gifted and successful teacher and became Housemaster in 1892 and, thus, as he observed, 'in loco parentis to some of the highest-born in the land.'

In July 1899, at the unveiling of the Benson Memorial in Canterbury Cathedral, he was invited by the Duchess of Albany, the Queen's representative, to travel back to Victoria Station in the royal coach. Already the Duchess's son, the Duke of Albany, was in Arthur's House, and Benson had stayed at Claremont, her Surrey home. Helen, Princess of Waldeck-Pyrmont – the Duchess – was the widow of Victoria's fourth son, Leopold. Her children were Alice, later Countess of Athlone, and Charles Edward, born in the year of his father's death (1884) and destined, ultimately, to leave Eton early to become Duke of Saxe-Coburg.

Arthur Benson enjoyed many subsequent meetings with the Duchess, and through her he was invited to the Mausoleum Service at Windsor in December 1900. Benson, recorded that he 'tried hard not to stare too hard at the Queen – very small and bent.' He took an instant dislike to the Prince of Wales, who was 'like an old fat fox.'

At this time Arthur Benson, indeed, was rendering regular service to Royalty by producing hymns, odes, etc., for various occasions. There was a wedding hymn in July 1896 for Princess Maud of Wales, a hymn for the Mausoleum Service – set to music by the Queen herself – a hymn for the South African War (*O Lord of Hosts*), an Ode to commemorate Victoria's visit to Ireland, and many other such examples. Benson had a remarkable facility with words and was never happier than when writing. When a hymn to celebrate the confirmation of Prince Leopold of Battenburg was requested, he dashed off two during the brief train journey from London to the family home at Horsted Keynes in Sussex. One could be forgiven for thinking that Arthur Benson, not Alfred Austin, was England's Poet Laureate.

Clearly his father's position was helpful to Benson's acceptability. He was, of course, author of the large-scale biography of the Archbishop. Friendship with Sir Henry Ponsonby, Secretary to the Queen and, especially, Ponsonby's wife Mary was another factor in his favour. At Windsor Castle on 24 May 1899, on the occasion of the Eton boys' annual madrigal concert, which marked the Queen's birthday, Benson was presented to Her Majesty: 'Her voice so slow & sweet – some extraordinary simplicity about it. Much higher than I had imagined and with nothing cracked or imperious', he recorded. In June 1899 he was invited to a Command Performance of opera (including *Pagliacci*) at the Castle; and in December, just after the publication of his biography of his father, he was invited to dine with the Queen at Windsor. 'No doubt it was the first time that a schoolmaster pure and simple – not a headmaster or clergyman – had ever sat at that table', observed Benson in his diary. The Queen was all attention and interest: 'How is your mother? Where is she living? She tried Winchester I think. Why did she leave that? Is Miss Tait still with you?'

Benson was captivated: '... she is so simple, motherly, shrewd, good.' Not so the Prince of Wales! At his accession he personified for Benson 'the vulgarity of the times.' In no time the 'Victorian atmosphere had gone completely ... When it was said that the Queen was coming ... courtiers ran about like frightened hens and were horribly afraid of her, knowing she would notice everything. Now no-one could be exactly afraid of the King!'

Benson continued at Eton until, in December 1903, he received yet another royal commission – to edit Victoria's letters (1837–61) for publication – that led to his resignation from the College. By nature he was not a natural courtier, and he observed that he would find it 'impossible' to live in the 'atmosphere of false deference and elaborate ceremony' that characterised Claremont. 'I can't really breathe there – it isn't my monde at all.'

Meanwhile Edward Elgar had in the very last years of Victoria's reign emerged from obscurity to fame. He had hoped for a royal dedication for his *Imperial March* Op.32 premièred on 19 April 1897. The *Variations*, Op.36, were to confirm his emerging eminence in June 1899, to be followed by *Sea Pictures* (premièred on 5 October 1899), then *The Dream of Gerontius* (premièred on 3 October 1900) and in same month – though Elgar purported to be lukewarm – he was informed of the proposed Cambridge Honorary Doctorate.

The première of *Sea Pictures* had been in Norwich and with Clara Butt singing, but within fifteen days Ada Crossley was performing two of the settings, by Royal Command, at Balmoral. Beforehand, Elgar had been approached by Sir Walter Parratt – Master of the Queen's Musick – regarding music for royal occasions. Parratt (1841–1924) had been organist to the Earl of Dudley at Witley Court, Worcestershire from

1861–68. There he met W.H. Elgar, tuner of organ and piano and the young Edward accompanying his father's rounds. In 1882 he was appointed to St George's Chapel, Windsor. He became Master of the Queen's Musick in 1893. Elgar had contacted him in 1898, regarding the business of getting permission to dedicate *Caractacus* to the Queen. Parratt agreed and his approaches were successful. He asked Elgar to set Frederic Myer's *To her beneath whose steadfast star* as an unaccompanied madrigal for the Queen: 'I am getting up a sort of Victorian Triumphs of Oriana, a tribute by the Composers and Poets of the day to the Queen.' [3] The occasion was to mark the Queen's eightieth birthday, and Elgar's piece, along with *Chanson de Matin* and *Chanson de Nuit*, was included in the concert in Windsor Castle on 24 May 1899.

In the course of the correspondence about the dedication of *Caractacus,* Parratt had assured Elgar that the Queen liked his music: 'I use your music constantly, and the Queen likes it. Have you done any more *small orchestra* things. They are most useful.' [4]

Clearly he was happy with the madrigal setting, since he was soon engaging Elgar to conduct a concert organised by Parratt at the Royal Albert Institute, Windsor. This took place on 18 October 1899 and Elgar conducted no less that ten of his own short pieces. Victoria was absent at Balmoral, but Princess Christian attended and Elgar stayed overnight in the Castle. He wrote enthusiastically to his sister Helen ('Dot') on 20 October: 'Yes it was a Concert at Windsor & 3 princesses were at it – they did *ten* of my pieces which I either conducted or accompanied – you shall see a gold programme! Very nice & I slept in the Castle!'[5] As Arthur Benson was emerging as an unofficial literary laureate so, at the same time, Elgar was being noticed at Court.

It has been suggested that Benson, too, was a keen amateur musician and 'deeply musical,'[6] but this is, perhaps, to overstate matters. He could certainly play the piano and organ, but his observations regarding a performance of Bach's B Minor Mass in Cambridge in 1910 was: 'I am no good at serious music.' We know, too, that he received scant parental encouragement. He had, however, already collaborated with composers, for example Parry's *Ode to Music* composed for the opening of the Royal College of Music. Subsequently he certainly admired Elgar's setting of the *Coronation Ode* and, indeed, *The Kingdom*: 'This comes nearer, in my mind, to being music than anything I know,' and *The Apostles*: '... a work of real genius ... end was really divine, a glimpse of heaven.' [7] In general he did not, however, think much of musicians: 'Their minds seem to be enclosed in a small park. They are without humanity, absorbed, fond of details, fond of bad jokes, desultory, apt to consider small things important.'[8]

Much later in life he found Elgar 'foolishly elated' on becoming Master of the King's Musick himself, and at a subsequent dinner at the Athanaeum Elgar was 'both stupid and discontented'.[9] Though it should be noted that Benson, almost unfailingly courteous in life, was almost unfailingly acerbic in his diary!

Benson did have a brief romantic attachment to the composer Arthur Somervell, a contemporary at King's, Cambridge; but the great exception to his low view of musicians was Walter Parratt. They were near neighbours and on Sundays Benson would frequently walk with Parratt. They had, indeed, collaborated in the settings of a Mausoleum hymn: 'It enables me to do something for the Queen, whom I regard with an extraordinary love and veneration ... and secondly it gives me many sights of Sir Walter Parratt, who is very high-minded, affectionate and able man – more suggestive and less limited than any musician I know.' As well as walks, Benson accompanied Parratt into the organ loft at St George's, where they would both play.

It is little wonder, given his relations with both, that it was Parratt who was destined to bring Benson and Elgar together. On 12 March 1901, Queen Victoria having died on 22 January, Elgar received a letter from Parratt enclosing verses of an ode for the Coronation: ' ... these words have been sent to me by Arthur Benson, son of the Archbishop, a genuine poet and known to the Royalties. Should it take your fancy – he would be honoured and most grateful if you could set it to immortal music.' About a week later, Benson sent a 'follow-up' letter to Malvern: 'I need hardly say that I shall be very proud if you decide to set them.'

As 'reward', Parratt became the dedicatee of Elgar's *Five Part-Songs from the Greek Anthology,* which was published in 1903, and within a year Edward had produced music, some of which certainly may now be described as 'immortal', and in so doing assured Arthur Benson of immortality too.

It has been suggested, incidentally, that Elgar emerged only as second choice as setter of Benson's words and that there had been an earlier approach to Stanford which was declined. Benson's biographer, David Newsome, tells of Stanford visiting Benson, and Benson's diary certainly records that in December 1901 Stanford ' ... came in to see me ... he was blowed if he wd write a line of music for the blackguards (ie Novello).' He predicted that the firm would ' ... come a cropper by miserliness soon; they have alienated Elgar'.[10]

Undoubtedly Stanford felt strongly about English music publishing;[11] but the outburst seems strange if related to a *Coronation Ode* project, since Novello did not have a monopoly in this area and Elgar was to deal in the matter of publication with Boosey. However, Stanford was surely correct in asserting that Elgar was at odds with Novello (see below); hence his dealings with Boosey.

However, it seems likely that Benson's diary entry refers not to his *Ode* but rather to a different piece, a *Coronation Hymn*. Benson had received an approach from Novello, who appear to have left him to find a composer for this project. Certainly Benson, never short of undertakings, was particularly busy with the approaching coronation – Wagner's *Kaiser March* with words provided by himself, was just one such project scheduled for the actual Coronation Service in the Abbey. In February 1902 he was able to mention that he had heard the setting of his hymn. With Stanford's refusal, C.H. Lloyd, precentor of Eton College, had been turned to and provided music, which 'trips along very blithely', observed Benson.[12]

Stanford remained discontented with matters concerning the Coronation. He was furious at being largely neglected and fired off letters to Frederick Bridge, organist at Westminster Abbey, who in turn attempted to blame Parratt as Master of the King's Musick. Benson had it from Parratt that: 'Stanford is simply furious & very undignified – but P. says that this is to him a deadly rankling insult. Parratt feels this acutely & sees in it the seed of much unhappiness & wrangling.'[13]

One can note in passing that when the Cambridge-based Stanford is recorded in Benson's diary as having made mention of Elgar to Benson, such mention is not usually complimentary. For example, in 1904 Benson recalls that: 'Stanford under cover of praising Elgar would make out that he has no melody.'[14] On a later occasion, when Elgar cancelled a speaking engagement at the last minute Stanford told Benson: ' ... he *always* does this if he is asked to speak – he accepts – & then can't face it.'[15] (Stanford was probably generally correct regarding the latter; but certainly not the former!)

Not that the Elgar/Benson collaboration was quick off the ground. It has been suggested[16] that Elgar was almost at a loose end at this time. It seems that there was plenty going on. Queen Victoria died on 22 January 1901 and Parratt wrote to Elgar about the *Ode* on 12 March. The Coronation of Edward VII was fixed for 26 June 1902. Between June 1901 and June 1902 Elgar conducted the première of *Cockaigne* and was considering the composition of a sequel to the overture, to be called *City of Dreadful Night.* He scored Brewer's *Emmaus,* which was performed at the Gloucester Three Choirs Festival in September 1901, along with the Prelude and Angel's Farewell from *The Dream of Gerontius* as well as *Cockaigne.* During the Festival, Elgar attended a house party at Hasfield Court. July and August had been time for cycling, welcoming Jaeger and Buths to Craeg Lea – the Elgars removing themselves to Birchwood – and the Llangranog holiday. Elgar nonetheless finished and orchestrated the first two *Pomp and Circumstance* marches. He agreed to and made a start on the provision of music for the play *Diarmuid and Grania,*[17] without either first reading the play or having a guarantee of payment! In October he attended the Leeds Festival where he conducted the *Variations.* On 19 October the first two *Pomp and Circumstance* marches were premièred in Liverpool, conducted by Rodewald. Elgar was present.

In December the commission for *The Apostles* was received. Meanwhile Elgar provided the pianist Fanny Davies with the *Concert Allegro.* He suffered from eye trouble. Later that month he was in Düsseldorf for *Gerontius.* At the opening of 1902 he was working on *Dream Children* and in February he was showing the third march to Ivor Atkins, and discussing plans for *Gerontius* at the Three Choirs; famously there were problems with the text. In the spring he abandoned a projected opera plan (Moore/Binyon), and at the same time was having to tell the organisers of the Norwich Festival that a promised cantata, *The High Tide,* could not be written, alleging continued eye trouble. He did, however, make his arrangement of the National Anthem. In the month before the projected Coronation, he conducted Parry's *The Lotus Eaters* in Worcester before venturing to Düsseldorf again for the Lower Rhine Festival performance of *Gerontius,* which was followed by a fortnight's holiday in Germany.

The *Coronation Ode* had to be fitted in among all this, and its composition was by no means the only issue.

It was at the Leeds Festival in October 1901 that the notion of adapting Benson's *Ode* for the celebrations of June 1902 was mooted, although to begin with it was the possibility of an operatic adaptation of *Caractacus* which attracted Elgar. Introduced by Frank Schuster to H.V. Higgins, Chairman of the Covent Garden Opera Syndicate, Elgar learned that Higgins was determined on a special event at the Opera House to mark the occasion. Benson's *Ode* was mentioned, but Elgar came up with a plan to revise *Caractacus,* a work dedicated to Queen Victoria and, no doubt, in his mind at this return visit to Leeds, the city of its first performance in 1898. He promised to send the score to Higgins for consideration.

It was not an idea that recommended itself to Jaeger, who wrote to Elgar in December:

> *Dont* cook up Caractacus for Covent Garden. It will never do. Write a *real* opera – WAIT a year or two. I cannot imagine Englishmen & women, however operatically 'Fashionable' or blasé[,] enjoying Britons being shown on the stage under the *Conqueror's Yoke!* Your labour will all be wasted & they'll *never ask You again* if the thing is a failure. You cant alter a Cantata into an opera. no one can. ... Think it over & dont make rash promises and dont waste your genius & Your time on a forlorn hope.
> Write a *new* work.
> I have studied Caractacus again & cannot see anything *operatically* effective in it except the Love Duet & the march (with Britons tied captive to the Conquerors' wheels!)
> DONT!!![18]

But, in fact, Higgins had already come to a separate view, that *Caractacus* would not do: '... in its present form ... unsuitable for dramatic representation on the stage.' However, he clearly remained keen on the Benson idea and continued in this letter to Elgar: 'There will undoubtedly be a gala performance at Covent Garden in honour of the Coronation: would you be prepared to undertake the composition of a *Coronation Ode?*'

Higgins wanted a work on a fairly large scale and soon Benson was agreeing to write further verses. The Bishop of Winchester, Randall Davidson, had given his view that the *Ode* was not sufficiently liturgical to form part of the actual Coronation Service, and so the Covent Garden plan seemed an admirable alternative. By 1 December Higgins was able to tell Elgar that the King had approved the proposal for an Ode to be performed at a Gala performance, and that it was understood 'Mr. Benson is to write the words.' While Benson was quick to assure the composer: 'I will gladly do what I can (ie in the matter of alterations) ... Parratt will tell you that I am quite the least stubborn of librettists.'

An intense postal collaboration between Elgar and Benson was soon under way. Already by 3 December Benson was able to forward an outline of the structure of the work comprising:

> i. An introductory passage – to England, comprising eight lines 'rather smooth in character.'
> ii. A Contralto solo, comprising eight to ten lines – on Freedom.
> iii. A Duet for Soprano and Tenor – on Art.
> iv. A Bass Solo – on War.
> v. Finale.

He included a draft of the bass solo 'England Ask of Thyself'. Elgar preferred 'Britain' for musical reasons. As Dr Moore has written: 'Elgar's private identification was very much with "England". It was merely that "Britain" would sing better – more forcefully – and provide the bass with an imposing effect.' [19]

It was the first of many amendments. Elgar took Benson at his word when he wrote: 'Please remember that I am a very willing librettist, & will rewrite & correct *to any extent* – so do not scruple to suggest that *any passage whatever* is unsuitable from the musical point of view.' In discussing the finale, Benson undertook to provide something '... on lines you indicate – though the metre is a hard one.' He asked Elgar to ' ... string together a few nonsense words, just to show me how you would wish them to run, I would construct it, following the air closely.' [20]

It is clear that in this case the music was already decided and Benson needed to find words to fit a pre-ordained tune – and a somewhat awkward one! That tune, of course, was the Trio of the first *Pomp and Circumstance* March, premièred triumphantly just a few weeks before. It had occurred to Elgar, or had been suggested to him, that words should be set to it and now the *Ode* presented the opportunity. On 10 December Benson forwarded the verses beginning 'Land of Hope and Glory'. Elgar did not ask for this to be changed.

While this was going on, Jaeger had heard of it and again counselled against. In a letter of 6 December he wrote:

> I say you *will have to* write another tune for the 'Ode' in place of the 'March in D' tune (Trio)[.] I have been trying much to fit words to it; that drop to E & the bigger drop after wards are quite impossible in singing ANY words to them[.] They sound downright vulgar: Just try it. The effect is fatal. No, You must write a *new* tune to *the* words & not fit the words to this tune. Consider this carefully & give no Choir a chance of scooping down. It will sound horrible. TRY IT (no extra charge).[21]

Elgar replied on 9 December, facetiously: 'My dear Jaeger: I haven't time to answer all your *impertinent* letters. Yah!'.[22]

Ultimately Jaeger and Elgar were of one mind – the composer reluctantly? – concerning the *Caractacus* idea but, so far as the march and *Land of Hope and Glory* were concerned Elgar, was not to be dissuaded. He was delighted with Benson's verses.

'Please don't thank me', wrote Benson, 'it is a most interesting and delightful task.'

The collaboration went on apace, including an alteration to the ending of the *Land of Hope and Glory* sequence. In March 1902 Benson observed: 'I don't approve at all of the Bell Couplet and I will try and write you one today to take its place.' On 2 April Benson proposed that 'Instead of the line about the *bells*, the last line but one, I would suggest – 'Hearts in hope uplifted, loyal lips that sing, Strong in Faith & Freedom we have crowned our King'.[23] And thus it remained.

The librettist continued to protest his compliance: 'Please make any criticism; I am as meek as Moses', he had written towards the end of December. The correspondence was, indeed, so regular that Benson took to regretting that they had never met. 'I hope we may some day meet after all our interesting correspondence. Are you by any chance going to be at the Royal College on the 24th? I am going and we might at least shake hands.' This was on 7 February 1902, hard upon an earlier hope of a meeting expressed a fortnight before. But Elgar was not going to the Royal College, and there was to be no meeting for quite a while yet.

It has been a commonplace of Elgarian folklore since the composition of the *Coronation Ode* – one of the classic pieces of Elgarian mythology – that the notion of setting the march trio to words came as a suggestion (virtual command even?) from the King. The chief evidence for this must surely be a letter of Elgar to Clara Butt dated 21 November 1927 stating bluntly that 'King Edward was the first to suggest that the air from the *Pomp and Circumstance* marches should be sung', and that its present form evolved 'via the Coronation Ode in which you were to have sung.' This letter is quoted by Dr Percy Young[24] and Michael Kennedy goes further in writing that the suggestion was 'probably' made at a 'meeting with his sovereign'[25] to which Elgar alluded in anticipation in a letter of 12 November 1901 to Jaeger: 'The Robes [Cambridge Doctorate Robes] have *not* come yet ... I *want* 'em now to appear at Court.'

Sir Walter Parratt had, indeed, arranged for a performance of the first *Pomp and Circumstance* March at a Royal Concert on 5 February 1902, but Elgar did not attend. There was, thus, no meeting with the King. One wonders whether his doctoral hood would have been appropriate dress in any case and, of course, the whole business of Elgar and Benson's correspondence about the use of the march tune had been completed two months previously. It is, in fact, possible that Elgar's reference to appearing 'at Court' was no more than a joke based on the remarkable success of the first two marches. Henry Wood has recorded that, uniquely in his experience, he had to grant a double encore at the London Queen's Hall performance on 22 October 1901. Elgar had become a celebrity.

In fact the King had at this time never met Elgar, and Dr Moore can find no evidence that he heard the march before February 1902.[26] Elgar's letter to Clara Butt is not published in either Dr Young's edition of Elgar's letters nor in Dr Moore's *Letters of a Lifetime*, rather suggesting that it has proved difficult to locate the original and that the whole claim might well depend on secondary authorities. In any case, the date of Elgar's letter was some twenty-five years after the event, and sometimes it is necessary to be on guard against evasions, 'red herrings' and economy with the truth when considering Elgar's letters and pronouncements. Elgar was not averse to the growth of legends around his life and work, and in later years assiduously promoted their currency.[27]

A different, and more likely, account is that Clara Butt attended a performance of the march on 26 November 1901 and sat with Elgar. She later claimed in an undated letter at the Elgar Birthplace, but possibly precipitating the November 1927 rejoinder: '*While* listening to the tune in *Pomp and Circumstance* [No.1] I asked you to write something like it for me & after a little persuasion on my part you said "You shall have that one my dear".' [28] Certainly the Butt story seems more plausible and the one which is gaining acceptance.[29]

By 15 April *The Daily Telegraph* wrote that: ' ... an interesting feature (of the new *Ode*) is to be its imposing finish – the theme of the Trio of the March in D from the composer's *Pomp and Circumstance*. In compliance with a request Dr Elgar has used it as representing the climax of national feeling.' Thus, perhaps, launching the notion of a 'request'. But from whom? Another, though minor, confusion is that J.F. Porte attributed the 'request' as coming from Queen Alexandra.[30] This theory seems to have been plucked – like Elgar's music is sometimes said to be – out of the air!

Perhaps it ought to be mentioned that there is some evidence that the King subsequently came to have a liking for the famous tune. On 16 August 1903 Parratt wrote to Elgar: 'The King has taken a great fancy to you. He commanded the *Pomp and Circumstance* [No.1] for one Court: which caused a comical incident. The Lord Chamberlain sent word up to me that it was too loud, and asked me to play it PP!! which I flatly refused to do!'[31] Lady Maud Warrender recalled in her *My First Sixty Years* a performance of the *Ode* in 1903 at the Albert Hall conducted by Elgar. She tells of being seated in a box adjacent to the Royal Box, in which the King had dozed off. Lady Maud managed to exchange seats with Alice Elgar to prevent Alice's noticing! But the King woke '... when 'Land of Hope and Glory' blazed forth, all was well.'

The version of *Land of Hope and Glory* that concludes the *Coronation Ode* is neither the only nor the most famous setting. In the *Ode* there is no reference to 'wider still and wider', rather we get the admirable sentiment:

> *Truth and Right and Freedom, each a holy gem,*
> *Stars of solemn brightness, weave thy diadem.*

In his *Edward Elgar: a guide to research*, Dr Christopher Kent not only gives copious details of sketches and scores of the *Coronation Ode* to be found in the British Library, but also *Land of Hope and Glory* (Song for voice pf.) arranged from the first *Pomp and Circumstance* March, Op.39 and the *Coronation Ode*. Dr Kent records that in BL Add.MS 63155 f.3 sk this is 'described by Elgar as: "the first sketch of the rest of the song/*Land of Hope and Glory* the principal theme of which first appeared in *Pomp and Circumstance* No.1/and afterwards in the *Coronation Ode*: It is entitled *National Song*" '.

It was this *National Song* which Clara Butt first sang on Saturday, 21 June 1902 at a 'Coronation Concert' at the Royal Albert Hall, five days before the date fixed for the Coronation (26 June) and just over a week before the scheduled première of the *Coronation Ode* (30 June). Benson's revised/additional words for this different occasion are as follows:

> *Dear Land of Hope, thy hope is crowned:*
> *God make thee mightier yet!*
> *On sov'ran brows beloved, renowned,*
> *Once more the crown is set!*
> *Thine equal laws by freedom gained,*
> *Have ruled thee well and long;*
> *By freedom gained, by truth maintained,*
> *Thine Empire shall be strong.*
>
> *Land of Hope and Glory, Mother of the Free,*
> *How may we extol thee, who are born of thee?*
> *Wider still and wider shall thy bounds be set;*
> *God, who made thee mighty, make thee mightier yet.*
>
> *Thy fame is ancient as the days,*
> *An ocean large and wide;*
> *A pride that dares, and heeds not praise –*
> *A stern and silent pride.*
> *Not that false joy that dreams content*
> *With what our sires had won;*
> *The blood a hero sire hath spent*
> *Should nerve a hero son.*
>
> *Land of Hope and Glory, etc ...*

It can be argued that this *National Song* was a celebration not only of the impending Coronation but also of the ending of the Boer War. Ironically, Benson was anything but a jingoist[32] and had been on record at the time of the Relief of Mafeking as 'severely deprecating' the attendant 'hysterics'. He was, it has been said, one who abhorred the 'popular taste for vulgar excitement'.

It seems likely that the inspiration for this fresh setting came from the publishers Boosey. Dr Moore writes: 'When they saw 'Land of Hope and Glory,' their [Booseys'] experience with ballads told them that it would make a hit. At their request, author and composer revised it as a solo song for separate publication.' [33]

Of course, Elgar too, knew a good tune when he heard one – ' ... a tune like that comes once in a lifetime' [34] – and was certainly never averse to exploiting commercial opportunity. At all events Benson was in discussion with Elgar about the separate song proposal before the end of April 1902. Boosey & Co. had been in touch with him and Benson wrote to Elgar: 'I am quite ready to try and do what I can ... I don't think I have got quite the popular ring – but I should like to try very much.' [35] By 26 April he had despatched his draft version.

Butt had been envisaged as singing in the première of the *Ode*, as correspondence between Elgar and Higgins makes clear, but this fell through. Her Albert Hall performance, however, was a triumph. *The Morning Post* reported that Butt sang ' ... a new song by Dr. Elgar, 'Land of Hope and Glory',' and was ' ... several times recalled at the close.'

No sooner had the vocal score of the *Ode* been completed, at the end of March 1902, than Benson was struck by an afterthought. He wrote to Elgar that he had realised: ' ... on a lonely walk yesterday that there was not a word in the Ode about Queen Alexandra. This is a grave omission. So I have written a tiny two verse lyric, which I enclose, in the hopes that you may approve.' He undertook to alter anything in it to suit Elgar, but clearly hoped he would not be required so to do: ' ... you will see that it is all balanced, and I will confess it will not be very easy to pull it about.' [36]

Perhaps even this most compliant collaborator was tiring of Elgar's constant revision proposals; a state of affairs exacerbated when Henry Higgins of Covent Garden kept insisting on adding his views. In January he had told Elgar that he would wish to see Benson's libretto 'before you commence your task.' Such a suggestion was, of course, scarcely to be reconciled with Elgar's approach to word-setting and the continuing nature of his collaboration with the librettist. Clearly, however, some material was forwarded, since by 2 February Higgins was telling Elgar that he liked 'the scheme of it, but some of the lines appear to me very halting.' He went on to mark passages which he found weak, and suggested that Elgar might 'delicately' ask for changes.

So far as the Queen Alexandra passage was concerned, however, Benson and Elgar agreed, that it must form a separate, additional movement to follow the first. Benson summed it up: 'I don't think that the illusion would have come well in the first *piece* because the King is *symbolic* there – indeed there is so little that is romantic or distinguished about the King personally (with all due respect) that one cannot linger on the personal side – but with the Queen one can.'

Benson was able to report by 9 September, after the Coronation, that the Queen was to accept a special copy of the verses 'Daughter of the Ancient Kings.' Later – on 11 November – she was to tell Lady Mary Lygon:

> It was very kind and nice of you to send me that very pretty bit of music by Dr Elgar – a greeting to myself in the Coronation Ode – which alas I have not yet heard. Please tell the great Master *how* much I appreciate his having sent it me and how grateful I am to you for having pointed out that the Chorus of "Ancient Kings" is the prettiest and most effective one in the composition.[37]

Certainly, though Ernest Newman found it 'lacking in distinction, and unworthy of a place in the work', opinion has generally been favourable toward the interpolation. Dr Moore speaks of its 'disarming simplicity [which] raised Benson's capable verses to a level of genius,' [38] while Dr Robert Anderson writes of its 'simple chords, heartfelt and very beautiful.' [39]

Any satisfaction felt by Elgar, however, was given a jolt when Dora Penny told him that she recognised the beginning since it closely resembled a hymn in *Hymns Ancient & Modern*. This was No.528 'Not For Our Sins Alone' to the tune *Waltham* by W.H. Monk. At Elgar's invitation she played the first line of the hymn on his piano, he having denied any knowledge of 'your hymns.' His retort to the piano demonstration was: 'Well, I can't help it. I've never heard the wretched hymn in my life' sounds as if Dorabella had successfully made her point.[40] Anyone listening to the opening bars of the hymn and the opening of 'Daughter of Ancient Kings' must surely agree.

Composing the *Ode* was by no means the only task demanding Edward's attention. The various complications surrounding the mounting of the work proved among the most traumatic of any Elgar première and, indeed, concluded in cancellation.

At least the business of publication went on amicably. At this time Edward was at odds with Novello following a protracted dispute concerning royalties on *The Dream of Gerontius*, occasioned apparently by a misunderstanding between the firm and G.H. Johnstone, an official of the Birmingham Festival Committee. Novello were loath to be generous since, as Alfred Littleton wrote to Johnstone: 'Unfortunately for us the work is a commercial failure & we have no anticipation of ever realizing our initial expenses.' [41]

It is perhaps interesting to note in passing that Benson and Parry had discussions about *The Dream of Gerontius*, Parry informing Benson that he had himself rejected Cardinal Newman's poem as 'impossible.' Benson agreed, somewhat acidly, that 'the cigar and the yacht were hardly compatible' (with *Gerontius*),[42] a verdict rather hard on Parry who Delius felt would have set the entire Bible had he lived long enough.[43]

At all events it was Boosey to whom Elgar offered *Cockaigne*. Boosey accepted with alacrity and paid well. Similarly the first two *Pomp and Circumstance* marches went to Boosey for fifty and twenty-five guineas respectively, plus a royalty. Novello had missed out on a hugely successful venture. Now it was to Boosey that Elgar turned once more, Novello having to be content with an arrangement of the National Anthem.

Boosey agreed to pay a fee of £100 plus a royalty, as well as being responsible for printing publicity material for Covent Garden. By mid-April the vocal score was well advanced. The publishing manager at Boosey, James Leighton, proved to be, as Dr Moore writes, 'a man after Elgar's own heart',[44] and sent lengthy and informal letters, signing off one such, for example:

> 'I feelweaddernuff.
> Yrs very Sincly & gratitudinaciously,
>   Jas. Leighton.' [45]

Elgar was delighted and presented Leighton with a signed photograph.

There was some discussion about the pricing of the vocal score and, thus, Elgar's royalty. Arthur Boosey observed in a letter of 18 April that: '3/6 I am afraid is too much ... If we make it 2/6 we could pay you a Royalty of 4d.' [46] Indeed, 2/6 was the price at which the vocal score was marketed, though Elgar appears to have secured a royalty of 5d per copy. Boosey also agreed to supply a book of words to be presented to members of the Covent Garden audience. Arthur Boosey told Elgar that he felt: ' ... we must look upon this performance purely as an advertisement';[47] hence there would be no charge, or royalty, for this. Quite how Benson emerged from these dealings is unclear.

In May there were some further dealings, regarding an arrangement of the *Ode* for military band.[48] While it is interesting that when Boosey approached Elgar for two songs, on 30 June 1902, suggesting that 'Mrs. Elgar will find you some words', the words used were, in fact, by Benson. Elgar supplied the songs – *In the Dawn* and *Speak Music* – at the end of August.[49] George Boosey, Arthur's younger brother, was enthused, and Elgar received twenty-five guineas for each plus a royalty. One feels that A.J. Jaeger must have worked hard at this time to prevent Elgar's total abandonment of Novello in favour of Boosey.

Elgar found more problems when it came to agreeing the forces that would present the work. He was clear that the Sheffield Chorus must be engaged. The Sheffield Triennial Musical Festival had been inaugurated in 1896 as a two-day event, and the Second Festival, in 1899, was extended to three days. That year Elgar had conducted *King Olaf* and had been delighted with the results. Indeed, even on the evidence simply of a rehearsal, he had written to F.G. Edwards of *The Musical Times* on 20 July 1899: ' ... do you know that the chorus is absolutely the finest in the world! Not so large as Leeds but for fire, intelligence, dramatic force they are electrical. *Do* go to the Festival – for the first time in my life I've heard *my* choral effects (Olaf) & very terrifying they are. Laus Deo! (& Cowardus).' [50]

This last was a reference to Henry Coward, the remarkable Sheffield choral conductor, whom Elgar met for the first time in 1899. Indeed Edward stayed at Coward's home during the Festival and *Gerontius* was no doubt discussed. Coward always imagined that some of that work was written at his house, and was immediately determined to secure a performance for the 1902 Festival with Elgar conducting; and this was duly agreed. Thus, when composing the *Coronation Ode*, the Sheffield Choir was much in Elgar's thoughts and high in his estimation.

By March Higgins had been in touch with E.W. Frith, Secretary to the Sheffield Choir and, though the date of the performance had yet to be finalised, was able to tell Elgar that month that it (the performance): ' ... would be a full State one,' and the chorus 'exclusively a Sheffeld chorus.' In early April he had a 'very satisfactory' meeting with Frith, and engaged in negotiation with Elgar about the numbers concerned. Elgar's preference was for as many as possible: ' ... all maybe of those who sang before for me.'

However, in the end he settled for 160 (forty-four sopranos, thirty-four contraltos, forty-two tenors, forty basses), no doubt all that the Covent Garden stage could comfortably accommodate. Coward assured Elgar in a letter of 25 April that: 'You may be sure I have chosen those whose ability and enthusiasm will do full justice to your work.' In fact the 'difficult and delicate' task of choosing about half of the 300-plus-strong choir and disappointing the rest was achieved partly by Coward's nomination and partly by ballot – 'drawn by hand' by the city's Mayor. This solution seems to have satisfied all but five choristers, who resigned. When Elgar visited Sheffield on 12 June for a rehearsal he was 'received as a conquering hero.'

In his subsequent *Reminiscences* Coward speaks of the 'seventh heaven of anticipation' which activated the choir as they awaited the great day when they were to perform before 'a gathering of emperors, kings, queens, potentates, powers, diamonds, tiaras, pendants, bracelets, rings, flowers – £5,000 spent in floral decorations alone – and our worthy selves would be there to see this regal splendour, surpassing anything in the Arabian Nights.' [51] The outcome, of course, was to be different.

Casting the soloists proved more troublesome than fixing the Choir. Ultimately Melba, Kirkby Lunn, Ben Davies and Ffrangcon-Davies were settled upon, but not without much argument. Higgins's policy was outlined in a letter as early as 19 December 1901: 'As regards singers, we must, of course, as far as possible utilise singers who will be engaged at Covent Garden.' Shortly after, on 7 January 1902, he wrote to Elgar to advise that Clara Butt had refused an engagement at the Opera and: 'I do not wish to bring any outsider to sing at the gala performance, more especially as I have the very best opinion of Kirkby Lunn.' Elgar, naturally, gave scant priority to this argument, preferring Butt, and Higgins was still having to justify Kirkby Lunn at the end of April who: ' ... without having so fine a voice is a far better singer.' He also reiterated the argument that Lunn was a member of the Covent Garden Company.

Nor did Elgar seem totally at ease with Melba as soprano, Higgins having to write testily to him: ' ... no sane person would hesitate between Melba and Albani.' Elgar must, one feels, surely have been content with Ffrangcon-Davies, not only a regular singer in Elgar's music but also a determined and effusive correspondent.[52] Indeed he seems to have suggested him at an early date. Nonetheless, this did not prevent the name of Andrew Black being floated, and once more it was Higgins who was the objector: 'I am not at all an admirer of Black who in addition is not engaged at the opera.'

So far as the tenor was concerned, Elgar's preference for John Coates was made very clear, and Higgins had to have recourse to proclaiming a *fait accompli*: 'I have already written to Ben Davies and could not therefore withdraw the part from him unless he refuses it.' So it appears that there is much evidence that none of Elgar's preferred line-up (Coates, Black, Albani, Butt) was engaged. This was a clear victory for Higgins.

On one matter, however, Elgar did stand firm. He was determined to conduct not only the *Ode*, but also his own new arrangement of the National Anthem. Higgins was eager to obtain this crumb for Mancinelli, 'our principal conductor for fifteen years.' As late as 20 June, with the performance due within ten days, he was still reporting plaintively that Mancinelli was anxious to conduct *God Save the King*.

The King might have approved the proposal of an *Ode* back in December 1901 but, in March 1902, Higgins had still not been able to confirm a date for a Royal Gala Performance or even if there was to be such a performance. 'I think you could perfectly well announce that the Covent Garden directors have requested you to write an ode for performance on this Gala night if there be one', he advised Elgar in a letter of 7 March. Indeed he was doubtful in his letter of 11 March whether the status of Royal Gala would be granted earlier than 'a fortnight before the performance'.

By 20 March, however, he was able to tell Elgar that the performance would, indeed, be a 'full state one', though almost a month later – 16 April – he still had no date. The performance seemed fairly certain to be in the last week of June or the first week of July –though not on Thursday, 26 June, the day of the Coronation, or the day following. Rather the 24th seemed 'likely'. As late as 29 April, Benson was still unclear about a date and proposed asking Sir Walter Parratt to present a copy of the *Ode* to the King, possibly in the hope of expediting matters. In fact the date of the performance was finally fixed for Monday, 30 June. This continuing uncertainty cannot have assisted in the engagement of singers. Moreover, it is clear that this confusion has sometimes bemused later Elgarians. Dr Percy Young states that the *Ode* was due to be performed on 25 June, the day prior to the Coronation,[53] as does David Nice[54] – that is, five days too soon.

It was not only the question of casting the *Ode* that exercised Higgins. At the end of April, Benson had invoked Elgar's assistance in the matter of actually getting into Covent Garden once the performance date had finally been fixed. Elgar received the remarkable information from Higgins on 2 May that there were no complimentary tickets to be had even for Alice Elgar let alone Benson. He would however: ' ... see that Mr. Benson has a Balcony Stall; i.e., a Dress Circle Ticket, also that Mrs. Elgar has the same. This is the best I can do.'

Presumably Henry Coward's 'kings, queens, potentates, etc.' were expected in number and, it would seem, had priority over the librettist and the composer's wife. One wonders, too, if Higgin's equating of 'Balcony Stall' and 'Dress Circle' was accurate. It is certainly not true today, nor has it been during the past fifty years at least, in an auditorium virtually unchanged since 1902. At any event, Benson was not prepared to let the matter rest and wrote to Elgar on 20 May indicating his intention of seeking the intercession of Lord Esher, 'a friend of mine, who is on the Executive Coronation Sub-Committee'. Perhaps he was encouraged, by having heard that the King had, in principle, accepted the dedication of the *Ode.* This, in turn, raised another issue, the form of words to be used. Benson wrote to urge Elgar that the words 'and Subjects' be added to 'Servants.' This was 'customary' and 'besides, I rather prefer being a subject to being a servant.' Indeed, in the dedication Elgar and Benson are recorded as being: 'Loyal and Devoted Servants and Subjects.' [55]

Benson, in fact, was nothing if not pedantic and had, for example, informed a doubtless uninterested Elgar on 9 April that the very title *Coronation Ode* was dubious since the word 'Coronation' was 'strictly speaking' not an adjective. Fortunately Benson recalled other usages such as 'Wedding March,' 'Birthday Present' and 'Dettingen Te Deum,' so he was prepared to let matters stand.

The saga of the tickets, however, continued. In mid-June Benson was informing Elgar: 'I have done my best to get Mrs. E. a better place (and myself as well) but it seems very difficult'. By 20 June he was reporting the latest strategy: 'I *hope* to have a chance of seeing a friend of mine who is a good deal with the King just now, and has a great deal to do with the Coronation arrangements', though he conceded that caution was needed since the King: ' ... doesn't like to think he is being dictated to – "These gentlemen seem to forget it is *my* Coronation".' One can easily imagine that Edward VII had more on his mind than the Elgar/Benson seating arrangements at Covent Garden.

Benson, though, went on and on. It would, he maintained, be mentioned to the King 'if it can be', but explained that on medical advice the King was not to be 'fussed or bothered.' The whole affair, asserted Benson, was 'very humiliating – not personally but from the point of view of art.' He went so far as to float the possibility that he might absent himself from the performance and simply attend the rehearsal.

Ultimately all Benson's efforts were of no avail and Higgins was, once more, the victor. On 23 June, just a week before the performance date, Arthur wrote to Alice Elgar that it would be a great pleasure to meet the Elgars on the 30th, 'all being well,' and went on to observe: 'I think I would as soon be in the front balcony row as anywhere in the House.' Of course, all was not destined to be 'well'.

Alice's ticket may still be seen at the Elgar Birthplace – number 17 in the Balcony Stalls. Dr Jerrold Moore states that Edward purchased 'two stalls' at twenty guineas each. As we have seen they were not actually 'stalls' and one wonders whether Edward expected reimbursement from the well-to-do Benson for one of them. However, one does not doubt Dr Moore's conclusion that 'There was no shortage of money in the Elgar household when the occasion was imperious.' [56]

There remained one final matter to be settled. As early as the beginning of December 1901 Higgins had suggested a twenty-minute limit on the length of the work. In his letter of 7 March he told Elgar that the King was: '... very anxious that the evening's performance should be as short as possible.' He went on to suggest that Elgar limit himself to fifteen minutes. In fact the *Ode* lasts just over half an hour (about thirty-three minutes in the Gibson recording and thirty-one in the Ledger recording).[57]

Higgins returned to the matter in early June, with rehearsals about to get under way. He emphasised the need for cuts: 'I know you will not think I am saying anything rude when I say that I do not think it will prejudice you in any way if your work is not done in its entirety – I do not think we can possibly allow more than 25 minutes inclusive of "God Save the King".' On 11 June Higgins wrote again to Elgar: 'I am much obliged to you for meeting our views as you have done.' It sounds as if Elgar had agreed to fall into line. Had the performance taken place the matter of what was to be left out would have become clear.

At all events if, as it appears, Elgar lost out on the matters of soloists, tickets for the performance and 'cuts', one may conclude that Higgins was, indeed, a redoubtable opponent. Almost the only 'victory' Elgar could claim was that Higgins, perforce, accepted that since the Cambridge honorary degree (22 November 1900) he was dealing with 'Doctor' Elgar and that this was what the Gala's programme should – and did – acknowledge: 'I quite understand about the "Doctor" – you are quite right', he conceded in his letter of 11 March 1902.

On 24 June Alice Elgar's diary records: 'E. out cycling again. Heard the dreadful news of the King's illness and postponement of the "Coronation".' Rosa Burley confirms that she was cycling with Elgar on that day: ' ... we visited Stretton Grandison, a village just off the old Worcester–Hereford main road, where there is a fine church.' After looking at the church, they obtained tea at the local inn. It was a hot day. Alice and Edward were due to leave for London the next day. Edward and Miss Burley discussed the approaching Coronation: 'Edward agreed that to attend a gala performance immediately after reviewing the fleet at Spithead ... might prove a strain to one who, like the King, was known not to be strong.'

At this point the innkeeper's wife burst in with news that the King had been taken seriously ill and that the Coronation and attendant celebrations had been postponed *sine die*. It was, Rosa Burley goes on, ' ... a terrible disappointment for Edward,' who returned home in gloomy anticipation that Alice would feel the blow all too keenly, an eventuality which Rosa Burley confirms – 'the worse sufferer of the two.' [58] Although on the following days Alice's thoughts were ostensibly with the King rather than her own disappointment: 'Intense anxiety for news of the King,' is her diary entry.

On what should have been the eve of the Coronation *The Times* announced that *Tristan und Isolde* with Van Dyck and Nordica would replace the Coronation Gala. Higgins wrote to Elgar on 28 June expressing the hope that the *Ode* was merely 'deferred.' However, there was no revised arrangement made for performance at Covent Garden. Cancellation was a blow to Boosey also, but Arthur Boosey wrote stoically to Elgar on 30 June: 'Make your mind easy about the Ode. We are quite happy & it will come along all right later on – What a blessing to the Country it is that The King is going on so well.' [59]

Elgar put on a brave face. He told Rosa Burley that it meant that he was now available for more cycling, and he took the same line with Jaeger:

> Don't, for heaven's sake, *sympathise* with me – I don't care a tinker's damn! It gives me three blessed sunny days in my own country (for which I thank God or the Devil) instead of stewing in town. *My* own interest in the thing ceased, as usual, when I had finished the M.S. – since when I have been thinking mighty things! I was biking out in Herefordsh: yesterday & the news reached me at a little roadside pub: I said 'Give me another pint of cider'[.] I'm deadly sorry for the King – but that's all. [60]

Ivor Atkins was another to get a similar response. Atkins had written on 1 July in conventional fashion: ' ... very great disappointment ... when it does come off it will be with added zest ... great personal disappointment to me but your music will grow bigger in the meanwhile ... ' [61] Elgar replied:

> Many thanks for your very kind letter. I have had too much experience of 'things' to worry at all, at all! I have been Biking wildly – but not too well – during the last 10 days & playing Bach, who heals and pacifies men & all things. However it was good of you to write & I thank you. I am now plotting GIGANTIC WORX of which more anon.[62]

Elgar's gigantic work in prospect was, assuredly, *The Apostles.*

Benson was another who learned of Elgar's relaxed reaction to the cancellation. After congratulating Edward on his philosophical acceptance of the situation, he goes on in a letter of 8 July: 'Bach and bicycling! I have myself returned to construing and correcting ... I do not suppose there was ever an occasional writer who so entirely had the wind taken out of his sails as I – 'Coronation Ode', 'The Loyal Ode' (for the King's visit here) the 'Kaiser March' for the abbey and two Coronation Hymns – all fell straight into limbo.' In discussion at this time with a colleague, H.V. Luxmoore, Benson reiterated his unenthusiastic view of the King, finding it 'ironic' that: ' ... this bourgeois, ungraceful, small-minded, gross, kindly man (had had) ... the cup (which he made no pretence of not enjoying) dashed from his lips.' [63]

Of course, unlike the Covent Garden Gala, the Coronation was only postponed and Benson's Westminster Abbey contributions were given. It was not so with the *Ode* and one feels that, notwithstanding his persistent talk of cycling days in rural Worcestershire, for Elgar the loss of this vastly prestigious occasion must surely have been deeply felt. The sort of philosophical acceptance on which Benson now congratulated him did not come readily to Elgar, and it was not so long ago that he had made the immortal declaration: 'Providence denies me a decent hearing of my work: so I submit – I always said God was against art & I still believe it,' and his heart was ' ... shut against every religious feeling & every soft, gentle impulse *for ever.*' [64] Such was his immediate reaction to the inadequate première of *The Dream of Gerontius.* Edward's apparent public reaction to the cancellation of the Covent Garden Gala is among the most remarkable features of the entire episode.

Nor can his equanimity have been other than tried when he was passed over in the Coronation Honours List. 'I noticed the omission of your name from a certain list but I do not think you will lose anything by waiting a little,' wrote Higgins on 28 June. *The Pall Mall Gazette* reported on 30 June that Stanford was to be knighted, though ' ... some may have doubted if Stanford has ever done a really *big* work.' Parry was to receive a baronetcy. The *Gazette's* view was that: 'We should have approved with more complete whole-heartedness if we did not rather miss one name upon whose inclusion some had very confidently counted – Edward Elgar.' Dr Moore puts forward the perfectly feasible notion that so confident might Elgar have been about matters that the 'mighty things' of which he wrote to Jaeger, and upon which his thoughts were fixed, was royal recognition rather than *The Apostles*.[65] Elgar eventually received his knighthood in 1904, a few weeks after another Covent Garden occasion, the three-day Elgar Festival.

Elgar was not alone in taking the cancellation in his stride. A fashionable weekly, *Lady's Realm*, had gone to press in advance of the event and despatched an issue to distributors containing observations on the Gala performance notwithstanding that it had not taken place. Moreover, the author, writing under the pseudonym 'The Daughter of a Peer' (she 'appears to have peered a little too far into the future' punned *The Musical Times*) was highly critical: 'The gala-night at the opera was a disappointment to many. Seldom have we heard a worse chorus, and even stars of song must shine less brilliantly as years go on. The unrivalled Jean has not the wonderful power he had once, and if Melba is as delicious as ever she is no better. As for Caruso he is a distinct disappointment.'

The Musical Times wondered what the Sheffield chorus had to say regarding this calumny. While so far as Jean de Reszke was concerned – 'the unrivalled Jean' could apply to no other – he had not even been advertised to sing in the Gala and, indeed, had ended his Covent Garden career two years previously, in 1900.[66] Caruso certainly was billed to appear as the Duke in Act II of *Rigoletto*, which along with excerpts from *Carmen* and *Tannhäuser* made up the operatic portion of the programme. *The Musical Times* hinted at forthcoming libel actions, but sadly did not report the outcome.[67]

Not that *The Musical Times* was itself always free from error. When the postponed Coronation actually took place, on Saturday, 9 August, we are told that its editor was 'very properly' allotted a seat and was able to give a lengthy 'eye-witness description.' We learn in passing that: ' ... the service music proper had all been published in one volume by Messrs. Novello. It included Elgar's *Coronation Ode* conducted by the composer.' This, of course, is total nonsense. The *Ode* was never to be part of any Coronation Service and was certainly not performed at the Abbey on 9 August. Elgar was not even present, much less conducting.[68]

Benson, however, was in the congregation, doubtless to his surprise, since a month earlier – on 8 July – he had expressed to Elgar his doubt at the King's survival: 'I did not imagine that the King had more than a very outside chance of recovery.'[69] Indeed, appendicitis/peritonitis was a serious matter in 1902 and the King was not a young man. It has been said that his remarkably rapid recovery 'put appendectomy into surgical fashion.'

Benson left a detailed account of the Coronation in his voluminous diary – 'one wonders', writes David Newsome, 'if a fuller account of this splendid occasion has ever been recorded.' Typically Benson noted those elements which were absurd and even grotesque. The aged and almost blind Archbishop of Canterbury, Frederick Temple, for example, had difficulty fulfilling his high function. Having knelt in homage to the King, he was unable to get up and the King had to seize his hands and try to lift him, the while appealing to nearby Bishops for assistance. Temple was then carried to a chair – 'by main force' – and the Bishop of Winchester made an unrehearsed entry to the Service with the words: 'Can I get you anything? There is some sal volatile close at hand.' There were other mishaps involving the unfortunate Archbishop, culminating in the moment of Communion when he could not see where the King was, went to 'quite the wrong place' and almost 'put the bread on the carpet.'[70]

Nor was the musical side of things ideal. The Westminster Scholars were misinformed about the King's entrance to the Abbey and shouted 'Vivat Rex Edwardus' prematurely, which in turn led to an early rendition of Parry's anthem 'I was glad'.[71] Both had to be repeated. While so far as the valedictory Wagner was concerned, the words to the *Kaiser March* were spoiled because the Choir was so anxious to see the King depart that they did not much bother to sing and the result was 'awfully feeble', ruining Benson's contribution. He was still bemoaning this in a letter to Elgar over ten years later. He recalled the 'feeble moaning', and asserted that if he were to collaborate with Elgar again (a proposal to set words for a Coronation March in 1911) 'the choir must be made to sing it.'[72]

It seems that Elgar with his visit to Bayreuth, a holiday at Rodewald's home near Chester, his involvement in the Three Choirs Festival and his work on *The Apostles*, was well out of matters at Westminster.

At the end of April Elgar had received approaches from Sheffield suggesting that the second performance of the *Ode* take place there along with *The Dream of Gerontius* at the Festival in October. There was every confidence that the Sheffield Choir would return in triumph from Covent Garden, and that a repeat performance on home ground seemed a natural arrangement. It was pointed out that, in Sheffield, the whole Choir, not just a contingent, could be involved – 'all could learn the work.' It was specifically asked that there be no performance between the Gala première in London and the Sheffield performance.

The *Coronation Ode* was therefore actually premièred in Sheffield on Thursday, 2 October. *The Dream of Gerontius* was given in the morning and was followed in the afternoon by the *Ode* as the climax to a concert that included Ysaÿe playing the Beethoven Violin Concerto. The Concerto was conducted by Henry Wood; Elgar conducted his own works. The soloists for *Gerontius* – John Coates, David Ffrangcon-Davies and Muriel Foster – joined Agnes Nicholls in the *Ode*. Foster was, in fact, a substitute in *Gerontius* for an indisposed Marie Brema. Thus in the first performance of the *Ode* only Ffrangcon-Davies survived from the projected London soloists.

The première was a triumph. 'Magnificent performance of Ode – immense enthusiasm,' Alice recorded in her diary. *The Times* referred to a 'serious and masterly composition.' *The Musical Times* wrote of 'a performance which must have afforded him as much pleasure as his music gave to the audience,' while the *Sheffield Daily Telegraph* reported 'loud and prolonged cheers for everybody concerned.'

Arthur Johnstone, the distinguished music critic of the *Manchester Guardian* wrote a long and thoughtful piece. He found the *Ode* to be: ' ... popular music of a kind that has not been made for a long time in this country,' and was totally supportive of the use of the *Pomp and Circumstance* tune, a melody which ' ... I beg to suggest is as broad as "God Save the King", "Rule Britannia" and "See the Conquering Hero", and is perhaps the broadest open-air tune since Beethoven's "Freude Schöner Götterfunken".' He was astonished that anyone should criticise Elgar for re-using the tune and echoed Elgar himself, when he observed: ' ... such tunes are composed less frequently than once in 50 years ... The chorus enjoyed themselves over it and so did the audience.' Johnstone's view, writes Michael Kennedy (correctly it seems to me), 'is surely the commonsense view', and he describes the work as a masterpiece, which, notwithstanding the Coronation Honours List, 'set the seal on Elgar's "official" status.' [73]

Elgar was delighted, despite some slight mix-up with the chorus at the beginning of *Gerontius*. He jovially consoled one apologetic chorister: 'My dear girl, I am older and uglier than you are and I shall never hear better singing than that to which I have listened today until I get to Heaven.' If he had to choose a chorus to sing the *Coronation Ode* he 'should not hesitate to come to Sheffield.' Four days after the performance, he wrote presenting a copy of *The Dream of Gerontius* score to the Sheffield Free Library.

Elgar's only complaint during these days seems to have been about the toothache he contracted the Saturday before going to Sheffield – as a result, he thought, of his cycling. He obtained temporary attention on 29 September, but was complaining to Jaeger in a letter three days after the Sheffield performance: ' ... now it's really awful again ... Oh! this tooth is awful. I've lit a pipe now so I can't swear without sacrificing some smoke (Sanford's tobacco) So a more Xtian atmosphere prevails.' [74] The tooth was removed later the same day. 'E. had gas & the tooth out. E. conducted "Gerontius" all the time he was under gas,' recorded Alice. This last, quite clearly describes Elgar's involuntary gesticulations while semi-conscious/ unconscious, and is not a reference to his performance at the actual première of the *Ode* as has been assumed by one author!

The Sheffield visit enabled Elgar to meet Charles and Alice Stuart Wortley, who were patrons of the Festival, for the first time. Together with Lord and Lady Edmund Talbot, the Stuart Wortleys attended a dinner party with Schuster and Elgar at the Festival's conclusion. Lord Edmund Talbot was brother to the Duke of Norfolk, England's leading Roman Catholic layman, and there was much talk about the overlong absence of *The Dream of Gerontius* from London. The seeds of the London première at Westminster Cathedral in June 1903 were then sown. [75]

Elgar clearly recovered rapidly from his tooth extraction since, within a couple of days, he was conducting another performance of the *Ode* in Bristol. In the autumn of 1902 performances proliferated, and by early November Jaeger could count up to six in a matter of four weeks with audiences numbering from 3,000 to 5,000. 'Elgar has 'knocked 'em' at the Queen's Hall,' [76] he observed. The first of a veritable run of performances at this venue took place on 26 October at a special *National Thanksgiving Concert* arranged by Henry Wood. The *Ode* was the climax to a programme of, for the most part, items inspired by the Coronation. There were, for example, Coronation Marches by Cowen and Mackenzie. A large contingent from the Coldstream Guards band ensured an authentic rendition.

Willie Reed was among the Queen's Hall Orchestra violins and left an account. At the close, enthusiasm was so high that Elgar was recalled five times to the platform and a voice from the gallery shouted, 'Let's have the last part again,' [77] and this, indeed, happened. Adrian Boult, a boy at Westminster School, was in the audience and recalls that Robert Newman, promoter of the Queen's Hall Concert, had to announce that Elgar would conduct the desired encore and that, moreover, he promised there would be a further performance on Sunday 9 November, the King's birthday.[78] *The Morning Leader* reported that Elgar was ' ... received with such applause that one may believe the British public is at least interested in one of its composers.'

David Ffrangcon-Davies repeated the bass part which he had sung at Sheffield and immediately after the Queen's Hall performance wrote to congratulate Elgar ' ... on the superbly strong impression you made on that mass of British humanity in Queen's Hall today. You stirred them all to genuine enthusiasm, and one felt that the heart of them beat in unison with your own.' He goes on, however, to suggest 'with all diffidence' that both at Sheffield and now in London he, himself, had 'failed to get the full effect' of the bass solo and that he would like to 'take just a shade more time with the words, and to make the phrases a trifle broader.' [79]

It was at the later performance on Sunday, 9 November that Benson was finally able to escape from Eton, get to hear the work and meet Elgar at last. On 7 November he wrote to Alice Elgar indicating that he would try to get to the performance but could not accept an invitation to lunch. Perhaps understandably Benson assumed he need only turn up to gain admission, but clearly his provisional hope expressed to Alice was not taken as a firm 'booking' and he found himself facing a queue at the box office when he arrived at the last minute. He seems to have spied an acquaintance – presumably towards the front of the queue – whom he persuaded to buy him a ticket.

Benson sat through a March by Saint-Saëns and a Tchaikovsky Concerto – 'my idea of music' – and then came the *Ode*. He described Elgar as: ' ... taller and shapelier than I have imagined ... a long nose – red hands – large cuffs. He conducted with smiling aplomb – has a funny fumbling movement of the hands after [the] end of [the] piece. The *Ode* did both please and impress me very much; it is wizard-like music – I like the softer parts best.' Indeed, elsewhere he observed: 'The last movement I don't care for.' After the performance Benson went to the 'Premier Artists' room and was admitted immediately on giving his name: 'I found Elgar with his artists. I ought to have thanked them – but I was too stupid – and just had three pleasurable words with E., who was very genial and pleasant. Once or twice I detected a twang I thought.' [80]

On 24 November Benson wrote to Elgar to repeat that the *Ode* had given him 'enormous pleasure'. He owned to not knowing much about music technically: ' ... but I have very strong preferences – now No.4 seems to me to have a sort of magical quality about it – it is all fine and you can imagine the kind of pleasure it was to me to hear the words thus glorified.' By 'No.4' one imagines Benson meant 'Hark, Upon the Hallowed Air', followed by 'Only Let Thy Heart Be Pure'. He goes on, almost a year since their lengthy collaboration had begun, to suggest that in correspondence they could, perhaps, drop 'formal prefixes.'

There was to be further collaboration – and abortive collaboration – between the two, as well as occasional further meetings. Benson called on the Elgars while they were in Rome at the end of December 1907 and recorded unvarnished impressions of Alice and Carice[81] as well as Edward – 'socially always a little uneasy – he has got none of Parratt's courtesy or Parry's geniality.' Though in the end, 'the kindness of the party won my heart.' The worst thing about Elgar was 'the limp shake of his thin hand.' In fact few people could be more 'genial' than Elgar when in the right mood.

Earlier in 1907 Elgar had greeted Benson as 'his old friend and collaborator' when in Cambridge to conduct *The Kingdom*. Such meetings, however, were rare, though there was one in 1924: ' ... what a pleasure it was to meet you again,' wrote Benson on 8 March; 'I used to find you the most generous and considerate of collaborators.' These were words which Elgar might more appropriately have used of Benson.

Although Jaeger was a dissenting voice, describing the *Ode* as 'brilliantly effective but by no means great' and bemoaning the propensity of audiences to 'shout themselves hoarse over the weak stuff he (Elgar) has written', the *Ode* was clearly a great success and much admired. Today, too, writers such as Robert Anderson and Jerrold Northrop Moore find much to say in its favour. Michael Kennedy has described it as a 'masterpiece' and that is my view also. However, by its very nature the *Coronation Ode* could hardly be other than a very occasional piece. By the summer of 1904 Elgar wrote to Boosey: ' ... the ode is naturally dead & I shd. Think the song won't go much further.' [82] As so often Elgar moved via exaggeration into nonsense. 'The Song' – *Land of Hope and Glory* – has not stopped running since, thus rendering the letter one of his most absurd. There is, however, evidence that Elgar was not dissatisfied with his work: ' I did not intend the thing to lie on the musical antiquary's shelves, but wanted the "people" – in the best sense of the word – to enjoy themselves: and they are doing so', he wrote to Benson at the end of 1902.[83]

In May 1904 the *Strand Magazine* published Rudolph de Cordova's celebrated interview with Elgar. Edward's 'delightful and most acute sense of humour' emboldened de Cordova to ask about his 'musical crimes'. 'Oh,' replied the composer,

> you mean the *Cockaigne*, the *Coronation Ode* and the *Imperial March* especially. Yes, I believe there are a good many people who have objected to them. But I like to look on the composer's vocation as the old troubadours or bards did. In those days it was no disgrace to a man to be turned on to step in front of an army and inspire the people with song. For my own part, I know that there are a lot of people who like to celebrate events with music. To these people I have given tunes. Is that wrong? Why should I write a fugue or something *which* won't appeal to anyone, when the people yearn for things which *can stir them?* [84]

Let Benson have the last – and as usual apposite – word. After hearing the *Ode* he wrote to Alice Elgar: 'I felt like the fly on the engine who said "How fast I run, and how everything gets out of the way for me" – only, unlike the fly, I know I was not the motive power.' [85]

Postscript
Elgar, Benson and 1914

Despite his observation in 1904 that he did not think 'the Song' (i.e., *Land of Hope and Glory*) would 'go much further', Elgar, perhaps to his surprise, found that it was his greatest success. So it happened, and no doubt under pressure to rise to the occasion, that within a few days of the outbreak of War in August 1914 he wrote to Benson asking for fresh words appropriate to the situation. Perhaps, he suggested, some reference to a 'scrap of paper' [86] might be made. At all events 'wider still and wider' should come out: 'It is liable to [be] misunderstood now.' [87] Edward enclosed a copy of the American poet John Hay's *God's Vengeance* as an example of the sort of sentiment he had in mind:

> *Saith the Lord, 'Vengeance is Mine;*
> *I will repay,' saith the Lord,*
> *Ours will be anger divine,*
> *Lit by the flesh of his word.*
> *Right and Wrong; – both cannot live.*
> *Death-grappled which shall we see?*

> *Strike! Only justice can give*
> *Safety to all that shall be.*
> *Shame! to stand faltering thus,*
> *Tricked by the balancing odds.*
> *Strike! God is waiting for us!*
> *Strike! for the vengeance is God's.*

Arthur Benson, a Fellow of Magdalene College, Cambridge since 1904,[88] proved less enthusiastic than in his previous collaboration with Elgar and the *Coronation Ode*. In a letter of 25 August he replied: 'I'm not strong in the *Vengeance* line & indeed I don't see what there is to revenge as yet – we have hemmed in Germany tight all round for years ... & the cork has flown out! ... What I do feel with all my heart [is] that *bullying* must be stopped – but bullying musn't be met by bullying.' [89]

Notwithstanding his 'establishment' connections, Benson was radical in some things and certainly of independent mind. He was, moreover, not a 'political' person. He seems to have had little inkling of impending war; the Sarajevo assassination did not disturb him unduly. It is not until 30 July that his friend Percy Lubbock, back in Cambridge from the Continent, managed to persuade him that the situation was serious: 'It seems as if we might be plunged in war for simply nothing at all, and when no direct interests are involved. There's an awful fatality about it, and none of our statesmen seem able to do anything', he wrote in his diary on the 31st. On 2 August he signed a peace protest, which begged the Government not to be 'egged' into war. When on the same day Germany declared war on Russia and France, Arthur's diary verdict was 'a sort of *madness*'. He came to accept the inevitability of British involvement. It was, however, absolutely typical of Benson that he should come up with the schoolboy image of 'bullying'. This – the plight, for example, of Belgium – was what moved Benson, still the schoolmaster at heart.

At all events Benson's sensibilities soon had Elgar backtracking and agreeing that 'vengeance isn't the issue' in a letter apologizing for: '... my stupidity in not making clear what I wanted to suggest from Hay's poem viz:– if it is God's work it is our place to do it.' Benson, despite his misgivings, agreed to Elgar's suggestion and, through August, drafts arrived at Severn House. 'Wrote two more stanzas for Elgar of "Land of Hope and Glory" – I don't know if I ought to. Very evil Dreams of the deaths of friends' [90] recorded Benson. Nonetheless a satisfactory conclusion appeared to have been reached:

Dear Land of Hope, our helm of pride
Upon thy brow is set.
Thy keen-eyed navies span the tide;
Be strong, be patient yet!
Then let thy thunders' rolling smoke
O'er echoing seas be borne,
To shatter with their lightning stroke
The braggart sons of scorn.

Land of Hope and Glory, Mother of the free,
How shall we uphold thee, who are born of thee?
Gird thee well for battle, bid thy hosts increase;
Stand for faith and honour, smite for truth and peace!

The gage is flung, the secret hosts
Pass out in serried throng,
They gather on the far-seen coasts,
To do thy comrades wrong.
Then leap to battle for the right,
Rise, haste thee, be not blind!
Heave up thy sword of old to smite
The tyrants of mankind.

Land of Hope and Glory, etc.

Benson remained downcast: 'I wish I felt more like *singing* – I don't mean that I'm in serious doubt about the end of it all (the war), but it's a Pilgrim's Progress at best!' he observed in a letter to Elgar in September. Though, in fact, few others felt like singing when it came to the new words. The nation seemed perfectly content with the original version. Clara Butt, it was proclaimed, would sing 'Land of Hope and Glory' all over the realm. Elgar noted that 'on all the circulars [were] printed the old stanzas.' In a letter of 9 September to Benson he called a halt.

So it was that Elgar, specially released from police duties by permission of one Chief Inspector King of the Hampstead Special Constabulary, joined Bridge, Cowen, Stanford, Landon Ronald and Henry Wood at the Grand Patriotic Concert in aid of the Queen's 'Work for Women Fund' at the Royal Albert Hall on 10 October 1914, in order to conduct Clara Butt in the well-loved, familiar version of *Land of Hope and Glory*. Benson's original words, indeed, were quoted at the head of the programme:

Not that false joy that dreams, content
With what our sires have won;
The blood a hero sire hath spent,
Should serve a hero son.

Two other Elgar works were performed. A 'new' Marching Song entitled *Follow the Colours* with words by Captain de Courcey-Stretton:

Some will return and some remain.
We heed it not, we heed it not.
Something's wrong, to put it right's
The soldier's lot, the soldier's lot.

This martial number was sung, according to *The Daily Telegraph*, under the composer's direction, 'with great vigour' by the Royal Choral Society. It had, in fact, been performed as long ago as May 1908 at an Empire Concert in the same Hall. It was accompanied now by a contralto song, *The King's Way*, with words by C. Alice Elgar. It transpired that this 'Militant song in excelsis' (*Daily Telegraph*) also had a previous history. The words were written originally in 1909 and inspired by Alice's recollection of the comparatively mundane occasion of Edward VII's opening of the well-known London thoroughfare some four years previously. Dr Percy Young has described it as a 'stirring, chauvinistic ballad – a proper piece for a Major General's daughter.' [91] Elgar had used the trio tune from the fourth *Pomp and Circumstance* March – though as Robert Anderson observes, 'the words scarcely enhanced the tune,' [92] and it was premièred in January 1910 at the Alexandra Palace. Boosey were delighted to publish it: 'Song causes delight' was the text of the firm's telegram to the composer. Lady Elgar herself received a small royalty of three guineas for copyright of the verses. The inevitable climax of the 1914 Concert was reached when the audience of 12,000, which included Queen Mary, joined in the *Land of Hope and Glory* refrain.

Meanwhile, Arthur Benson determined to lie low and get on with life as normally as possible in Cambridge. 'I was made for peace, I am useless in war,' he observed. However, these were not 'normal' times. Although not a pacifist, Arthur was happy to assist young conscientious objectors in the presentation of their cases and, thus, found himself listed as a 'pacifist' in *The Times*. He was determined to avoid controversy – 'I have no taste for martyrdom' – but found this well nigh impossible. When he was bold enough to publish an article in the *Church Family Newspaper* urging readers not to believe newspaper stories about German atrocities, he found himself denounced both nationally (*The Daily Express*) and locally (*The Cambridge Daily News*). The latter advised him to recant or expect public demonstrations against him. 'I represent rather an unpopular figure', observed Benson sorrowfully.

Elgar famously 'did his bit' for the War effort by enrolling in the Hampstead Volunteer Reserve and seems to have been prepared to do more. On 12 September 1914 he completed a 'Householder's Return' for a Parliamentary Recruiting Committee to the effect that there was no member of the household qualified to enlist, but 'I will do so if permitted.' [93] At fifty-seven he was five years older than Benson, who makes no such offer of involvement. His main activity outside Magdalene College in 1914 was to continue to serve on a committee meeting regularly at Church House in London for the purpose of revising the Prayer Book Psalter, and which brought together various Anglican divines. The nearest he got to the 'War Effort' was to attend a Government-sponsored gathering of eminent writers at Wellington House, Buckingham Gate, the aim of which was to unite British authors in counteracting German propaganda. Benson made no contribution to the discussion whatsoever, but left his usual sardonic account of such things in his diary. Wells, we are told, was 'fat, brown and perky', Hardy 'very old and faded',[94] Trevelyan 'very dark and gloomy', Barrie 'small and insignificant', Chesterton 'enormous, streaming with sweat' and Arnold Bennett 'looking every inch a cad.' Benson's diary provided a secure safety valve. To it he confided his view: '...if there is such a thing as Hell, I feel that Northcliffe is safe of a place there.'

A letter to *The Times* from the Bishop of Pretoria,[95] describing Germany as 'the Devil Incarnate', might have been understandable from a tradesman but certainly not a Churchman, Benson felt. Such letters were 'on the side of Caiaphas – not Christ.' Nor did Arthur readily forgive those for whom the War was an opportunity for self important interfering, such as the Cambridge philosopher who became a special constable and in military cap prowled round the town checking lights![96] He was dismissed as 'a fat sneak.' Just as well, perhaps, that Elgar's beat was as far away as North London! It was in his diary, too, that Benson tells us: 'I am against war in any guise, I think it an anachronism in civilized nations.'

On 15 August 1915 he was again in correspondence with Elgar about a possible fresh collaboration, which, in the event, came to nothing. In passing, he recalls the amended *Land of Hope and Glory* and that it had never appeared, observing, 'I think it just as well it didn't.'

This essay is an expanded version of a lecture given to the London Branch of the Elgar Society at Imperial College, London on 4 November 2002.

Text

No 1. CROWN THE KING! INTRODUCTION,
(SOLI AND CHORUS)

Crown the King with Life!
Through our thankful state
Let the cries of hate
Die in joy away;
Cease ye, sounds of strife!
Lord of Life, we pray,
Crown the King with Life!

Crown the King with Might!
Let the King be strong.
Hating guile and wrong;
He that scorneth pride,
Fearing truth and right,
Fearing nought beside;–
Crown the King with Might!

Crown the King with Peace;
Peace that suffers long,
Peace that maketh strong,
Peace with kindly wealth,
As the years increase,
Nurse of joy and health;–
Crown the King with Peace!

Crown the King with Love!
To his land most dear
He shall bend to hear
Every pleading call;
Loving God above,
With a heart for all;–
Crown the King with Love!

Crown the King with Faith!
God, the King of Kings,
Ruleth earthly things;
God of great and small,
Lord of Life and Death,
God, above us all!
Crown the King with faith!

God shall save the King,
God shall make him great,
God shall guard the state;
All that hearts can pray,
All that lips can sing,
God shall hear today;–
God shall save the King!

No 2. DAUGHTER OF ANCIENT KINGS
(CHORUS)

Daughter of ancient Kings,
Mother of Kings to be,
Gift that the bright wind bore on his sparkling wings,
Over the Northern Sea!

Nothing so sweet he brings,
Nothing so fair to see,
Purest, stateliest, Daughter of ancient Kings,
Mother of Kings to be!

No 3. BRITAIN ASK OF THYSELF
SOLO (BASS) AND CHORUS (TENOR AND BASS).

Britain, ask of thyself, and see that thy sons be strong,
Strong to arise and go, if ever the war-trump peal;
See that thy navies speed, to the sound of the battle-song
Then, when the winds are up, and the shuddering bulwarks reel,
Smite the mountainous wave, and scatter the flying foam,
Big with the battle-thunder that echoeth loud and long;–
See that thy squadrons haste, when loosed are the hounds of hell:–
Then shall the eye flash fire, and the valorous heart grow light,
Under the drifting smoke, and the scream of the flying shell,
When the hillside hisses with death, – and never a foe in sight.
So shalt thou rest in peace, enthroned in thine island home;–
Britain, ask of thyself, and see that thy sons be strong!

No 4.(I) HARK, UPON THE HALLOWED AIR.
SOLI (SOPRANO AND TENOR).

Hark, upon the hallowed air,
Spirits pure of sight and sense,
Hovering visions, rich and fair,
Lend their radiant influence!
Airy powers of Earth and Sky
Bless our meet solemnity!

Music, sweetest child of heaven,
At thy touch the heart is free,–
Ancient wrongs by thee forgiven,
Cares uplifted, healed by thee,
Listen smiling, borne along
In the sacred tide of song.

Music of the poet's heart!
Widening yet the echoes roll;
Fiery secrets, winged by art,
Light the lonely listening soul,
Till the aching silence rings
With the beat of heavenly wings.

Magic web of woven hues,
Tender shadows, linked line,
Sweet, mysterious avenues
Opening out to Light Divine!
Painter-poet, thou canst teach
More than frail and faltering speech.

(II) ONLY LET THE HEART BE PURE
(QUARTET)

Only let the heart be pure,
Pure in steadfast innocence;
Stainless honour, strong and sure,
Stem the ardent tide of sense!
So shall Wisdom, one with Truth,
Keep undimmed the fires of youth.

Strong to conquer, strong to bless
Britain, heav'n hath made thee great!
Courage knit with gentleness
Best befits thy sober state.
As the golden days increase,
Crown your victories with peace!

No 5. PEACE, GENTLE PEACE
QUARTET AND CHORUS (UNACCOMPANIED)

Peace, gentle Peace, who, smiling through thy tears,
Returnest, when the sounds of war are dumb,
Replenishing the bruised and broken earth,
And lifting motherly her shattered form;
When comest thou? Our brethren long for thee.

Thou dost restore the darkened light of home,
Give back the father to his children's arms;
Thou driest tenderly the mourner's tears;
And all thy face is lit with holy light;–
Our earth is fain for thee! Return and come!

No 6. LAND OF HOPE AND GLORY
FINALE (CONTRALTO SOLO AND TUTTI)

Land of hope and glory, Mother of the free,
How may[97] we extol thee, who are born of thee?

Truth and Right and Freedom, each a holy gem,
Stars of solemn brightness, weave thy diadem.

Tho' thy way be darkened, still in splendour drest,
As the star that trembles o'er the liquid West.

Throned amid the billows, throned inviolate,
Thou hast reigned victorious, thou hast smiled at fate.

Land of hope and glory, Fortress of the free,
How may we extol thee, praise thee, honour thee?

Hark, a mighty nation maketh glad reply;
Lo, our lips are thankful, lo, our hearts are high!

Hearts in hope uplifted, loyal lips that sing;
Strong in faith and freedom, we have crowned our King!

Bibliography

Allen, Kevin: *Elgar the Cyclist* [Malvern, 1997].
Allen, Kevin: *August Jaeger: Portrait of Nimrod* [Ashgate, 2000].
Anderson, Robert: *Elgar* [London, 1993].
Atkins, E. Wulstan: *The Elgar–Atkins Friendship* [Newton Abbot, 1984].
Baily, Leslie: *Land of Hope and Glory* in *Leslie Baily's BBC Scrapbook* [Allen & Unwin].
Benson, E.F.: *Final Edition* [London, 1940].
Bennett, Joseph: *Coronation Ode – Analytical Notes* [Novello, 1902 – Reprinted *Elgar Society Journal,* March 2002].
Boult, Adrian: *Boult on Music* [London, 1983].
Burley, Rosa and Carruthers, Frank C: *Edward Elgar: the Record of a Friendship* [London, 1972].
Ffrangcon-Davies, Marjorie: *David Ffrangcon-Davies: his life and book* [London, 1938].
Hodgkins, Geoffrey: 'Oh, That Sheffeld Chorus' [*Elgar Society Journal,* November 1999].
Kent, Christopher: *Edward Elgar: A Guide to Research* [New York and London, 1993].
Lewis, Gareth: 'Henry Coward' [*Elgar Society Journal,* September 1982 and January 1983].
Moore, Jerrold Northrop: *Edward Elgar: a Creative Life* [Oxford, 1984].
Moore, Jerrold Northrop: *Edward Elgar: Letters of a Lifetime* [Oxford, 1990].
Moore, Jerrold Northrop: *Edward Elgar: The Windflower Letters* [Oxford, 1989].
Moore, Jerrold Northrop: *Elgar and his Publishers: Letters of a creative life* [Oxford, 1987].
Newsome, David: *On the Edge of Paradise: A.C. Benson the Diarist* [London, 1980].
Newsome, David: *Edwardian Excursions* [London, 1981].
Nice, David: *Edward Elgar* [London, 1996].
Kennedy, Michael: *Portrait of Elgar* [Oxford, 1987].
Knowles, John: *Elgar's Interpreters on Record* [London, 1985].
Ponder, Winifred: *Clara Butt* [London, 1928].
Porte, J.F: *Elgar and his Music* [London, 1933].
Powell (nee Penny), Mrs. Richard: *Edward Elgar: Memories of a Variation* [London, 1937 and Aldershot, 1994].
Reed, W.H: *Elgar* [London, 1939]
Redwood, Christopher (ed): *An Elgar Companion* [Ashbourne, 1982].
Rosenthal, Harold: *Two Centuries of Opera at Covent Garden* [London, 1958].
Scholes, P.A: *The Mirror of Music* [Oxford, 1947].
Ward, Yvonne M: 'Gosh! Man I've Got a Tune in My Head' in *The Court Historian,* Vol.7, [2002].

Williams, David: *Genesis and Exodus: A Portrait of the Benson Family* [London, 1979].

Young, Percy M: *Elgar O.M.* [London and New York, 1973].

Young, Percy M: *Letters to Nimrod* [London, 1965].

Young, Percy M: *Alice Elgar: Enigma of a Victorian Lady* [London, 1978].

Quotations from the diaries of Arthur Benson are made by kind permission of the Masters and Fellows of Magdalene College, Cambridge, who also gave permission for the reproduction of the portrait of A.C. Benson.

Letters to Elgar from Arthur Benson, H.V. Higgins and others were to be found at the Worcester Public Record Office, whose Elgar collection is now housed in the Elgar Birthplace Museum archive at Broadheath.

Notes and References

1   See Newsome, David: *On the Edge of Paradise* [London: John Murray, 1980] 13.

2   William, D.: *Genesis and Exodus: a portrait of the Benson family* [London: Hamish Hamilton, 1979] 113, and Benson, E.F.: *Final Edition* [London: Hogarth Press, 1940] 12–13.

3   Parratt to Elgar, 20 July 1898 in Moore, J.N. (ed): *Edward Elgar: letters of a lifetime* [Oxford: OUP, 1990] 65.

4   Parratt to Elgar, 20 July 1898 in Moore: *Lifetime, op.cit.,* 65.

5   Elgar to his sister Helen, 20 October 1899 in Moore: *Lifetime, op.cit.,* 80–81.

6   Moore, J.N.: *Edward Elgar: a creative life* [Oxford: OUP, 1984] 365 and Moore: *Lifetime, op.cit.,* 484.

7   See diaries of Benson A.C. (Magdalene College, Cambridge), Vol.82, 67–68.

8   Newsome, *op.cit.,* 106.

9   See Benson diaries (Magdalene College, Cambridge) Vol.173, 51 and Vol.174, 35.

10 *ibid.,* Vol.9, 17–18 and Newsome, *op.cit.,* 104.

11 See his essay 'The Ethics of Music Publishing in England' in his *Studies and Memories.*

12 Ward, Yvonne, M.: 'Gosh! Man I've Got a Tune in My Head', *The Court Historian,* Vol.7, No.1 [2002] 22.

13 Benson diaries, Vol.13, 21–22.

14 *ibid.,* Vol.52, 66–67.

15 *ibid.,* Vol.143, 46.

16 Moore: *A Creative Life, op.cit.,* 350.

17 The correct title of the play – Elgar reversed the names. See Chapter 3: Newton, C.: *Now He Belongs to the Big World: The Historical Elgar.*

18 Jaeger to Elgar, 9 December 1901 in Moore, J.N. (ed): *Elgar and his Publishers: letters of a creative life* [Oxford: OUP, 1987] Vol.1, 318.
19 Moore: *Lifetime, op.cit.,* 108.
20 Benson to Elgar, 3 December 1901 in Moore: *Lifetime, op.cit.,* 107–108.
21 Jaeger to Elgar, 6 December 1901 in Moore: *Publishers, op.cit.,* 317.
22 *ibid.,* 319.
23 Benson to Elgar, 2 April 1902 in Moore: *Lifetime, op.cit.,* 110.
24 Young, Percy, M.: *Elgar O.M.* [London: White Lion Publishing, 1973] 99.
25 Kennedy, Michael: *Portrait of Elgar* [Oxford: OUP, 1987] 169.
26 Moore: *A Creative Life, op.cit.,* note 9, 364.
27 e.g., the one about his preferring horse racing to music!
28 Moore: *A Creative Life, op.cit.,* 364.
29 Anderson, Robert: *Elgar* [London: Dent, 1993] 53 and Ponder, Winifred: *Clara Butt* [London: Harrap, 1928] 188.
30 Porte, J.F.: *Elgar and his Music: an appreciative study* [London: Pitman, 1933] 92.
31 Parratt to Elgar, 16 August 1902 in Moore: *Lifetime, op.cit.,* 134.
32 See Bury, D.: 'Was Arthur Benson a Jingoist?' in *Elgar Society Journal* [November 2002].
33 Moore: *A Creative Life, op.cit.,* 367.
34 Quoted in Young, *op.cit.,* 289.
35 Benson to Elgar, 21 April 1902.
36 Benson to Elgar, 2 April 1902 in Moore: *Lifetime, op.cit.,* 110.
37 Copy letter held in the Elgar collection in the Worcester Public Record Office 705: 445 Parcel No.16. XV. No.5912–1902.
38 Moore: *A Creative Life, op.cit.,* 367.
39 Anderson, *op.cit.,* 193.
40 Powell, Mrs. R.: *Edward Elgar: memories of a Variation* [London: OUP, 1937; 4th edn: Aldershot: Scolar Press, 1994] 72.
41 Moore: *Publishers, op.cit.,* 249.
42 Benson diaries, Vol.42, 24–25.
43 Fenby, Eric: *Delius as I knew him* [London: Bell, 1981] 124.
44 Moore: *Publishers, op.cit.,* 347.
45 Leighton to Elgar, 23 April 1902 in Moore: *Publishers, op.cit.,* 348.
46 Arthur Boosey to Elgar, 18 April 1902 in Moore: *Publishers, op.cit.,* 348–349.
47 Boosey to Elgar, 24 April 1902 in Moore: *Publishers, op.cit.,* 349.
48 See C.T.Boosey to Elgar, 7 May 1902 in Moore: *Publishers, op.cit.,* 350.
49 Benson Diaries, Vol.40, 68. See also Moore: *Publishers, op.cit.,* 371.
50 Elgar to F.G. Edwards, 20 July 1899 in Moore: *Publishers, op.cit.,* 131.
51 Quoted in *Leslie Baily's BBC Scrapbook.* 'The Story Behind Land of Hope and Glory' [London] 78.
52 Letters from Ffrangcon-Davies to Elgar are to be found in Ffrangcon-Davies, Marjorie: *David Ffrangcon-Davies: his life and book* [London: John Lane, The Bodley Head, 1938] 31–46.

Portrait of A.C. Benson by R.E.F. Maitland.
[Reproduced by permission of Magdalene College, Cambridge]

Above left:Queen Victoria; above right: King Edward VII;
below left: Queen Alexandra; below right: Sir Walter Parratt.
[Photos: David Bury collection]

A

Coronation Ode *soloists for Covent Garden:*
Above left: Nellie Melba; above right: Louise Kirkby Lunn;
below left: Ben Davies; below right: David Ffrangcon-Davies.
[Photos: David Bury collection]

Above: Elgar and Shaw at Malvern in 1929.
[Reproduced by courtesy of the Sir Barry Jackson Trust]

Below: Elgar, Shaw and guests at Sir Barry Jackson's garden party at Lawnside, Great Malvern in August 1929, for the opening performance of Shaw's The Apple Cart.
[Photo: Elgar Birthplace Museum]

Facing page: Sir Barry Jackson, 1879–1961.

Shaw, Elgar and Mrs Claude Beddington at Lawnside on 31 July 1932.

53   Young, Percy, M.: *Letters to Nimrod* [London: Dobson, 1965] 165.
54   Nice, David: *Edward Elgar* [London, 1996] 52.
55   The Dedication reads:–

Dedication
To
His most gracious Majesty
This
Coronation Ode
Is by special permission
Dedicated
By his Majesty's loyal and
Devoted Servants and Subjects
Arthur Christopher Benson
And
Edward Elgar

56   Moore: *A Creative Life, op.cit.,* 368. It is with some sense of 'deja-vu' that one notes in June 1911, as a fresh Coronation approached, and in view of which some amendments had to be made to the *Coronation Ode,* Benson is to be found writing to Elgar in plaintive fashion once more on 22 June 1911: 'I hope the *Ode* will go well. I have received no invitation to be present … but I am very anxious to hear how the new strophe is treated.'
57   Sir Alexander Gibson, Scottish National Orchestra and Chorus: Chandos 1977. Philip Ledger, New Philharmonia Orchestra, Cambridge University Musical Society, Choir of King's College, Cambridge: – EMI 1977.
58   Burley, Rosa: *Edward Elgar: the Record of a Friendship* [London: Barrie & Jenkins, 1972] 158–159.
59   A. Boosey to Elgar, 30 June 1902 in Moore: *Publishers, op.cit.,* 360–361.
60   Elgar to Jaeger, 25 June 1902 in Moore: *Publishers, op.cit.,* 360.
61   Ivor Atkins to Elgar, 1 July 1902 in Atkins, E. Wulstan: *The Elgar–Atkins Friendship* [Newton Abbot: David & Charles, 1984] 75–76.
62   Elgar to Atkins, 2 July 1902 in Atkins: *The Elgar–Atkins Friendship, op.cit.,* 76.
63   Benson diaries, Vol.14, 48–49.
64   Elgar to Jaeger, 9 October 1900 in Moore: *Publishers, op.cit.,* 244.
65   Moore: *A Creative Life, op.cit.,* 371.
66   Jean de Reszke (1850–1925), Polish operatic tenor. He and his brother Edouard (1853–1917) a bass, are mentioned by Sherlock Holmes on the final page of Arthur Conan Doyle's *The Hound of the Baskervilles.*
67   Scholes, Percy, A..: *The Mirror of Music 1844–1944. A Century of Musical Life in Britain as reflected in the pages of The Musical Times* [Oxford: OUP, 1947] Vol.2, 882.
68   *ibid.,* 883.
69   Benson diaries, Vol.14, 49–50. 'I have no hope for his life, or very little – Even my poor Ode won't be performed – it will go down to Limbo. – I can't

Chapter Five

Windflowers

John Kelly

There is a mystery here; I shall stay to un-riddle it. (*Gil Blas*)

Shall we rouse the night-owl in a catch that will draw
Three souls out of one weaver? Shall we do that?
(Shakespeare: *Twelfth Night,* II. iii)

In October 1905, when giving an interview to *The Hereford Times,* the Austrian Violinist, Fritz Kreisler, said, 'If you want to know whom I consider to be the greatest living composer, I say without hesitation, Elgar. Russia, Scandinavia, my own Fatherland, or any other nation can produce nothing like him … I wish Elgar would write something for the violin. He could do so, and it would certainly be something effective.'[1]

Kreisler had been born in Vienna where he entered the Conservatory at the age of seven, taking up a career as a soloist in New York when still a teenager. However he returned to Europe to study medicine in Vienna and art in Rome – two subjects, which coincidentally might be identified as 'hidden themes' in Elgar's Violin Concerto composed in 1909 and 1910. Kreisler resumed his career as a violinist in 1899 and at the time of his appeal to Elgar to write 'something effective' for the violin was aged thirty. Kreisler was unlikely to have been aware that Elgar had attempted to write a concerto already, in 1890, and that he had destroyed it – a step which we might consider unusual, when we remember that Elgar was an inveterate hoarder of notebooks, themes, and musical ideas. What was it that dissatisfied Elgar with that first attempt? Could it have been that such a work with all its associations demanded more of him than he felt able to express adequately at that early stage of his career? A perfectionist, he had perhaps been disappointed with his first efforts, particularly as the violin was his own instrument. Or was there some other deeper reason?

Because of Elgar's later success as a composer, it is sometimes forgotten that he began his career as a violinist and teacher of that instrument, with

1 – Notes and references for this chapter appear on pages 167-169.

this extending for many years. When he played the violin in the Three
Choirs Festivals and in Stockley's Orchestra in Birmingham he must surely
have acquired a special love for that instrument. It has been said that
Elgar did not like to be seen in the street carrying his violin case, but there
is other evidence that he had no inhibitions about being a violinist. For
instance on a letter to his sister Lucy which he wrote on hotel headed note
paper from Paris in 1880 there is affixed a picture of a violin which
identifies his affinity to this instrument in a particularly personal manner.[2]
Interestingly too, in the 1881 and 1891 censuses, the first in Worcester,
and the second in London, Elgar is recorded as a 'Professor of violin', both
entries presumably at his own instigation. We know that he did not enjoy
teaching this instrument, yet how pleased he must have been in later years
to see one of his pupils, Marie Hall, achieve success and fame. He
recorded the Concerto with her in 1916, albeit in an abbreviated form,
having to make adaptations to the score, due to the limitations of the
recording process, which was then in its infancy.

In his early years Elgar entertained hopes of taking up a career as a
professional soloist. Much is made of Elgar being self-taught – yet it
should be remembered that as far as the violin is concerned, he considered
it desirable to have lessons. So he saved up and spent some time in
London to take instruction from Pollitzer, the leader of the New
Philharmonic orchestra. Pollitzer thought him a good pupil, but after
Elgar attended a concert and heard Wilhelmj play he realised that he
himself would never reach sufficient standard as a soloist. In later years
Elgar's playing of the violin was described as 'hard and cold',[3] yet Carice,
his daughter recalled how, when he played the piano, he could make that
instrument sound like a whole orchestra.

The violin was also the instrument played by Helen Weaver, Elgar's one
time fiancée, or 'Braut', as he described her in a letter to his friend in
Yorkshire, the cellist, Dr Charles Buck. Elgar had had ambitions to study
music in Leipzig, but family finances did not allow this, whereas Helen,
who was three years younger than Edward, was better placed. The Weaver
family ran a boot and shoe business in Worcester High Street, not far from
the Elgars' music shop. Helen (whom Elgar called Nelly), and Edward
probably knew each other from their early years. Elgar dedicated several
of his small Powick pieces to her: *Nelly, La Blonde* and *Helcia*. When
Helen went with a friend to study in Leipzig at the Conservatoire, Elgar
visited them there in the New Year of 1883. Together they went to concerts
in the Gewandhaus, with its Mendelssohn connections and around that

time it appears that they came to an understanding as to their future together. For reasons which we can now only surmise that was not to be, and their engagement was broken off in the following year, possibly because of differences in religion, as Helen was a Unitarian, Elgar a Catholic. However, a possible different reason will be suggested in this essay. Elgar wrote about this failed love affair to Buck in the summer of 1884, saying, 'My prospects are worse than ever and to crown my miseries my engagement is broken off and I am lonely ... I have not the heart to speak to anyone ... Once more accept my good wishes for your happiness; these I can give you the more sincerely since I know what it is to have lost my own forever.'[4] Worse still shortly afterwards, Helen emigrated to New Zealand to seek a new life and hopefully a cure for the tuberculosis which she had developed.

At the time Elgar seems not to have spoken about this broken engagement or her illness to anyone other than Buck, but later on he may well have confided something of his past romance to a few of his women friends such as Miss Burley, the Malvern Headmistress, and almost certainly to Alice Stuart Wortley. His friend, Ivor Atkins, the organist at Worcester Cathedral knew about it, and after Elgar's death found himself in a dilemma, not knowing whether to reveal his knowledge or not. So he arranged for the facts to be published fifty years after Elgar's death, and his wishes were carried out by his son, Wulstan in 1984. It is therefore only in comparatively recent times that Helen Weaver's importance in Elgar's life has been properly appreciated. Fifty years is a long time to keep knowledge of a secret, particularly when the event itself took place another fifty years previously.

Ernest Newman, the music critic, guessed that there was something in Elgar's past, which was of great significance. In *The Sunday Times* on 18 November 1956, writing of the Romanza Variation '(***)' of the *Variations*, he said: 'He, Elgar, was here dwelling in imagination on something and somebody the parting from whom had at some time or other torn the very heart out of him.' Indeed, one of the impressions made on Newman when he first met Elgar was that he was a secretly unhappy man.

So, returning to the year after his broken engagement, 1884, one conclusion stands out: with an ambition to have a career as a violin soloist abandoned, and with his expectations of a happily married life with a female violinist frustrated, Elgar's experiences in his sensitive early twenties were, to put them at their lowest, sad and disappointing.

Some twenty years later, in 1905, in response to Kreisler's call, Elgar began work on a concerto, but he made little progress and put it away until 1909. Then, in 1910 Kreisler's wish was answered when Elgar's Concerto for Violin and Orchestra in B Minor, Opus 61, received its first public performance with Kreisler as the dedicatee and soloist. However, after the dedication on the score Elgar created another of his mysteries, when he also added a Spanish phrase 'AQUI ESTA ENCERRADA EL ALMA DE.....' (1910). This was a quotation, which could have been taken from the introduction to the novel *Histoire de Gil Blas* by the French author Le Sage or from the use of the text by the English Victorian poet W.E.Henley in his *Echoes*. When asked to explain this Spanish phrase by his friend Nicholas Kilburn, Elgar stated that it could be translated: 'Here, or more emphatically *in here*, is enshrined or simply enclosed – buried is perhaps too definite – *the soul of* .....? The final 'de' leaves it indefinite as to sex or rather gender. Now guess'.[5] (An attempt to understand the significance of this phrase is complicated by the fact that Novello, the publishers of the score, have wrongly and consistently printed 'encerrada' as 'encerra' since 1910, but no ulterior motive on Elgar's part seems likely. Moreover, initially Elgar used the word 'del'(as in the novel), changed it to 'de la', but finally must have accepted 'de' as printed by the publishers.) The use by Elgar of five dots to hide the identity of the 'soul' has generally been accepted as indicating the name of a person consisting of five letters, otherwise the more usual setting of three dots would have been used by the printer, whatever the size of a missing word. Basil Maine, writing in 1933, stated that he had been told by Elgar that he had a feminine spirit in mind.[6] On 23 May 1939, Ernest Newman wrote to Clare Wortley, Alice Stuart Wortley's daughter: 'I am pretty sure I know the name: the whole facts of the case were given to me by a correspondent (unknown to me personally) who was an intimate, long ago, of both Elgar and "....." I myself had for many years been sceptical about the "Lady Mary Lygon" as the subject of the 13th. Variation but I hadn't any information that could give point and body to my suspicions. After receiving the information about the "....." I asked my correspondent whether the person "enshrined" here was the same as the one covered by the three asterisks (Romanza) and I was told that they were one and the same ... The details are very <u>curious</u> and <u>sad</u>'.[7] (This author's emphasis). Thus it is intriguing to note that the reviewer of the first performance of the Violin Concerto in *The Times* of 11 November 1910 wrote: 'There is a theme in the fine movement called by the analyst the fourth of the first "subject group"(i.e. the first windflower theme) which reminds us strongly of a theme in the last of the *Variations* and it is hard to believe that the same individual

a Counterpoint

has not inspired both.' This could well be the motif in that variation which is heard at Cue 65, described by Julian Rushton as new, and by Roger Fiske as 'music that seems to have very little indeed to do with Elgar's theme'.[8] But let us keep those two adjectives of Newman's – 'curious' and 'sad' – in mind.

For many years there seemed to be little doubt as to who was the person represented by the 'soul', as 'Dorabella' in her biography of the composer recalled hearing sketches of the Concerto during its composition:

> The windows were wide open and the curtains drawn back, and lovely scents came in from the garden. I think I must have heard most of the sketches for the Violin Concerto that evening, and how I loved it, every bit of it, from the beginning.
>
> A year later I heard the revised Concerto, played all through to me from a printed proof copy, and I thought I had never heard anything more beautiful. What sadness and regrets, what high hopes and dreams was he describing? Alone in the study, just before leaving for home, I found the copy on the table and turned at once to pages which I had not noticed while I was busy with turning over. Having examined the title-page I came next to the Spanish quotation on a page by itself. I knew no Spanish, but the word 'alma' struck me – was it not 'soul'? – and then the blank space with five dots caught my eye and a name immediately sprang to my mind. The door opened and the Lady came in, She came and stood by me, saw what I was looking at, and translated the Spanish sentence: 'Herein is enshrined the soul of .....' Then she went on to fill in the name – that of a personal friend – and asked me never to reveal it. I promised her that I never would. My guess was right. I think it may be conceded that there must be, in practice, a time-limit to the value of such a promise as the one I gave to Lady Elgar in 1910. Writing as I do now, in 1946, I feel that the limit in this case has been reached. Carice Elgar-Blake agrees with me and it is with her full consent that I make known that the five dots in the Spanish quotation have concealed the identity of Mrs. Julia H. Worthington, a most charming and kind American friend. She was known to intimate friends by another name – also of five letters, and I cannot say definitely whether the composer had this name or her first Christian name in mind. Nor does this matter; the gap is now filled.[9]

That is reasonably definite! But wives do not always know what their husbands are thinking. However, it is understandable that Alice Elgar should have thought that Julia Worthington was the inspiration for the Concerto. Her 'other name' was 'Pippa'. She was a wealthy American with whom Elgar had become friendly and when staying at her rented villa, the Villa Silli, in Florence, Elgar had returned to the composition of a violin concerto and his work there ultimately became what we now know as the Andante, the slow movement, which meant so much to him.

Carice recorded some memories of their time in Florence: 'Careggi proved an ideal place, a long drive out of Florence opposite Fiesole . . . It was wonderful summer weather, & the nightingales sang all night & if they ever paused, the frogs filled in the gap. Pippa arranged for a carozza to be at our disposal every day, so some one of the party could always go to Florence for shopping or sightseeing. My father was thoroughly happy here & wrote music which always seemed to me to be in a different vein of its own, viz, *Go Song of Mine* (Op.57), and *Angelus* (Op.56).' [10]

But, all could not have been happiness and joy for as it was here that Elgar received news of Jaeger's death from the tuberculosis, which had troubled him for some years, although rather surprisingly Alice's diary does not record this. However, Elgar wrote: 'I am overwhelmed with sorrow for the loss of my dearest and truest friend.' [11]

Elgar's choice of key for the Concerto was B minor – a key which Beethoven had described as 'the Black key', used in Baroque music by Handel and others to represent tragedy, sadness or pain. It was in B Minor that Mozart wrote an Adagio on the death of his father and Bach's Mass is also in the key of B minor. But having said that, there does not appear to be any special connection with Jaegar's memory in the Concerto, and what significance there is in this area of key, lies, it seems, elsewhere.

Robin Legge the music critic of *The Daily Telegraph*, recalled an incident at a rehearsal of the Violin Concerto in September 1910 at the Gloucester Festival, writing to his wife: 'What the Adagio means *au fond* to Elgar I cannot guess of course, but at the end of it the tears were pouring down his face. The whole man and his life is in his composition'.[12]

Despite the fact that Elgar once said that the soul was feminine some commentators have wondered whether it was Elgar himself who was represented by the five dots. Professor Charles S. Terry of Aberdeen University, a friend of Elgar's who was to become recognised as a leading Bach scholar, attached a note dated 12 November 1910 to the first proof copy of the score, which Elgar gave him. This was two days after the first performance and his assessment was that whilst he had never before heard Elgar speak of the personal note in his music, the Concerto was the one exception. 'Of it I heard him say more than once when he was playing it over as it was produced: "I love it" ', he wrote.[13] This point was reinforced in 1956 by Newman who, when writing of Elgar's reluctance to talk about his music generally, stated: 'The case is different however with regard to that other outpouring of Elgar's inmost and profoundest human self, the violin concerto. We find him in his letters of 1910 speaking of this new work of his with a frankness that has no parallel anywhere else in his references to his own music.' [14] He could have added that two years later Elgar wrote to Alice Stuart Wortley saying significantly: 'I have written out my soul in the Concerto, Sym II & the Ode & you know it … in these three works I have *shewn* myself.' [15]

But with this complicated man and composer it is perhaps significant that just before its first performance Elgar wrote in a letter to Alice Stuart Wortley: 'How I detest its being made public'.[16] Yet conversely, to Ivor Atkins that he said that he would like a bar from the Concerto inscribed on his tombstone.[17] (This is 5 after 53 in the second movement, and is marked *nobilmente* in the orchestra. Interestingly in the solo part the next bar is reminiscent of the Mendelssohn quotation as heard in Variation XIII, unusually for Elgar marked *vibrato*. Played quickly here in performance it is almost lost to the listener).

Whilst considering what the Concerto meant to Elgar, it might be helpful to digress briefly and look at his method of composition – such as it was. W.H. Reed, in his biography of Elgar, states that Elgar had no method,

> in the ordinarily accepted sense of the term, he conceived his music at all times – in the middle of the night, out walking, in a crowd, or in solitude – scribbling his ideas on any piece of paper that came handy, to be noted more fully on music paper and considered from all possible points of view in various keys and in varying moods. Like Beethoven, he allowed an idea, which may have occurred to him as a short phrase to germinate and transform and throw out branches. He rarely started anything at the beginning. He worked at a theme and brought it perhaps to a climax; for then, as he said to me, he knew to what he was leading.[18]

Elgar himself said that he 'japed them up' to make a coherent piece.

It was this japing which Billy Reed experienced when he visited Elgar, at his request, at his flat in New Cavendish Street, where he found the musical ideas pinned on the backs of chairs, or stuck up on the mantelpiece ready for him to play in various orders.[19] Elgar had asked Reed to assist him, an incident that shows his humility as well as his genius. A perfectionist, who desired to be absolutely right in his scoring for the violin, he revealed his self-doubt too in turning to a professional violinist for support. His later gesture to Reed, in September 1910, in asking him to play the Concerto for the first time at a private party before the Gloucester Three Choirs Festival also says much about Elgar's kindly nature to other performing musicians.

In looking at Elgar's methods we should remember what he told his first biographer, R.J.Buckley in 1904. Speaking of *The Apostles* he said, 'When I compose such a work as this <u>I first of all read everything</u> I can lay my hands on which bears on the subject directly or indirectly, <u>meditating on all that I have sifted out as likely to serve my purpose and blending it with my musical conceptions</u>. Every personality appears to me in a musical dress. I suppose that all who read novels form mental pictures of the characters. So with me: I involuntarily give to each a musical character, clothe each with a musical expression ... I never sit down and say "Now I will compose", the thing is inconceivable to me. What comes, comes of itself; of course I am often thinking in music.' [20] (This author's emphasis). Elgar's statement is worth keeping in mind when considering a solution to the 'soul enigma'.

First, however, we must look at the facts concerning the person who today is accepted by most musicologists as the 'soul,' Alice Stuart Wortley, a friend with whom the composer developed such a close relationship whilst composing the Concerto, referring to it as 'our Concerto'. He wrote to her, 'I go on working and working and making it all as good as I can for the owner';[21] and '... all stands still until you come & approve!' [22]

Michael Kennedy makes out an extremely strong case that Alice Stuart Wortley was the 'soul'.[23] He recalls what Elgar once told Alice after she had missed a musical evening at his London home. Somebody had asked him: ' "*Where on earth* is Mrs. W. in all this music?" ' Elgar had said to himself: ' "Everywhere – and alas! nowhere" ' adding, 'But you see they all thought it was nothing without you and so did I.' [24]

It seems likely that Elgar first met Alice Stuart Wortley in 1897 [25] at Sheffield and that they renewed their acquaintance from time to time in the early part of the century. Alice was the daughter of the Pre-Raphaelite painter Millais, and at the time of their first meeting she was thirty-five, five years younger than Elgar. She was the second wife of Charles Stuart Wortley, the Conservative Member of Parliament for the Hallam Division of Sheffield. Charles had had a daughter, Bice, by his first marriage, and so Alice became a step-mother upon her marriage. Later Charles and Alice had their own child, Clare. Both Charles and Alice were keen music lovers and Alice was an accomplished pianist. She had learned to play from an early age and had regularly played for her father, Millais, whilst he was painting. Such was the reputation earned by Millais that he eventually became the first painter to receive a baronetcy.

Elgar's association with Alice became more frequent in 1909 and 1910, and they met often with other friends in a 'set', which included *The Daily Telegraph's* art critic, Claude Phillips, who was to become the first Keeper of The Wallace Collection and to receive a knighthood.

Also in the 'set' was Frank Schuster, a wealthy Jewish German Banker who owned a magnificent property at Bray near Maidenhead, The Hut. It was there that Elgar put the finishing touches to the second movement of his Concerto.

Art as well as music, was a topic of conversation when these friends met, and this was a subject in which Elgar took a close interest. He frequently visited galleries in London and other towns, and Percy Young reminds us that Elgar 's interest in art was similar to that of Handel's.[26]

This author's knowledge of art was virtually non-existent until he began researching the background to the composition of Elgar's Violin Concerto and what little he now knows has been one of the many rewards in recent years from this activity. So the reader can imagine his delight when rummaging in a junk shop he came upon a copy of a painting, *The Angelus* by the French artist Millet. This, he subsequently learned, is a famous painting, and at first he confused the French artist, Millet, with the English artist, Millais. That was a mistake, and yet perhaps here we have the explanation why in 1910 Elgar dedicated his short piece *The Angelus* to Alice Stuart Wortley, whose maiden name had been Millais. The similarity in the pronunciation and spelling of surnames could well have appealed to Elgar, in view of their mutual love of art. (It will be recalled that Carice referred to Elgar writing this at Careggi).

Elgar took care to ensure that the wording of the dedication to her of *The Angelus* would be entirely acceptable to Alice and this may have been because three months previously in March 1909 he had addressed her as 'Carrie', which was a name used by her friends. But she did not like Elgar's use of this nickname, and so Elgar wrote:

> I want to bring * the enclosed little remembrance of Careggi *. Had no time, alas! & ask if your name may go on it: please look at the title carefully and tell me if I have it right and tell me how to amend it or to remove it

Masshead
(Langfellar's Hyp.

altogether – it looks GASTFULLY formal. Also you may not like the words – so I enclose them and you can censor them – but they are of the place and not far from your own monastery on the Fiesole Road of which CBSW has memories also. Anyway it would give me the greatest pleasure to put your beloved name on it if you both allow it.

Much love to you all.

Yours ever. Edward.' [27]

Alice made one amendment to Elgar's suggestion, and the dedication finally read: 'To Alice/Mrs Charles Stuart-Wortley.'

In November Edward wrote to Alice from York addressing her as 'My dear Alice'. He began, 'You see how dull my inventive powers are in the presence of acute emotion and <u>I have found no name for you yet!</u>' [28] (This author's emphasis).

It is clear from this letter and earlier correspondence that Elgar was searching for a 'pet' name for her, and so we might ask: *Why did Elgar ultimately decide upon the name 'Windflower' for his themes and for her?* Suggestions that it described a lovely flower and so was appropriate for a graceful lady seem completely unconvincing as Elgar chose or invented names for well considered and appropriate reasons – Mr Phoebus for his bicycle, (Phoebus being a Greek sun god, the bicycle being a Sunbeam), – Carice for his daughter, (an amalgamation of his wife's two Christian names, Caroline Alice), – Craeg Lea for his house in the Wells Road, (an anagram), – and Nimrod for his friend and mentor, the publisher's agent A.J. Jaeger, (German for hunter). So, why 'Windflower'?

The first evidence of the use of this name can be seen in a letter he wrote in the spring of 1910, when on 21 March he addressed her as: 'Dear Windflower (nemorosa)'. [29] What is particularly important for the purposes of our exploration is Elgar's identification, in parenthesis, of the specific variety of windflower to which he was referring, by the use of its botanical name. Bearing in mind Elgar's uncertainty about the choice of a different name earlier, it seems quite probable that prior to this letter there could well have been a conversation between them in which Elgar tested Alice's reactions to his suggestion and explained his reasoning. On 18 April Elgar wrote again saying: 'Please take care in the cold wind. Your name does not mean that you *like* cold winds.' [30]

Clare Stuart Wortley, Alice's daughter, many years later in 1940, claimed: 'He ultimately called her Windflower after the themes – not the themes after her.' These themes were those in the Concerto which had come as a sudden inspiration to Elgar in the February of 1910 after an evening with the Stuart-Wortleys and after she had persuaded him to continue composition of the Concerto at a time when in a mood of depression, he was threatening to abandon it, just as he had once before in 1890.

Clare's recollections, now in the Birthplace Museum state:

The "First Windflower theme", and the "Second Windflower theme" must be the Windflower themes mentioned in Sir Edward Elgar's letters to my mother April 27th and 28th, 1910. He says only "the tunes stick, and are not Windflowerish at all, and that he is working hard at them, and she must come and approve. The Windflower themes appear to be those which she liked best in the first movement of the Concerto, which was the first-fruits of her persuasion of him to continue writing the Concerto in February, 1910, after he had already written, and threatened to abandon, the second movement, written by itself at Careggi in 1909. He dedicated the Windflower themes to her in gratitude.

The Windflower at 1.0 (2) (*sic*) had its anniversary frequently kept on February 7th (see its own sketch dated February 7th, preserved herewith).

The Windflower theme at (4) (*sic*) was frequently copied – the first two bars of it, in his letters to her. I believe he ultimately called her Windflower after the themes – not the themes after her.' [31]

In her note Clare referred to both themes applying to her mother, but the case about to be made in this essay is that Clare's surmise of the <u>two themes</u> referring to Alice was incorrect, for when Elgar addressed Alice in musical notation in letters, he used only the second theme. For reasons which will be explored, it is this writer's belief that the first theme does not refer to Alice Stuart Wortley at all. But certainly the moment of inspiration for the composer, in February 1910, the day following the dinner at Schuster's with the Stuart Wortleys, was of immense importance to Elgar. He noted on the score ' Feb 7: 1910 6.30pm.' and added 'This is going to be good! Where Love and Faith meet There will be Light'.[32] And henceforth the 7th February was kept as a special celebration by Alice and Edward, as far as was possible in their separate and busy lives. What the precise relationship was between Edward and his 'Windflower' we shall never know, but there can be little doubt that he was at that time in love with her, and expressed that love in his music, if not in other ways. There is the added mystery of the destruction of almost all of the letters Elgar received from her. Most of his letters to her are preserved and we can get a good flavour of their correspondence from Jerrold Northrop Moore's *The Windflower Letters*. What is clear is that undoubtedly Alice Stuart Wortley was essential to Elgar in those months in 1910 when he made good progress with his composition.

So, from a mood of depression in mid December when he had written: 'The music is not fit to see or be seen', he swung to the other extreme and wrote on the score: 'This is going to be good!' and later, in a letter to Schuster: ' ... it's *good*! awfully emotional! too emotional but I love it:' [33] His wife Alice recorded in her diary that Elgar was working feverishly on the Concerto and Elgar became so immersed in the third movement that he had to confess to Schuster that he could not see his way to finishing it. Apparently he loved it so much he just went on and on, composing new music and recapturing the themes of the first movement in the wonderful Cadenza with his inventive approach of an accompaniment from the 'thrumming' orchestral strings.

Throughout the summer and autumn he worked on the orchestration at Plas Gwyn in Hereford, correcting the printer's proof copies. Following the private performance at Gloucester when Billy Reed was soloist, came the first public performance, on Thursday 10 November, at a Philharmonic Society concert in Queen's Hall. Kreisler was the soloist and Elgar conducted. Kreisler spoke of the Concerto in glowing terms and exclaimed: 'I will shake Queen's Hall'. But for an assessment of the Concerto by a modern day soloist the words of Ida Haendel when interviewed a few years ago speak for all lovers of this Concerto. Somewhat tongue-in-cheek she disagreed with 'Sir Edward Elgar's view that the Concerto is too emotional. Emotion is what music is all about', she claimed. 'Music is tears, music is expression, and music is part of the soul of the human being, so why not express it in that way?' For her the Violin Concerto is one of the greatest works ever composed, and she absolutely adores playing it.[34]

The audience greeted the Concerto with enthusiasm and indeed this was the high point of Elgar's relationship with his public, for this was the last occasion when a new composition from him was received so appreciatively. The critic Ernest Newman summarised the new work in the words: 'Human feeling so nervous and subtle as this has never before spoken in English orchestral or choral music.' [35]

Alice Elgar wrote ecstatically in her diary – as always when describing her husband's work: 'At Frank's. To Rehearsal at 10 – Very Wonderful – Back to Lunch. E. pestered A. and Frank to see flat. No good. – To Concert with Frank in car. Poured in desperate torrents. Crowd enormous. Excitement intense. Performance wonderful. Enthusiasm unbounded. Shouts. E. walked backwards and forwards bringing Kreisler. But his England wanted <u>him</u>, and he had to come by himself. He looked beautiful and Kreisler fine and dignified – A wonderful event.'

After the performance Schuster had arranged a party for about forty persons, amongst who were the Elgars, Kreisler, the Stuart Wortleys, Landon Ronald and a young musician, F.S.Kelly, soon to be killed in the First World War.[36] Four tables had been arranged in the shape of a letter **E** and Schuster surprised Elgar by arranging for his male voice *Five Part-Songs from the Greek Anthology*, to be sung by choristers from St. Paul's and Westminster Cathedrals. Menus were headed with three themes from the Concerto. Adrian Boult, then aged twenty-one, was present and later recalled, in his autobiography, hearing Elgar say to Claude Phillips, the art critic, – 'Well, Claude, did you think that was a work of art?' [37] – a reference almost certainly to an article which Phillips had written in *The Daily Telegraph* in April. Due to Professor Trowell's remarkable detective work, it is known that the article, 'Love in Art', was once pasted to the score at the <u>second</u> windflower theme and later removed.[38] Professor Trowell's conclusions are important, but for this author, Elgar's question to Phillips at the party seems to propose that just as 'Love' is portrayed in its many forms within paintings, so in this, his music, he, Elgar, had portrayed his love for 'The soul enshrined herein'. Elgar was claiming to have created in music, that which artists through the ages have painted on canvas by way of the obvious and visible, as well as by disguise and allusion.

The time has come therefore, to look more closely at windflowers and to suggest answers to the question: why did he call Alice 'Windflower' and why did he refer to windflower themes? It appears that few people, – and surprisingly few Elgarians – know that a windflower is the nickname given to an anemone flower, although they may be forgiven for not realising that there are as many as one hundred and fifty varieties both wild and cultivated. Some years ago on a visit to a friend's home the author was browsing through a gardening book[39] when he found mention of one variety called 'Alice', and it may have been that incident which stimulated his further interest in this area of the mysteries in Elgar's Concerto. Surprisingly, over the years, however, he has been unable to find any other mention of this particular cultivar. Some anemones are popular today in gardens; e.g. *Anemone blanda*, and the cultivars of *Anemone coronaria* ('St. Brigid' and 'De Caen') are often seen for sale in florist's shops. All kinds carry the nickname 'windflower' but it is the wild white woodland species with which we are particularly concerned – *Anemone nemorosa*. This is the plant's Latin botanical name, which Elgar specifically identified when he wrote to Alice on 21 March 1910 at which time *Anemone nemorosa* would just have been coming into flower in the woods of Herefordshire and Worcestershire.

A naturalist who for a period of thirty years observed the dates on which various flowers came into bloom in the spring, noted that the wood anemone never blossomed earlier than March 16 and never later than April 22. (One wonders if this still holds good in these years of alleged global warming?). So when Elgar wrote to Alice Stuart Wortley on 21 March, he may well have just seen his first wood anemone of that year.

Botanically, *Anemone nemorosa* is a member of the buttercup family (Ranunculaceae). It grows ten or twenty centimetres in height and its flower consists of six or eight white or pink tinged hairless sepals, although the curved seed-pods are slightly hairy. The blossom is of little attraction to insects as it only gives off pollen and not nectar, so that only a few seeds develop and after falling into dry woodland do not germinate. Hence the growth of *Anemone nemorosa* is dependent on its unseen slender creeping root, which spreads a few centimetres each year. In the British Isles the plant is found in most parts except the Outer Hebrides, the Orkneys and Shetland; nor is it found in the Channel Islands or Ireland. When picked *Anemone nemorosa* soon droops and dies. Its sepals, as the petals are more correctly called, are white, but are occasionally tinged with pink or red on the outside and more rarely the whole sepal is sometimes brightly and delicately coloured pink or purple-ish. A wild sky blue variety may now be extinct (var: caerulea) and this was probably the type referred to in a *Times* article of 1923, as being found by Farrer in a Cornish wood. In Wayland Wood, Norfolk – the home of the Babes in the Wood legend – there is a purple variety.

All parts of *Anemone nemorosa* are poisonous and can cause blistering if crushed in the hand by a person with a sensitive skin. The poison is called protoaneimonine.[40] An elderly book seller in Malvern once told the author how he and his friends when young, used to gather the plant and chew the stems and leaves, presumably as a 'dare', but found that they had to spit them out. The seventeenth-century herbalist Culpepper (1616 –1654), himself a sufferer from tuberculosis from which he ultimately died, used to advise his patients to chew the root as it 'purgeth the head mightily and is therefore good for lethargy'.[41] How many of Culpepper's patients remained 'on his books' after taking this remedy is not recorded!

Whilst researching the medicinal properties of the plant this author was fascinated to read about and to speak to researchers at Aberystwyth University and elsewhere who were analysing the DNA of the wood anemone in their efforts to develop a new drug to cure tuberculosis, as strains of this disease resistant to existing medicines have re-appeared in this country.[42] The scientists' work has been stimulated by recent developments in the field of DNA engineering and they are in consequence re-examining wild flower and herbal remedies used by country-folk in former centuries. They noticed that in folklore, particularly in Wales, the wood anemone was used as a cure for leprosy, lethargy and consumption. It is a matter of speculation as to whether or not Elgar was aware of these matters, for knowing of his wide interest in out of the way subjects that would seem quite feasible, and indeed, in that 'sweet borderland' of England and Wales – Herefordshire and Worcestershire – such matters may not have been at all 'out of the way.'

There is even a possible visual link between a wood anemone and a sufferer from tuberculosis, like Helen Weaver. The body and limbs of a patient grow thin, and the face pale. When racked with coughing, the head shakes, as in a wind, and if blood is expectorated red stains can be left on the features, like the pink reddish tinge on the wood anemone sepals. In an advanced state of the illness a pink flush can appear on the face of a patient with fever, and this author has memories of such sights from a short period in his life when he was employed as a nurse in a sanatorium. Elgar too is likely to have seen such distressing symptoms when Helen nursed her own step-mother in the last days of her life, as Helen had to return to Worcester from Leipzig to take care of her and never afterwards resumed her studies abroad. Helen probably caught the disease from her stepmother, who was only ten years older than Helen.

The nickname 'Windflower' comes from the Greek word 'anemos' – meaning wind, and refers to the flower's nodding movement in even a light breeze. Hence Elgar's reference to the name and to his advice to Alice to take care in cold winds. The word 'nemorosa' also comes from the Greek – the word 'nemos' meaning 'wood'. In Latin 'nemus' is a grove and we get the adjective nemorose in English from this source, meaning growing in groves or full of woods. *Anemone nemorosa* is so called because it appears in spring in country environments, especially in woods, although it can also occasionally be seen on shaded grassy banks by the roadside. Indeed one such location is only a few hundred yards from the Elgar Birthplace Museum – an area which possibly was woodland some one hundred years or so ago. Readers do not need to be reminded of Elgar's love of his woods – particularly those surrounding Birchwood and Brinkwells.

As well as knowing about the windflower botanically, Elgar is also likely to have known the country names for the flower around Worcestershire. Even fifty years ago, when one of the author's friends was at school there, the wood anemone was known as the 'Wooden Enemy' and 'Granny's Nightcap', because the flower shuts and droops at night or on a dull day. In Gloucestershire it is called 'Lady's Nightcap', 'Nemony' or 'Windflower'. A vice-president of the Elgar Society, Vernon Handley, known to all as 'Tod' since his childhood days, might be surprised to hear that one country name for a windflower is 'Tod's Weed'! Another name is 'Smell Foxes', because of its faint bitter scent, reminiscent of leaf mould and foxes. It is also known as 'Prairie Smoke', as the smoke from the burning seed-pods was used to revive a person from a faint. In Stanley Wood, Derbyshire, it was called 'Moggie Nightgown', and possibly here is one explanation for the drawings of cats and the name 'Caterina' which Elgar doodled on his score. Apparently there is also a link with girls and their chemises and smocks, and the bad habits of cuckoos and snakes. Indeed it is surprising how extensive is a list of country names from counties all over England. Included in such, *inter alia*, would be: bow bells, candelmas caps, chimney smocks, cuckoo-flower, cuckoo-spit, drops of snow, Easter flower, granny thread the needle, Jack o'Lantern, lady's milkcans, lady's petticoat, lady's purse, milkmaids, moll o' the woods, moon-flower, Nancy, nedcullion, shame-faced maiden, shoes and slippers, silver bells, soldiers, soldiers buttons, white soldiers, and star of Bethlehem.[43]

In 1923, thirteen years after the Concerto was composed, an article was published in *The Times* from 'a correspondent', and Jerrold Northrop Moore identified the correspondent as Elgar himself, although he did not give any reason for that deduction. However, Carl Newton has suggested that the author was one A. Grove, possibly Alfred Grove, a Lecturer in Zoology at Sheffield, from 1919 to 1929. Gardening was one of his interests.[44]

Whatever the truth of the matter, Elgar certainly sent a copy of this article to Alice whom he was still calling, and would continue to call, 'Windflower' for the rest of his life. Indeed it had become his habit to send her the first windflowers he could find each year.

The article about windflowers, 'The Vernal Anemones: A Beautiful Native', published in *The Times* on 28 April 1923, states:

> The pleasant legend which couples the tears of Venus with the anemone is not one that need try the receptive imagination very high, for in its simple, graceful beauty the flower may well have had a celestial origin. The little group of anemones commonly called windflowers are happily named too, for when the east wind rasps over the ground in March and April they

merely turn their backs and bow before the squall. They are buffeted and blown, as one may think almost to destruction; but their anchors hold, and the slender-looking stems bend but do not break. And when the rain clouds drive up, the petals shut tight into a tiny tent, as country folk tell one, to shelter the little person inside.

Our native windflower, *Anemone nemorosa,* is often overlooked by gardeners, who think of it, perhaps, as always white, as in many places it is. But there are wild colonies of it where it "sports" through French grey into pink and lavender, and then to blue. Although the wood-anemone does not challenge the liquid blue of the infant's eye like its cousin of the Apennines, sometimes, since there is a tell-tale leavening of pink in the flower, there are some fine colour forms of it.

The article refers to Farrer finding a blue anemone in a wood, and it was Farrer who in 1909 (!) wrote his book *In a Yorkshire Garden*. This book may have caught Elgar's notice as it is dedicated 'In memoriam Aliciae'. Chapter XIV, 'Alice's Garden in the Wood' opens with the words: 'Alice lies in her garden now; many years before her time'.

Carice once said that the windflowers which her father sent to Alice were blue,[45] another mystery as we have seen that Elgar initially named his Windflower person after the white woodland species (*Anemone nemorosa*). It is strange that Carice should have thought that her father sent blue anemones to Alice Stuart Wortley. *The Times* article refers to the blue anemone and this may have misled her. Another explanation is that Elgar may well have been happy for Carice and others to believe that his flowers were blue, for confusion was part of his disguise, and we should remember that he was often at pains to dismiss or disown his interest in those matters which were closest to his heart. More simply he may have sent more than one species, as in 1923 he wrote to Alice from Kempsey, Worcester, saying, 'Here are some Windflowers from the garden: a different kind from the Stoke sort – they grow wild in the shrubbery here'.[46] *The Botany of Worcestershire* (1909) by Messrs J. Amphlett and C. Rea notes that the blue mountain anemone, (apennine), was first recorded in the locality in 1858 and was announced to the Malvern Naturalists' Field Club in that year. In 1909 they recorded three localities in Worcestershire where it could be found, which included Malvern Link and Tunnel Hill, Upton-on-Severn.

In *The Times* article there is a reference to the 'pleasant legend about the Tears of Venus', and in that phrase there could lie one of the most important clues we have to an understanding of the mysteries buried in the Violin Concerto. When *The Times* correspondent wrote of Venus he was referring to the Roman name for Aphrodite, who at one time was worshipped as the Goddess of the Sea and Seafarers, or as the Children's Britannica interestingly describes her: 'the Goddess of Calm Seas and Prosperous Voyages'! Later Aphrodite was known as the Goddess of Flowers and then, as we know her now, as the Goddess of Love and Beauty. The Greeks say that Aphrodite was born out of the Mediterranean Sea, onto the shores of Cyprus, having been blown there by Zephyr, the West Wind. Her birth is captured in Botticelli's painting, which would have been well known to Elgar, Phillips and Alice, bearing in mind the revival of interest in Botticelli's works, particularly by the pre-Raphaelites, in the late nineteenth century. This painting, *The Birth of Venus*, shows the Winds blowing the Goddess Aphrodite ashore as she is born from out of the sea, with Flora, the Goddess of Flowers, waiting to adorn her with a gown bedecked with flowers. The painting is in the Uffizi Gallery, Florence and Alice Elgar's diary records visits there in 1909 when the Elgars stayed at the Villa Silli with 'Pippa' – Julia Worthington. In particular, the entry for 20 May 1909, records: 'E. C. & A to Church at q. Very hot. E.A.& C. to lunch with Mr. Harris. Walked up steep old St. Mr. Horne learned in art and Botticelli there. – Very pleasant time. Saw garden etc.' So who was Mr Horne? There can be little doubt that this was the scholar who, in the previous year, had written a book on Botticelli, which today is still regarded as a standard work, even though – perhaps because of its size – only two hundred and fifty copies were printed. It can be seen in the Victoria and Albert Museum Art Library. Elgar was indeed fortunate to meet Horne in Florence, and to be told about Botticelli by an expert. He would have learned that *The Birth of Venus* had been painted on canvas in about 1484/6, probably upon a commission from the artist's patron Lorenzo, whose mistress could well have been the model for Venus. Elgar may have been told that she died at the age of twenty-three, from tuberculosis, or as it was called then and for some centuries subsequently, 'The Decline'. According to the story she was so beautiful that at her funeral, Lorenzo caused her body to be borne through the streets of Florence so that everyone could see her face, uncovered in all its beauty, even in death. A poet is recorded as crying out: 'Her soul hath passed into a star'. Elgar might also have been told a story about Botticelli's neighbours. These were cloth-makers or weavers. Sometimes, at night they would run their looms and the noise kept Botticelli awake, or if he was working, he could not concentrate on his painting. So he threatened to destroy their looms by having a large boulder placed on the wall which divided his studio from their workshop yard, and which he said he would topple upon them if they continued to annoy him.

Despite the fame that subsequently came to Botticelli, he spent his life living in these humble surroundings, in what we might call 'The Weavers' District'. However, his reputation diminished after his death, but interest was renewed by the pre-Raphaelites in the middle of the nineteenth century, and much fun was then made of the name Botticelli in the magazine *Punch,* and in other spheres.

There is another famous depiction of Venus' birth, by Ludovisi in 460 B.C., which shows Venus being carried out of the sea to the shore by sea nymphs or Naiads. Is it just a coincidence therefore that the overture at the concert when the Concerto had its première was *The Naiads,* by Sterndale Bennett, who had connections with both Mendelssohn and Leipzig? When Bennett first visited Leipzig in 1836 he took the new overture with him, and in 1837 it was performed at the Gewandhaus under Mendelssohn's auspices. In 1844 Mendelssohn chose to perform it together with his own *Midsummer Night's Dream* music at a concert, which he conducted in England. *The Naiads* overture is rarely played these days, but a listener might find a similarity in the opening theme of this overture, the four bars immediately after the *Calm Sea and Prosperous Voyage* quotation in Variation XIII of the *Variations,* and the music in the Concerto five bars before 71, and four after 100, where it forms the lead-in to the cadenza.[47] It is possible that Elgar suggested this work as a suitable piece to open the programme and he would have been amused about his private reasons for such a choice.[48] Elgar may have also known Edgar Allan Poe's poem *To Helen,* which contains the lines, 'Thy Naiad airs have brought me home to the glory that was Greece, and the grandeur that was Rome'.

The 'pleasant legend' referred to in *The Times* article is about an event later in the life of Venus, of how she heard of the death of her lover, Adonis, after she had implored him not to go out hunting. Adonis ignored her warning, and was killed by a wild boar. There is a famous and beautiful painting of this incident by Titian. Upon hearing the news, so the legend goes, Venus wept so bitterly that her tears which fell on his grave turned into anemone flowers or windflowers – subsequently called 'The Tears of Venus'.

Alas the Paphian! Fair Adonis slain!
Tears plenteous as his blood she pours amain.
But gentle flowers are born, and bloom around,
From every drop that falls upon the ground:
Where streams his blood, there blushing springs the rose;
And where a tear has dropped, a windflower blows.

This grief is similar to the description Elgar gave to a phrase in his Second Symphony, part of which was written concurrently with the Concerto He referred to its being 'like a woman dropping a flower on the man's grave'.[49]

Elgar's favourite painting, according to Alice Elgar's diary, also concerned the death of a lover. It is based on a poem *Isabella or The Pot of Basil* by Keats, a man ravaged by tuberculosis. The painting by Alice Stuart Wortley's father, Millais – in private competition with other pre-Raphaelites – depicts a scene of a family meal, but is full of allegory and foreboding. Elgar went to see it at Liverpool on New Year's Eve 1910 when he was there for a performance of the Concerto. The poem tells of two young lovers, Lorenzo, and Isabella. Her brothers were jealous of Lorenzo and so murdered him, burying his body in a forest. Guided by a dream, Isabella searched for him and when she found the 'murderous spot she seemed to grow, Like to a native lily of the dell'. Digging fervently she found the body, then cut off its head, and took it to hide at home in a pot of basil, keeping the plant watered with her tears.

Thus her grief and tears reminds us of the Venus and Adonis myth and her digging at the site of a grave has echoes of the search by the wiser of the two journeying scholars who found that stone engraved with the words ' Aqui esta encerrada el alma del licenciado Pedro Garcias' as described by Le Sage. How right Professor Trowell is to speak of Elgar being both elusive and allusive! Troyte Griffith described him as 'a very complex character'.[50]

Elgar had a deep interest in Greek mythology, and he probably knew of the myth in which Anemone was a lovely nymph who was loved by the God of the West Wind, Zephyr. Zephyr's love caused the Goddess of Flowers, Flora, to become jealous as she wanted Zephyr for herself, so she turned Anemone into a little windflower, and Zephyr thereafter took no further interest in Anemone, abandoning her to Boreas, the North Wind, who woos her early in the spring. It is from this myth that the anemone is said to represent all those who have been <u>forsaken</u> or who are <u>forlorn</u>.

Winds, clearly, have considerable relevance for the Concerto, and it was in 1910 that Troyte Griffith designed an aeolian harp for Elgar at his request. The harp can now be seen in the Birthplace Museum and on it, studded in pearl, are the names of the four winds. In Greek mythology Aeolus was the Father of all the winds, and on 18 September 1910 Elgar wrote to Newman about the cadenza saying, 'The sound of a distant Aeolian harp flutters under and over the solo'.[51]

Aristotle wrote that the Orphic verses record that 'the soul comes in from space as we breathe, borne by the winds' and Pythagoras stated that 'the facilities of the soul are winds'. In the Greek myths there are also references to impregnation by the winds.

Turning to Flora, Elgar and his Windflower, Alice, could hardly have failed to take an interest in her in 1910, for in that year there was a huge controversy in the art world concerning a wax bust of a Flora, which had been discovered in Berlin. Some claimed it was by Leonardo da Vinci, whilst others said it was a fake. Claude Phillips wrote about it in his *Daily Telegraph* article of 25 October, and Elgar sent a copy of this to Alice saying, 'You do not see the Telegraph so you never see Claude's articles which are splendid. Here is one.' [52]

There is perhaps, another relevant Greek Myth – that concerning the Judgement of Paris and the origins of The Trojan War, as described in *The Iliad*. There we read that Paris, a Trojan shepherd, but who was in reality the son of King Priam, had to award an apple to one of three goddesses presented to him. Aphrodite bribed Paris by promising to give him that most desirable of all women, Helen, should he choose her, Aphrodite, – which of course he did. Indeed, Helen and Aphrodite are often linked in mythology.

Perhaps all this explains why Elgar was so pleased when at the party after the first performance of the Concerto, Schuster unexpectedly chose and arranged for Elgar's *Five Part-Songs from the Greek Anthology* to be sung. A strange choice, but perhaps not so far removed from the hidden impulses behind the composition of the Concerto. Schuster may have been aware of these or just very knowledgeable about the composer's mind and its associations, which may themselves have been conscious or subconscious.

In 1903 the English artist J. W. Waterhouse, a follower of the pre-Raphaelite school, painted *Windflowers*. It was reproduced in the Christmas Edition of 'The Art Journal' in December, 1909, when the whole of that month's edition was devoted to his works. For many years the painting was in the Walker Gallery, Liverpool, which Elgar visited, and was exhibited at The Royal Academy in 1903. It is now in a private collection. The painting shows a young girl blown by the wind and holding anemone flowers, not *Anemone nemorosa* but *Anemone coronaria*. It is highly probable that Elgar viewed this painting when it was exhibited, and that he saw a copy of the December edition of 'The Art Journal'. It may well have been a topic of conversation with Alice and Claude Phillips. If so, it could have been a trigger in his mind – three months before he began calling Alice 'Windflower' – to choose that special name for his themes and for the muse who meant so much to him at that time.

There certainly seems to have been some significance in the question Elgar put to Claude Phillips, the art critic, at the party: 'Well, Claude, did you think that was a work of art?' which was overheard by the young Adrian Boult and recalled many years later.[53] In 1996 a companion painting, *Boreas* – the North Wind, which had been missing for many years, came to light and was put up for auction, selling for £848,500. Waterhouse used the same model as in *Windflowers*, and the painting showed a young girl and flowers blown by the wind. In 1904 it too was exhibited at the Academy. Another painting, *March Winds* is still missing. Intriguingly, there is another Waterhouse painting, *Mariana in the South*, which depicts a scene from the poem of the same name by Alfred, Lord Tennyson. Mariana was a lady jilted and abandoned by her lover, who is mentioned also in Shakespeare's *Measure for Measure*. Can it be that the overture *In the South (Alassio)* contains hidden mysteries too?

The anemones in Waterhouse's paintings are of the *coronaria* species called crown anemones, and there may be a link here with what Elgar wrote to Alice in 1916 after her husband, Charles Stuart-Wortley, was raised to the Peerage: ' I gave you a coronet long ago – the best I had but you may have forgotten it – now you will have a real one, bless you!'[54] Indeed it may be that Elgar and Alice had agreed that 'her windflower' should be the *Anemone coronaria*, for as early as 16 June 1910 Elgar wrote to her saying, 'Here is one of your own flowers.[55] If, as seems likely, he enclosed an actual flower with his letter it would not have been *Anemone nemorosa* so late in the season. Perhaps this is why Carice remembered blue anemones!

There may also be religious connections. Jesus asked his followers to 'consider the lilies of the field – how they grow – they toil not neither do they spin', reminding them that 'even Solomon in all his glory was not arrayed like one of these'.[56] Peake's *Commentary on the Bible* states that the Lilies of the Field were anemones and the reference by Christ is to the 'Song of Solomon' in the Old Testament, where a youth and a maiden speak with longing of their rustic bower and the youth replies to his beloved that her beauty is indeed like a lily (an anemone) amongst thorns (brambles).[57] A few chapters later on in the 'Song of Solomon' there is a line used by Bach in his *St Matthew Passion*, 'Whither is my beloved gone. O thou fairest amongst women?'[58] Elgar knew his Bach well – indeed in

1911 he co-operated with Ivor Atkins in a new edition of the *St Matthew Passion* and Elgar's first beloved had literally gone to the ends of the earth, to New Zealand to seek better health.

Another connection can be made too, as Sterndale Bennett, composer of *The Naiads* overture, had been the first man to conduct Bach's *St Matthew Passion* in England, being the founder of the Bach Choir.

However, it is submitted that any solution to our questioning lies not completely in the botany of the windflower, nor in Greek myths, nor paintings, although all seem to have some relevance. The breaking of Elgar's code, it is suggested, lies in the title of one of the earliest of Elgar's compositions – *The Language of Flowers*. The music of this short piece was composed when he was fourteen, although the words were not written by him; several biographies are incorrect here. The words were taken from a poem, *The Language of Flowers* by an American poet James Gates Percival (1795 –1856).[59] This poem referred to flowers and plants, which were of deep interest to Elgar's mother, who taught her children about them. Thus it was a natural choice for Elgar when he dedicated this piece to his sister Lucy on her twentieth birthday, 29 May 1872.

Percival's poem must have been well known in the Elgars' household and it seems that at a very early age Elgar had a good knowledge of this coded language so enamoured by the Victorians. Moreover, he knew the language's source, as in the first stanza it speaks of 'Eastern Lands'. At the top of the title page, presumably in Elgar's handwriting, there is written, 'Not for publication – by <u>special</u> desire', (this author's emphasis). One can speculate that he would not have written such an instruction at the age of fourteen, and if so, why did he express this wish later? Did he then want to guard against publicity for this piece that might provide a link with the Concerto or an explanation of windflower themes or persons?

The Language of Flowers can be traced back to ancient Greece and Rome. It is said that when Cleopatra wanted to show her love for Mark Antony she paid in gold for a room to be filled to a depth of two feet with rose petals. In more recent times, Ophelia, in Shakespeare's *Hamlet,* says, 'There's pansies – that's for thoughts'. Elgar wrote a work *Rosemary – That's for Remembrance*. The Language of Flowers was introduced to England by Lady Mary Wortley Montagu, the wife of the Ambassador to Constantinople (1716 –1718), an ancestor of Charles Stuart Wortley (maybe just another coincidence!) The Victorians were caught up in the code to an amazing extent and floral dictionaries became popular. Every flower had its own meaning, for there was significance and importance in the way in which a flower was positioned on a paper or in a display. The code gave men a means of expressing their feelings in correspondence, and women became able to indicate their inclinations 'secretly', to someone of the opposite sex. Numbers, days of the week, and even money, could be communicated by flowers.

An heraldic shield was made from flowers for Florence Nightingale, who was named Florence after Flora the goddess of flowers, for the city of Florence was chosen by her mother as the place where she wished to give birth. On the shield there are dock leaves, oak leaves, snow-drops, poppies, and strawberries. These represent patience, bravery, consolation and her kindly disposition. Florence's firmness is shown by the purple columbine, and the comfort she gave, by a red geranium. An anemone represents sickness.[60] This latter meaning came from the Egyptians and was later taken over by the Christians in symbolism to associate the flower with illness. We saw earlier that an anemone has a meaning as 'forsaken' or 'forlorn', and there is evidence that Elgar was aware of this, for in 1907, when he travelled to America without his wife, he sent a cable to her to announce his safe arrival, using 'anemone' to describe their respective states.

The Chinese called the anemone the 'Flower of Death', but *Anemone nemorosa* has also a converse meaning of curing sickness, for whilst in country folklore it was believed that simply to breathe the air which smelt of windflowers would cause sickness (the poisonous aspect), other country folk encouraged the picking of the first windflower as a remedy against disease. This was a reason for a jingle, which went: 'The first spring-blown anemone, she in his doublet wove, to keep him safe from pestilence, wherever he should rove'. So *Anemone nemorosa* has two meanings, this giving an important clue as to why two windflower themes appear in the Concerto. As well as meaning 'forsaken', and as well as representing 'sickness', the flower also carries the means of a cure from past or future ills.

There are those who believe that the identity of the feminine person, hidden by the five dots in the Spanish quotation, is Elgar's first love, Helen Weaver, and this author sides with them, whilst agreeing with Percy Young that no one can express finality about uncertain aspects of Elgar's life. Hence the ideas developed in this essay are simply to stimulate thought and to provoke interest in some unexplored areas.

Helen was a violinist and Elgar's 'Braut', the separation from whom he never overcame and in respect of whom, with the passing years and in his music he developed a deep psychosis. A windflower could have had a special significance for Elgar before he invented the name for Alice Stuart Wortley after the <u>second theme</u> in his Concerto, for Clare Stuart Wortley believed that Elgar called her mother Windflower 'after the themes', not the themes after her. It is this author's belief that the original 'Windflower' in <u>theme one</u> and the 'soul' hidden in the Concerto, was Elgar's first lost love. When their engagement was broken off, and Helen developed tuberculosis, subsequently emigrating to New Zealand, – as far away as one could get from Worcester and Elgar – he was shattered. Ernest Newman states that something in his life had torn the very heart out of him and from which he never fully recovered and we see much of that anguish in his Concerto.

A windflower represents both sickness and a cure and, after her emigration to New Zealand, Helen Weaver recovered from her tuberculosis, although her daughter, Joyce died at the early age of twenty-eight from the same disease. Helen had married John Munro, a bank clerk, and she had two children, Joyce and Kenneth, although it is not known if Elgar heard of these events. If he did, both meanings of a windflower are especially significant. If he did not, Elgar at least found some restoration of his mental health in his association with Alice Stuart Wortley.

Clearly there had been something of unique importance in the events of Elgar's first engagement and its termination, which perhaps, even now we can only guess. One can speculate whether it was Elgar who destroyed that future match, perhaps because he could not face up to Helen's illness and all its implications for himself and his ambitions for his own future. What was it that Elgar discussed with Dr Buck in their walks – did they talk about Helen's prognosis? If that were the case, and if Elgar had been responsible for the collapse of their plans, he could well have developed a serious feeling of guilt, especially if later, he heard of her recovery and realised that he could have married his first true love after all. Perhaps his mother had been right when in his childhood she had marked verses in a poetry book warning of the consequence of ambition.

It is hard for us now, at the beginning of the twenty-first century to appreciate just how much apprehension there was in the nineteenth century about pulmonary tuberculosis or consumption, as it was then called. A letter to which the author was referred in his research speaks of six members of one family dying from 'the decline' in the early 1800s. In 1882, just two years before Helen Weaver became its victim, the German scientist, Koch, had discovered the cause, when he identified the tubercle bacillus, spread by droplet infection, spitting, coughing, and kissing! Such was the fear of catching this killer disease that many relationships met their end – as well as most of the patients.[61]

When Elgar first attempted to write a violin concerto in 1890 his mind almost certainly would have strayed to his days of music making and courtship with Helen, the violinist. Perhaps in the first year of his marriage to Alice Roberts, he had felt it disloyal to his new wife to reflect on Helen in his composition, so that was why he destroyed it. But twenty years later he expressed all his old love for her, and his regret for the event in his life from which he had never completely recovered. The first windflower theme is sadder and more poignant than the second scored in a major key, which is clearly linked to Alice Stuart Wortley, as we know from Elgar's use of the notation and rhythm for her name when addressing her in correspondence. But surely the first theme could refer to Helen Weaver, if used similarly. It would 'go' just as well.

It seems that Elgar's mind was still working in this way in 1932. When he was with the young Menuhin, he added to the score a further dedication, 'to my dear Yehudi Menuhin' after the words 'Dedicated to Fritz Kreisler', and he wrote 'Yehudi Menuhin' over the six notes of the solo violin, where it enters for the first time in that unexpected way in the opening movement. Turning to Menuhin he said, ' You see, Yehudi, I thought of you ten years before you were born!' [62]

It is the case in this essay that the meaning of a windflower in the Language of Flowers, the Greek myths, the implications of the Botticelli painting of Venus, and that of *Isabella* by Millais, coupled with Waterhouse's *Windflowers* which was given prominence in an art journal just at the time when Elgar was trying to find a suitable private name for Alice, lead to no other conclusion than that the Concerto sums up his love for and loss of Helen Weaver. Professor Parrott was surely right when he once called this Elgar's most secret work.

But if the reader is still not convinced he is asked to consider this: why on 27 May 1910, when struggling to complete the third movement did Elgar write to Schuster saying: 'I want to *end* that Concerto but do not see my way very clearly to the end – so you had best invite its stepmother (this author's emphasis) to the Hut too. Do.'[63] He was referring to Alice Stuart Wortley who was of course stepmother to Bice, the daughter from Charles Stuart Wortley's first marriage. But Elgar would not have referred to Alice Stuart Wortley as a stepmother in this type of correspondence and his letter refers to its stepmother i.e. the Concerto's. This gives strong grounds for a case that Alice came on the scene in the Concerto later. She was not its birth mother, nor its natural mother. That mother was Helen Weaver, the violinist, and Elgar's one time betrothed. Elgar may have called the Concerto 'our concerto' in correspondence to Alice Stuart Wortley, but it is submitted that she was not the 'soul enshrined herein' as originally conceived.

In the last three years of his life, Elgar found a new muse, Vera Hockman, a violinist who was some forty years younger than himself. He called her his mother, child, lover and friend, and it seems now to be accepted that she was a motivating force as he attempted to compose a third symphony, just as Alice Stuart Wortley had been in respect of the Concerto. He and Vera played the Violin Sonata, written in 1918 – years before he had met her – and yet Elgar began to refer to the work as 'our sonata'. This was some thirteen years after he had composed that chamber work, yet he had no hesitation in ascribing the phrase, 'our sonata' to her, when, presumably it suited his amorous attentions. And so perhaps it had been with Alice Stuart Wortley when he used a similar phrase in calling the Concerto, 'our Concerto'?

On one occasion Elgar and Vera Hockman were listening to the proof records of the Menuhin performance which had only just arrived. Elgar turned to her in the pause between the second and third movements saying: ' This is where two souls merge and melt into one another',[64] surely an indication to her of the hidden secrets in the last movement just before it was played. (This author's emphasis). Moreover, in a letter to Vera after the recording sessions Elgar had written: '...I do not think there is anything quite like it, and some day perhaps it will be understood how much soul went into the making of it'.[65] It is in that last movement that a listener particularly hears the two 'windflower' themes merging and intertwining, especially in the Cadenza, that unique recapitulation of the first movement themes.

Professor Trowell has described his excellent detective work concerning the press cutting which Elgar pinned to the second of the two windflower themes and which cutting he gave to Alice, as recorded by her on 1 May1910.[66] This was the article referred to above. It ends with a description of what is believed to be Titian's last mythological painting now identified as Paris and Oenone. 'But the most wonderful love-poem of Venetian sixteenth-century art is perhaps the nymph and piping shepherd of the Imperial Gallery at Vienna – Titian's farewell, in extreme old age to life and love. ... It is twilight and soon will be night, with the lovers, who dally still in the sombre air shot with silver. <u>The poetry of the earlier years has come back</u> (this author's emphasis) intensified by something of added poignancy and of foreboding that is tinged it may be, with <u>remorse</u> (this author's emphasis). This last passion has something that the earlier passion had not; in one sense it is nearer to earth and earthiness; in another it is infinitely higher and more far reaching, more typical of the love that in its heights and depths, in its tender light and sombre, fitfully illumined shadow, is truly that which to the end of all things must hold and possess Man'. This cutting was removed from the manuscript score by someone, – an action which is highly significant and about which we would never have known, without Professor Trowell's invaluable research.[67]

From *The Daily Telegraph* cutting we can see the transfer of Elgar's old love for Helen Weaver to Alice Stuart Wortley, from the first 'Windflower' to the second, probably because Elgar had told Alice about his past love and all his associated problems. Alice had understood, comforted, and provided the encouragement that Elgar needed to continue working on his Concerto. Professor Trowell has written: 'By 1910, I think, turning to this Alice, Elgar may well have felt that the soul of Helen Weaver, in Lamb's words, "looked out of her eyes with such a reality of re-presentment, that I became in doubt which of them stood there before me" '.[68] But what may also be of significance is that earlier in this article Claude Phillips had made reference to the *Greek Anthology* and to Helen of Troy.

The article also refers to 'twilight'. It surely is more than coincidence that this is also the title of one of the three Parker songs set by Elgar in 1909/1910 and first performed at Jaeger's memorial concert in January 1910. Moreover, in some Greek myths Helen is referred to as the Dawn or as Twilight. In one verse of the Parker song we hear that: '<u>the Lilies of Love have a crimson stain</u>, And the old days never will come again. Adieu! Some time shall the veil between The things that are, and that might have been, Be folded back, for our eyes to see, And the meaning of all be clear to me. Adieu!' (This author's emphasis).

But here is an unexpected link: another country name for the wood anemone is 'Twilight'! So now we have a complete circle: Helen – Aphrodite – Windflower – Wood Anemone – Twilight.

At this time too Elgar began work on four songs where the words also were, unusually, written by himself. The first song he called *The Torch*, and intriguingly, one translation of 'torch' into Greek is 'helene'.[69] A line of the song recites: 'All my soul cries out for thee'.

Elgar once wrote: 'I have put it all in my music & much more that has never happened'.[70]

According to Professor Trowell, in the many books of poetry owned by Elgar, several poems were marked in pencil in the margin.[71] In one he drew a line alongside the last six stanzas:

> *My Past, whose light and life is flown,*
> *Shall live through memory for you still;*
> *Take all my Present for your own,*
> *And mould my Future to your will.*
>
> *One only thought remains apart,*
> *And will for ever so remain;*
> *There is one Chamber in my heart*
> *Where even you might knock in vain.*
>
> *A haunted Chamber – long ago*
> *I closed it, and I cast the key*
> *Where deep and bitter waters flow*
> *Into a vast and silent sea.*
>
> *Dear, it is haunted. All the rest*
> *Is yours, but I have shut that door*
> *For ever now. 'Tis even best*
> *That I should enter it no more.*
>
> *No more. It is not well to stay*
> *With ghosts; their very look would scare*
> *Your joyous, loving smile away*
> *So never try to enter there.*
>
> *Check, if you love me all regret*
> *That this one thought remains apart –*
> *Now let us smile, dear, and forget*
> *The haunted Chamber in my Heart.*

When she gave the letters which she had received from Elgar to the City of Worcester as a 'sacred bequest', and when she was instrumental in the establishment of the Elgar Birthplace Museum, Alice Stuart Wortley –

the 'Windflower' – took steps for which she will be gratefully remembered by Elgarians for all time. Indeed, without her encouragement of Elgar we might never have heard his Violin Concerto, – music which sings of 'memories and hope'.[72] But let us also never forget Helen, – a truly Grecian name – a windflower whose soul was deeply planted, enshrined, – 'encerrada' in the Concerto.

This essay is based on a lecture given to the London Branch of the Elgar Society at Imperial College, London on 5 February 2000.

Notes and References

1   *Hereford Times,* 7 October 1905.
2   Letter 11 August 1880, Elgar Birthplace, 9602.
3   Dora Powell to Clare Stuart Wortley, 15 May 1939 in Kennedy, Michael: 'The Soul Enshrined: Elgar and his Violin Concerto' in Monk, Raymond (ed): *Edward Elgar: music and literature* [Aldershot: Scolar Press, 1993] 82.
4   Elgar to Dr Buck, 20 July 1884 in Moore, J.N. (ed): *Elgar and his Publishers: letters of a creative life* [Oxford: OUP, 1987] Vol.1, 11.
5   Elgar to Kilburn, 5 November 1910 in Young, Percy M. (ed): *Letters of Edward Elgar and Other Writings* [London: Geoffrey Bles, 1956] 201.
6   Maine, Basil: *Elgar: his life and works* [London: G. Bell and Sons Ltd, 1933] Vol.1, 141.
7   Kennedy, *op.cit.,* 77.
8   Information given to the author by Dr M.E. Smith.
9   Powell, Mrs. R.: *Edward Elgar: Memories of a Variation* [London: OUP, 1937; 4th edn: Aldershot: Scolar Press, 1994] 105-6.
10   Young, P.M.: *Alice Elgar: enigma of a Victorian lady* [London: Dennis Dobson, 1978] 164.
11   Elgar to Isabella Jaeger, 21 May 1909 in Allen, Kevin: *August Jaeger: portrait of Nimrod* [Aldershot: Ashgate, 2000] 277.
12   Robin Legge to his wife, 8 September 1910 in Moore, J.N.: *Edward Elgar: letters of a lifetime* [Oxford: OUP, 1991]222-3.
13   Kennedy: 'The Soul Enshrined', *op.cit.,* 72.
14   *The SundayTimes,* 18 November 1956.
15   Elgar to Alice Stuart Wortley, 29 August 1912 in Moore, J.N. (ed): *Edward Elgar: the Windflower letters* [Oxford: OUP, 1989] 107.
16   Elgar to Alice Stuart Wortley, 5 November 1910 in Moore, *op.cit.,* 65.
17   Anderson, R.: *Elgar* [London: J.M.Dent, 1993] 352 and Kennedy: 'The Soul Enshrined', *op.cit.,* 81.   Overheard by Terry!

18   Reed, W.H.: *Elgar as I knew him* [London: Gollancz, 1973] 129.
19   *ibid.,* 23-4.
20   Buckley, R.J.: *Sir Edward Elgar* [London: John Lane, The Bodley Head, 1905] 75.
21   Elgar to Alice Stuart Wortley, 23 June 1910 in Moore: *Windflower, op.cit.,* 52.
22   Elgar to Alice Stuart Wortley, 27 April 1910 in Moore: *Windflower, op.cit.,* 46.
23   Kennedy: 'The Soul Enshrined', *op.cit.,* 72-82.
24   Elgar to Alice Stuart Wortley, 27 April 1916 in Moore: *Windflower, op.cit.,* 164.
25   Mackerness, E.D.: *'Somewhere Further North': a history of music in Sheffield* [Sheffield: J.W.Northend Ltd, 1974] 98.
26   Young, P.M.: *Elgar O.M.* [London: White Lion Publishers, 1973] 308.
27   Elgar to Alice Stuart Wortley, 23 June 1909 in Moore: *Windflower, op.cit.,* 29-30.
28   Elgar to Alice Stuart Wortley, 1 November 1910 in Moore: *Windflower, op.cit.,* 31.
29   Note by Clare Stuart Wortley, 1940.
30   *ibid.,* 44.
31   MS reminiscence of Clare Stuart Wortley held at the Elgar Birthplace Museum.
32   *ibid.,* 39.
33   Elgar to Schuster, 8 May 1910 in Moore, *Lifetime, op.cit.,* 220.
34   Radio interview with Ida Haendal [B.B.C., March 1995].
35   *The Nation,* 16 November 1910 in Moore, J.N.: *Edward Elgar: A Creative Life* [Oxford: OUP, 1984] 593.
36   F.S.Kelly (1881-1916), no relative of the author; however there would have been a different type of party at the same time in Ardwick, Manchester, where the author's mother would have been celebrating her seventh birthday.
37   Boult, Sir Adrian: *My Own Trumpet* [London: Hamish Hamilton, 1973] 19.
38   Trowell, Brian: 'Elgar's Use of Literature' in Monk, *op.cit.,* 250.
39   Hellyer, A.G.L.: *The Amateur Gardener.*
40   Freethy, R.: *From AGAR to ZENRY: a book of plant uses, names and folklore* [The Crowood Press, 1985].
41   *ibid.*
42   'Medecine goes back to Nature for Cures', *The Sunday Times,* 8 August 1999.
43   Grigson, Geoffrey: *The Englishman's Flora.*
44   Newton, Carl, *Elgar Society Journal,* Vol.11, No.1, March 1999, 64-5. Dr M.E. Smith (West Midlands Branch of the Elgar Society) has suggested that the author, A. Grove (nemus), would have been a perfect Elgarian jape if indeed the article has been written by Elgar.
45   Information given by Michael Kennedy to the author.
46   Elgar to Alice Stuart Wortley, 30 April 1923, in Moore: *Windflower, op.cit.,* 282.
47   Information given by Dr M.E. Smith to the author.
48   If there is any evidence as to how the overture was chosen, the author would be grateful to know.

49   Elgar to Alfred Littleton, 13 April 1911 in Moore: *Publishers, op.cit.*, Vol.2, 742.
50   A.T. ('Troyte') Griffith to Carice Elgar Blake, November 1937.
51   Elgar to Newman, 18 September 1910 in Moore: *Lifetime, op.cit.*, 224.
52   Elgar to Alice Stuart Wortley, 25 October 1901 in Moore: *Windflower, op.cit.*, 63.
53   Boult, *op.cit.*, 19.
54   Elgar to Alice Stuart Wortley, 20 December 1916 in Moore: *Windflower, op.cit.*, 172.
55   Elgar to Alice Stuart Wortley, 16 June 1910 in Moore: *Windflower, op.cit.*, 51.
56   St Matthew Chapter 6 v. 28-29.
57   Peake: *Commentary on the Bible,* Song of Solomon, Chapter 2 v.2.
58   *ibid.*, Chapter 6 v.1.
59   Nall, G., *Elgar Society Journal* [January 1985] 26.
60   Todd, P. and Penney, I.: *Forget-Me-Not: a floral treasury* [Bullfinch Press, 1993].
61   In the author's family an older cousin told how her father insisted that she stopped courting her boy friend when he contracted the disease in the 1930s.
62   Cutting from an unidentified newspaper at the Elgar Birthplace Museum.
63   Elgar to Frank Schuster, [27 May 1910] in Moore: *A Creative Life, op.cit.*, 581.
64   Hockman, Vera: *Elgar & Poetry* in Allen, K: *Elgar in Love* [Malvern, 2000] 75.
65   Allen, *op.cit.*, 75.
66   Trowell: 'Elgar's Use of Literature', *op.cit.*, 249.
67   *ibid.*, 250.
68   *ibid.*, 245.
69   *ibid.*, 318.
70   Elgar to Alice Stuart of Wortley, 5 March 1917 in Moore: *Windflower, op.cit.*, 176.
71   *ibid.*, 208.
72   Elgar to Alice Stuart Wortley, 16 June 1910 in Moore: *Windflower, op.cit.*, 51.

Chapter Six

Elgar's Passage to India

Robert Anderson

There are cuttings about Elgar's early career in his mother's scrapbook, which is now held at the Birthplace Museum; there is also much evidence of Ann Elgar's abundant curiosity. About 1880, when Elgar was living with the Graftons at 'Loretto Villa', she included a piece on 'Indian Art'. This cited an expert of the time, Dr George Birdwood, who described the collection of the East India Company when it was transferred to the South Kensington Museum (known from 1899 as the Victoria & Albert). Perhaps she showed Elgar the latest pastings in her scrapbook; possibly they discussed them. He had a more immediate introduction to things Indian in the spring of 1887, when he was taken to have tea with Lady Roberts at Hazeldine House. The Indian furnishings there were a product of Sir Henry Gee Roberts's career in the service of the East India Company. Born in 1800, he joined it as a cadet in 1818, married Julia Maria Raikes twenty years later, served under Sir Charles Napier on the northern frontier (1843), was political agent in Kutch when Caroline Alice was born, on 9 October 1848, bought Hazeldine House in 1 850, was promoted major-general in 1854, commanded the Rajputana Field Force during the Indian Mutiny (1857–8), was mentioned in a parliamentary motion of thanks on 14 April 1859, was created KCB, and died on 6 October 1860, three days before his daughter's twelfth birthday.

Lady Roberts died at the end of May 1887. After her marriage to Elgar two years later, Caroline Alice decided to sell the family home that was now spacious and expensive beyond her needs and inconvenient for her husband's work. There was a furniture sale at Hazeldine House, but much of the Indian legacy arrived at Forli on 22 January 1892. Ann Elgar visited six days later and was given a palm-leaf table. The following month Elgar spent some time on the general's arms, was particularly fascinated by a hide shield trophy, and eventually took swords into Worcester for cleaning. From time-to-time General Roberts occupied the attention not only of the Elgars but of a still-grateful nation. In the summer of 1895, when Elgar was working on the Organ Sonata, Alice was busy producing material on her father for the *Dictionary of National Biography*; and in June 1908 came the fiftieth anniversary of the Mutiny's collapse, so that the general was again prominent in the British press. At the time Elgar was much occupied by the First Symphony and depressed that the pleasure of cycling round Hereford was being spoilt by the increasing number of motor cars. By 1911, when he was awarded the Order of Merit and had long cultivated his own military appearance, Elgar clearly felt he had finally laid the general's ghost. On 17 July, he wrote to Ivor Atkins: 'Such things as K.C.B.'s are *very cheap* it seems beside O.M.' [1]

Lady Elgar's diary entry of 1 January 1912 marked the move to Severn House, Hampstead: 'Entered E.'s own House – may it be happy & beautiful for him'. The Indian furniture was still with them, and it so happened that the first music emanating from the London home was to be *The Crown of India*. On 8 January Elgar outlined the scheme to Alfred Littleton of Novello : 'The Masque is going to be very gorgeous and patriotic – Indian Durbar – & will last only 30 minutes : I shall write the music at once & it will not interfere with other things'.[2] The main commitment among 'other things' was *The Music Makers* for the following October. There was some confusion over publication. Elgar had already expressed unhappiness about his exclusive arrangement with Novello, but technically the agreement was still in force. He received, however, a tempting offer from Enoch of £600 against royalties and a rather improbable promise about continental performances. On the strength of this, he convinced himself that the proposed Masque was not really in Novello's line of business. Eventually Enoch published a libretto and vocal score of the work, while Boosey produced the piano score of an orchestral suite Elgar devised from the music.

The author of the Masque was Henry Hamilton, actor and playwright for many Drury Lane melodramas. Bernard Shaw gave little praise when he reviewed *Cheer, Boys, Cheer!* in September 1895. This was written by Hamilton in collaboration with Sir Augustus Harris and Cecil Raleigh: 'Give me Rosmersholm or The Master Builder, and I am in my depth : their comparatively simple, natural, sympathetic situations do not puzzle me at all; but in *Cheer, Boys, Cheer!* I not only do not understand, but I feel that I should go mad if I tried to'. A selective list of Hamilton's plays totals twenty-four, including a version of *Carmen* (after Mérimée), *The Devil* (from the Hungarian), a *Joan of Arc*, and *The Crown of India*. The main result of the 1911 Delhi Durbar, attended by George V and Queen

---

1 – Notes and references for this chapter appear on page 175.

Mary, was the shift of India's capital from Calcutta to Delhi; the rival claims of the two cities and the eventual settlement make the Masque's essential theme.

George V's announcement caused maximum sensation in India. *The Times* reported at once: 'The whole Durbar Camp is seething with excitement to-night. The dramatic announcement made by the King-Emperor has almost obliterated the recollection of the amazing spectacle which we witnessed this morning'. The reasons for the change of capital had not been announced and there was bewilderment. Moslems were unmoved by the implied tribute to the Moguls; Hindus feared more loss than gain; only the Rajputs, among whom General Roberts had conducted his Mutiny campaigns, were manifestly delighted: 'Princes were seen beaming with joy and shaking each other's hands over the prospect of the removal of the capital'. Despite a lack of enthusiasm, the announcement had greatly impressed 'all Indians with the power and attributes of the Crown'. Hamilton now had ready-to-hand the ingredients that required only mixing for the Masque.

When devising the music, Elgar ran through his sketchbooks. Any promising ideas were stamped 'COLISEUM MASQUE'. Thus he incorporated themes associated with an 'Antioch' scene originally intended for the 'Apostles' project, and considered others that ended up in *The Music Makers*. The prelude to the work begins with 'The sinful youth of Dan', inscribed in the visitors' book of George Robertson Sinclair under April 1903. Elgar incorporated into the Masque parts of *In Smyrna*, the piano piece written to remember his 1905 Mediterranean cruise; they appeared mainly in the 'Sacred Measure' and in Agra's song 'Hail, Immemorial Ind!'. The music for the 'Dance of the Nautch Girls' was headed *'Sneak's Noise'*, the tune beloved of Doll Tearsheet from Shakespeare's *Henry IV part 2* and therefore linked with *Falstaff*. The East India Company suggested 'pigtail stuff', to be enshrined in a Tempo di Menuetto played 'Maestoso antico'. The work was completed on 25 February. Soon John Austin arrived from Worcester to help with the checking of orchestral parts, and Hugh Blair was in attendance to make a vocal score. Lady Elgar described the final rehearsal in her diary entry for 10 March: 'dresses lovely, lights rather vague ... to Claridge's for lunch. Then back to rehearsal all rather better. Speeches & Calcutta's & Delhi's arguments much too long'. *The Times* had outlined the plot three days before, said the Masque was 'deliberately intended to be (in the best sense) popular', claimed wrongly it was Elgar's first time of writing 'for the secular stage', and mentioned that the 'orchestra will include a new gong contrived by Sir Edward Elgar for his special purpose'.

The first tableau of the Masque, which opened at the Coliseum on 11 March, revealed a temple typifying the 'legends and traditions of India', with a view of the Taj Mahal at the back. There were seats for India and her ten main cities, though Calcutta and Delhi were not yet in place. At the sides were a native musician with tom-tom and a couple of snake-charmers with pipes. After two files of nautch girls had executed their dance, India rose to praise her cities with a wealth of historical detail, recalling the distracted state of her empire previous to its unification under the Raj:

> *Into one nation welded by the West,*
> *That in the Pax Britannica is blest.*

India regretted the absence of Calcutta and Delhi and their constant bickering. Whereupon a fanfare sounded for Calcutta, who entered attended by Commerce and Statecraft, and there was a flourish for Delhi, accompanied by Tradition and Romance. As claim to be India's future capital Delhi pleaded her antiquity:

> *And wilt thou vaunt to me thy mushroom pomp*
> *Of new-made palaces? that wast a swamp*
> *One hundred years ago; when I a Queen*
> *Enthroned for forty centuries had been!*

Delhi summoned as witnesses the four greatest Mogul emperors, Akbar, Jehangir, Shah Jehan and Aurangzeb; Elgar marched them in. Calcutta relied on John Company and his minuet:

> *A strenuous Yesterday, a strong To-Day*
> *Are better than an aeon of decay,*
> *Barbaric splendours and bejewelled ease*
> *Adorned by Despots – and by Debauchees!*

For witnesses, Calcutta had such worthies as Clive, Warren Hastings and Lord Wellesley, with heroes of the Mutiny such as Sir Henry Lawrence, Sir Henry Havelock and Sir Colin Campbell, but unfortunately not Sir Henry Gee Roberts. Delhi then summoned as arbiter the spirit of English chivalry:

> *Thou that in Cappadocia's gloomy gorge*
> *Did'st beat the Dragon down – appear, St George!*

But the saint proved too chivalrous to make a decision 'Where either famous is and both are fair'. Instead he referred the matter to the King-Emperor, and proceeded to hymn the Flag of England, briefly citing *Land of Hope and Glory* in the last verse, at the words 'Dear Land that hath no like'.

A distant view of Delhi was the background to the second tableau, which symbolised the Durbar. The climax of the initial procession was the arrival of the royal pair:

> *He comes! he comes! Upon our dazzled eyes*
> *The Sun of Britain and of Ind doth rise.*

Meanwhile Queen Mary was praised as one who 'to our swooning Indian heats' brought 'The fragrant freshness of a Northern Spring'. In front of the assembled grandees George V had India pronounce his decision:

> *The Majesty of Ind his will proclaims:*
> *Delhi to be his Capital he names:*
> *And, of his Empire, further makes decree*
> *Calcutta shall the Premier City be.*

It was a diplomatic masterstroke, and Agra could now launch 'God save the King' with imperial words of homage:

> *God save the Emperor!*
> *Hear now, as ne'er before,*
> *One India sing!...*

There was general agreement that the women playing India, Calcutta and Delhi had expatiated at far too great length. Elgar had jotted down at the outset: 'N.B. There is *far too much* of this political business E.E.' Frances Colvin wrote two days after the première: 'I longed to stop those women shrieking & just have the music, & the wonderful colours to look at'.[3] *The Times* emphasised the symbolical nature of the Masque 'when a smooth-faced female figure heralded as "George, by the Grace of God, of that great name the fifth", enters in triumphal procession', heard that cuts had been made, and recommended more. At last Elgar and his daughter called on Oswald Stoll, owner of the Coliseum and whose brainchild the Masque had been. On 15 March Lady Elgar noted in her diary: 'E.& C. to Putney to see Mr. Stoll about cuts'.

In its own way Elgar's India had been as successful as that of General Roberts. Artistically well received, *The Crown of India* had been rewarding financially, as Elgar explained to Frances Colvin: 'When I write a big serious work e.g. Gerontius we have had to starve & go without fires for twelve months as a reward : this small effort allows me to buy scientific works I have yearned for & I spend my time between the Coliseum & the old bookshops'.[4] The extent of Elgar's library can be partially assessed from the Severn House inventory, taken in January 1913 for insurance purposes.

The Indian objects once collected by Lady Elgar's father have a separate section in the inventory and are catalogued in more detail. Among the general's furnishings were a 'carved Bombay rosewood square footstool', and 'Indian marble group of two elephants fighting', an 'Indian octagonal game board', a 'marble idol with dog,' a 'salver decorated with peacocks & foliage'. The military relics were recorded too: they included a 'general's sword in gilt scabbard', a 'trooper's sword in steel scabbard', 'cavalry swords' a 'Sikh dagger' 'Cingalese dagger', and the 'trophy comprising hide shield' that Elgar had admired twenty-one years previously. The furnishings were presumably dispersed when Severn House was sold and Elgar moved into his St James's flat. A letter at the Birthplace Museum suggests that the military equipment followed the East India Company's collection to the Victoria & Albert Museum. The letter is from the Town Clerk of the Borough of Monmouth to Carice Elgar Blake and is dated 11 August 1949. It advises her 'that the following Indian Armour has been received from the Victoria & Albert Museum, South Kensington' and goes on to itemise eleven objects that can be readily equated with the Severn House inventory. For the moment that seems to be the end of the story, as Monmouth now disclaims any knowledge of General Roberts and his weapons.

This essay is based on a lecture given to the London Branch of the Elgar Society at Imperial College, London on 7 November 1994.

Notes and References

1   Atkins, E. Wulstan: *The Elgar–Atkins Friendship* [Newton Abbot: David & Charles, 1984] 226.

2   Moore, Jerrold Northrop (ed): *Elgar and his Publishers* [Oxford: OUP, 1987] Vol.2, 760.

3   Moore, J.N. (ed): *Edward Elgar: letters of a lifetime* [Oxford: OUP, 1990] 243.

4   *ibid.,* 244.

Chapter Seven

Sleuthing the *Falstaff* Manuscript Diaspora

Arthur Reynolds

In the spring of 1992, I was surprised to find the following entry in Sotheby's catalogue announcing a Fine Printed Music sale to take place on 29 May:

> Lot 538: Elgar (Sir Edward) Autograph manuscript of part of the symphonic study *Falstaff*, Op. 68, being one page from the full orchestral score, numbered by Elgar "39" containing five bars, the first two altered by Elgar and pasted over the original version, notated in brown ink on thirty printed staves.

After Elgar's death, in 1934, his daughter Carice Elgar Blake distributed the manuscripts of his major works to sundry public collections. Where was the *Falstaff* autograph score and why was it incomplete? Would the score's institutional owner be bidding to acquire the missing page? If so, it would be inappropriate for me to compete; if not, the errant leaf might need rescuing.

In an effort to discover the manuscript's whereabouts, I contacted Wulstan Atkins and Jerrold Northrop Moore. Mr Atkins told me that the document had been mislaid shortly before Elgar's death and disappeared thereafter. Dr Moore said he had heard that the manuscript was somewhere in Cambridge but could offer no further information. Sotheby's gave me a clue in the form of another astonishing catalogue entry. Five other leaves of the *Falstaff* manuscript score had come up for sale in 1977. The catalogue entry describing Lot 94 in a sale dated 23 November 1977 reads as follows:

> Elgar (Sir Edward) Autograph Manuscript of *Falstaff*, Op.68, pages 1, 24, 99, 100 and 202 of the full score, in ink, on printed paper, some autograph deletions and corrections, pencil corrections and notes in another hand, rehearsal numbers stamped on two of the pages, unbound ... large folio 1913. The manuscript of *Falstaff* excluding these five pages is in Fitzwilliam College. *Falstaff* was first performed on 1 October 1913 at Leeds, Elgar conducting.

Sotheby's assert that the autograph manuscript is complete 'excluding these five pages', so why would a sixth page appear in the same sale room fifteen years later?

When I contacted Fitzwilliam College I learned that the manuscript resides not in the College but in the Fitzwilliam *Museum*. From a Museum representative I learned that Maggs, the London-located booksellers, had acted as agent for the Fitzwilliam in the purchase of the five leaves now restored to the rest of the text. When I contacted Maggs for confirmation that the firm intended to bid on behalf of the Fitzwilliam Museum in the forthcoming sale, I was astonished to learn that Maggs would not be bidding, because the Fitzwilliam Museum had declined to participate in the sale. Why? Because the Syndics who govern the Museum were concerned that they had been misled into using scarce resources to make the 1977 purchase by Sotheby's assertion that the restoration of the five leaves would complete the manuscript. Imagine their chagrin when another leaf came onto the market. How many more missing pages were there?

The answer is not complicated: simply compare the texts of the manuscript score and the printed score. Elgar's fair-copy version is notated in his hand on 230 pages of single-sided score paper. Each page has twenty-eight staves with four percussion lines and measures approximately 337 x 454 millimetres. Had someone acting for the Museum placed the manuscript score and a copy of the published score side-by-side, it would have been clear that page 39 was the sole missing part of the text.

Fearing that the errant leaf might disappear into some remote non-UK collection, I became the successful bidder and set out to discover why six pages of an important Elgarian manuscript had gone astray.

Elgar established the importance of *Falstaff* within his repertory during a 17 July 1913 interview with the journalist C.F. Kenyon, the pseudonym of Gerald Cumberland. Cumberland sought the interview to provide his readers with pre-première information about the work, because the first performance, in October at the Leeds Festival, promised to be a significant event on the musical calendar of that year. Cumberland's published piece appeared in the 18 July edition of *The Daily Citizen* and included this quotation from the interview:

> I have I think enjoyed writing it [i.e., *Falstaff*] more than any other music I have ever composed, and perhaps, for that reason, it may prove to be among my best efforts ... I have finished all the preliminary sketch-work, and of the actual scoring, only a little remains to be done. I shall say 'good-

bye' to it with regret, for the hours I have spent on it have brought me a
great deal of happiness.[1]

Initial response to the piece was lukewarm. Ernest Newman wrote this
after the first performance:

> The style of the score shows us quite a new Elgar, and one that the public
> used to the old Elgar will not assimilate very easily.[2]

In time, however, Elgar's friends and detractors alike came to share with
the composer a sense of the particular importance of *Falstaff*. Arch-foe
E.J. Dent gives grudging praise for the work in his notorious 'Englander'
essay published in the 1924 edition of Guido Adler's *Handbuch der
Musikgeschichte*. After fourteen lines of sneering denigration, the essay
surprises the reader with this comment:

> His most beautiful orchestral work is the symphonic poem Falstaff which,
> although weakened by an excessively close dependence on its programme,
> is certainly a work of great originality and power.[3]

Professor Dent's barb about the piece's excessive dependence on its
programme falls wide of the mark. Basil Maine had this to say about what
he called 'Elgar's finely imaginative achievement in *Falstaff*':

> The music's behaviour … is guided by an inner logic of its own rather than by
> a series of scenes and events, although it is still true the agreement between
> that inner logic and the 'programme' is a remarkable feature of the music.

Here is Jerrold Northrop Moore on the subject:

> The entire strength of pattern in … *Falstaff* came from its close thematic
> development – a prodigious skill of clothing consequent ideas in fitting
> orchestral dress that went beyond even the Second Symphony.[4]

Falstaff is a study of chivalry in decline. Elgar presents a musical canvas of
action and allusion into which he weaves a texture he called 'the
undercurrent of our failings and sorrows'.[5] The two Dream Interludes give
us a glimpse of what might have been, before the final theme descends
into what Elgar called 'The gargantuan, wide-composed *fortissimo*, first
given in the strings in three octaves, [that] exhibits his boastfulness and
colossal mendacity.'[6] Here is Newman again:

> The subject of the symphonic study is really the mad, pathetic mixture of
> contrarieties in us all, and the sense of something vast and inscrutable
> above us, putting an end – a harsh but perhaps bracing end of its own – to
> all our moral oscillations when the time comes …[7]

1 – Notes and references for this chapter appear on page 193.

Notwithstanding the pleasure it gave him, it is clear from the extant sketch material that Elgar's struggle with the composition was unusually arduous. Both the British Library and the Elgar Birthplace Museum house an extraordinarily large number of sketches. The fair-copy manuscript score shows an unusual number of paste-overs. The musicological features of these extensive revisions are admirably analysed in Dr Christopher Kent's essay, *'Falstaff:* Elgar's Symphonic Study'.[8]

Some of Elgar's revisions were more than could be accomplished by means of paste-overs. The composer Howard Ferguson gave me one example when I asked him if he had ever met Elgar. Ferguson replied that his one-and-only encounter with the composer took place at Ridgehurst, the home of Edward and Antonia Speyer, during the 1920s. A jovial Elgar strolled into the drawing room, where Ferguson and the rest of the Speyers' guests were assembled. He went straight to the piano and began delighting himself and his audience by playing an aria from *Norma*. Unfortunately, Edward Speyer managed to change Elgar's mood from ebullience to melancholy instantly and inadvertently by producing from a cupboard a draft full score of *Falstaff's* first Dream Interlude composed in a different key from the published version [G minor versus A minor]. Evidently, Elgar had forgotten he had sent the manuscript to Speyer in July 1913, and was embarrassed to be reminded of the transposition all those years later. The eight-page document remained in the family until 24 June 2003, when the Speyers' granddaughter consigned it for sale to Bonhams the auctioneers. When the bidding failed to reach an agreed reserve price, the Elgar Birthplace Museum stepped in to acquire the manuscript by private treaty.

Alice Elgar's diary makes clear that the active *Falstaff* composition period was April to September 1913. According to Alice, Elgar composed a substantial portion of the piece after July, when he told Cumberland he had finished the sketches and had nearly finished the scoring. As for the first performance, Alice's 2 October 1913 diary entry reads '... E rather hurried it & some of the lovely melodies were a little smothered ... E changed very depressed after ...'

Although Elgar frequently experienced depression after a première, in this instance the rushed rendition and subsequent gloom may have reflected his lingering doubts about whether or not the work was in its final form. If so, Alice certainly shared them. Her own first-edition copies of her husband's scores are normally truffled with laudatory exclamations. These are present in her *Falstaff* score, but in addition she annotated the text with numerous criticisms and emendation suggestions. Novello's must have been aware that Elgar was not wholly satisfied with the work, because the publisher printed an unusually small number of pre-performance copies of the miniature score.

Dr Kent's essay points out that 'Among Elgar's mature works, *Falstaff* is the only case where significant revisions were made to the printed score after the first performance.' [9] Kent provides a musicological explanation, arguing '... from a purely musical viewpoint the agile and economical textures of the work were a new departure requiring even greater deftness in their scoring.' [10]

Dr Kent suggests also that perhaps a deeper psychological necessity lay behind Elgar's uncertainty. The works of Elgar and Shakespeare share a preoccupation with loss of innocence. Shakespeare's later plays suggest that he was wary of his modern late-Elizabethan age. Elgar's later works indicate a wariness of post-Edwardian disillusionment. The two Falstaffs – Shakespeare's and Elgar's – represent the Merrie England that was, and was in the process of being lost.

'Construe the times to their necessities' is an anxious Shakespearean directive that Elgar took seriously. In the context of the *Coronation Ode*, Dr Moore writes: 'The composer as much as any man is the creature of his time. The time shares equally with the individuality in shaping an expression to define them both.' [11] If we agree with Dr Moore that Elgar's sensibility functioned as a litmus test of his times, consider the state of Elgar's world while he was composing *Falstaff*.

History confirms that 1913 was a dying-swan-song of a year. Domestically, Britain lay in the grip of violent social upheaval. There was the dark shadow of the Irish Question. The mooted Home Rule Bill divided the nation, and the Ulster Protestants began to arm themselves. Industrial action was ferocious. The first eight months of 1913 saw more trade disputes than in any previous year. That is damning indeed, considering that during 1912 one million miners walked off the job in a strike that threw the country into darkness and cold.

If industrial strife was not bad enough, the militancy of the suffragette movement reached its apogee in 1913. Militant ladies planted bombs, set letterboxes on fire, poured acid on golf courses, and even horsewhipped visiting politicians. The British public's attention was riveted on an event that took place at Epsom Downs in June. During the Derby, Emily Wilding

Davison, a thirty-two-year-old zealot for women's suffrage, ran onto the course at Tattenham Corner, just ahead of the thundering hooves. She grabbed the reins of Anmer, the King's colt, bringing down both horse and jockey. Miss Davison was injured so badly that she died a few days later. Her sister suffragettes organised an immense funeral on 14 June, about which Dame Ethel Smyth wrote:

> How they execrated Emily Davison! Some critics actually remarked "Such bad manners to the King!" apparently not grasping that the King's horse would call attention as no other animal could do to the strange fact that, for the sake of women in general, one particular woman was ready to let herself be trampled to death. Again others said, "Why, she might have killed the jockey!" though after all, this one must have seen what was coming, and jockeys are trained to fall.[12]

Alice was content to remain in an 'old-world state'. On the day of Miss Davison's funeral, she and Carice went to a local cinema to view a film depicting the life of Wagner. Her diary reads as follows: 'June 14 ... A & C to Cinema of Wagner. Hindered by crowd looking at Suffragette Funeral – Cinema wonderful ...' [13]

Meanwhile, Europe was on the brink of war. The previous year Bulgaria, Serbia, Montenegro and Greece had launched a joint attack on Turkey in the hope of seizing the latter's European lands. The Continental Powers shared with Britain an acute concern that Austria might intervene to prevent her rival Serbia from acquiring Turkish territory. While Elgar was at work on *Falstaff,* Sir Edward Grey, the Foreign Secretary, met every day the ambassadors of France, Germany, Russia and Austria, to form a joint policy they hoped they could impose on the Balkans. '1913 was dark with omen', wrote French President Raymond Poincaré, 'and in every effort to preserve peace one seemed to be frustrated by incidents that forbade it. The conference of ambassadors and of the Balkan delegates sat on in London, but ... the diplomats saw no solution.' [14]

The dark omens of art must have appeared to Edward Elgar and his generation no less worrying than the omens of war. The logical dissonance that would trap diplomacy into the Great War seemed to be providing the prevailing direction of new music.

London's musical year started off favourably enough. Despite much controversy, the first performance of *Der Rosenkavalier* took place in January. The opera had been considered for the Gala Performance of

1911 to celebrate the coronation of King George V and Queen Mary, but was turned down on grounds of indecency. 'I hope', wrote Queen Mary's aunt, the Grand Duchess of Mecklenburg-Strelitz, 'this novelty will not be selected, for it is the most improper opera in existence, even the male singers declared their horror at having to sing those words, and the females were more than scandalized!' [15] The January 1913 performance at Covent Garden was sold out, and the conductor, Sir Thomas Beecham, received a standing ovation.

What was Elgar listening to while he was working on *Falstaff?* He often went to the opera, where he heard new, predominately chromatic works such as Claude Debussy's *Pelléas et Mélisande,* which, Alice's diary says, he 'liked much'. But what particularly attracted his attention were the Russian operas Sergei Diaghilev brought to Drury Lane that year. Collaborating with Beecham, Diaghilev produced three works new to Londoners: *Boris Godunov* and *Khovanshchina* by Modest Moussorgsky, together with Nicolai Rimsky-Korsakov's *Ivan the Terrible.* Chaliapin sang the eponymous *Boris* role and overnight became the darling of London musical society, captivating Elgar, who watched a performance from Lady Maud Warrender's box and subsequently described Chaliapin to Sidney Colvin as '… the finest artist I have ever heard.' [16]

In 1913, Diaghilev presented three dark works as well: Florent Schmitt's *La Tragédie de Salomé,* Debussy's *Jeux,* and Stravinsky's *Le Sacre du Printemps.* The difference between the Paris and London receptions of the Stravinsky work is telling. First performed at the Théâtre des Champs-Elysées on 29 May, the composer's 'revolutionary' score, combined with Nijinsky's bizarre choreography, which required the dancers to move awkwardly to the unconventional rhythms, stirred the audience to hiss and jeer the work as musical anarchy. Camille Saint-Saëns was seen to shake his head in disgust. Critics and fellow musicians united to share Saint-Saëns's view, regretting that Stravinsky had deserted Holy Russia for a primeval place and time when people performed unspeakable rites to appease an unknown God.

The tails and tiaras in the London audience responded to their first performance of *The Rite of Spring* quite differently from Paris's *beau monde.* London greeted the work with professed fascination. After the première, Lady Ripon, a society hostess, entertained Nijinsky at Coombe Court, and the popularity of Britain's entente with Russia soared among the artistically inclined members of the Establishment. In these circumstances, Elgar must have sensed that the old diatonic basis of his music-making was becoming *vieux jeu*, which may partly explain why his *Falstaff* themes are chiefly chromatic.

According to Alice's diary, Elgar made the last of his changes on 18 October, after which Novello's dispatched the proofs to F.M. Geidel, the engravers in Leipzig. Unfortunately, Elgar did not see the final published score for six years, because the Geidel copies could not leave Germany until 1919, owing to the intervening war. Without engraved copies, Elgar was obliged to use the manuscript score to conduct the work.

The manuscript remained with Elgar until his death. Carice Elgar Blake did not appear to know how many pages were missing when she lent the score to the Fitzwilliam Museum in 1934 and converted the loan to a gift in 1968. A note in her hand left with the manuscript declares that '... the first page is missing, and the work begins at bar four ...' suggesting that even the composer's daughter was unaware that, apart from the cover page, five additional leaves were missing as well.

An examination of the errant pages produces a number of small mysteries. Page 1 is peculiar because Elgar has written the title twice. The first 'Falstaff' is centred at the top of the page – which is the way Elgar habitually inscribed the title on page 1 of a manuscript score. But then in the centre of this manuscript's page 1, the title appears again; the second 'Falstaff' is written in a darker ink and in very large letters, heavily underlined.

There is another puzzle: page 1 together with pages 99 and 100 bear drawing-pin holes in their four corners. No such holes appear in any of the other leaves.

If we presume that Elgar deliberately separated the six leaves, and if we believe that Elgar's love of puzzles was such that he would never make such a separation at random, what do the six leaves have in common? They all seem highly illustrative passages, showing actions or definite personal allusions, and they are all linked in terms of tonality.

1. **Leaf 1**, the opening, presents a typical fascinating feature of Elgar's later music: his postponement of the tonic key. The title at the top of the page reads: *Falstaff: Symphonic Study in C minor*. Yet the opening and the central thematic idea are based on G minor. In fact, there are very few points in the work where C minor figures significantly. The big tune at

figure four is in E flat, which largely dominates the first section, and the secondary material at figure seven is in E minor. The first important allusion to C minor does not occur until the section from figure 36 to figure 55 and from figure 55 to figure 59. Thereafter, Elgar abandons C minor for G minor.

2. **Leaf 24** [printed score pp. 16–17] presents the 'Impetuous Rush' music that ends the scene a few bars later, tying in neatly with Leaf 1 in that this page of the score ends the section begun by Leaf 1, and, significantly, concludes it in G minor. The instruction *Piu animato* effectively delineates the first section's coda.

3. **Leaf 39** [printed score pp. 28–29] has strong illustrative reasons for being chosen. This page presents the 'Honest Gentlewoman' at Eastcheap Inn. Structurally it occurs at the end of a more developmental passage. The theme fluctuates between 6/4 of A minor [the final key of the 'Falstaff Chasing Women' motif developed in Leaves 99 and 100] and a 6/4 F

minor, tonalities that play an important role in the work. A minor is also the key of the Interlude at figure 77.

4. **Leaves 99 and 100** [printed score pp 63, 64, and 65] are linked to Leaf 39 in that they pick up where 'Honest Gentlewoman' left off with 'Falstaff Chasing Women' about the tavern.

5. **Leaf 202** [printed score p. 132] gives us Prince Hal's regret at the seventh bar after Cue 130. The link is again one of tonality. The tonality shifts markedly at this juncture for two bars before reverting to Falstaff's material in an hysterical two-part counterpoint – again in G minor. This tonal statement parallels that begun in Leaf 1 and closed in Leaf 24.

No further analysis could be accomplished without the co-operation of the person who consigned the six leaves to Sotheby's. Auction houses have strict policies designed to protect sellers' identities. But Sotheby's did agree to pass on a 'To Whom It May Concern' letter from me. Auctioneers say that sellers rarely reply. Having braced myself for disappointment, imagine my surprise when I received a telephone call from a voice immediately familiar from the airwaves. It was Steve Race, who introduced himself as the former owner of the six pages. When I asked Mr Race how they came into his possession, he sent me a tape recording that provided my next clue.

The tape was a recording of Talk Number Thirteen in Mr Race's 'Like Old Times' series broadcast by the BBC Home Service on 22 September 1966. Programme Thirteen consisted of a series of interviews with sundry people who had known or who had encountered Sir Edward Elgar. Among them was the Duchess of Leinster, née Denise Orme. The Duchess told the following story:

A Royal Academy of Music violin scholar shortly before World War I, Miss Orme grew bored with her instrument and decided to try her luck with her voice. A vocal scholarship was on offer across town at the Royal College, so she went to the examination and found herself facing three adjudicators: the knights Walter Parratt, Hubert Parry and Edward Elgar.

The panel was evidently unaware of Miss Orme's instrumental prowess, which would have given her sight-reading capabilities not normally available to debutante students of the voice. They reacted with surprise when their candidate sight-read every piece placed before her. The Duchess described with relish her attempts to assure the adjudicators that she had not previously seen most of the music they had asked her to sing. Finally, Elgar broke the deadlock. 'I'll give her something she cannot have seen before,' he said as he took from his pocket a sheet of paper and wrote out a number of bars of music with words. Miss Orme took up the music and sang the song through without hesitation. From the stunned silence that followed, she drew the correct conclusion that she had won the scholarship.[17]

Steve Race ended the interview with this comment: 'What a pity she didn't put that piece of manuscript music into her pocket. Who knows what it might have become?'

Shortly after the broadcast, Mr Race received a letter from an East Sussex listener declaring that he possessed a few pages of Elgarian manuscript. Might these pages include the lost song? The listener's name was Bernard Gimber. Mr Race visited Mr Gimber, examined the manuscript material and realised that these were strays from the fair-copy score of *Falstaff* and as such were far more important than the sketch of an obscure vocal piece. So Mr Race purchased them. A decade later he consigned all but one of them to Sotheby's sale rooms. Having framed page 39 and hung it on his wall, Mr Race kept that leaf for another fifteen years before consigning it for sale in 1992. He shared the proceeds of both sales with Bernard Gimber, who had found the leaves among the papers of his late father, William Gimber.

Along with the manuscript material, Gimber gave Race his father's relevant files. The material in the files provided my next clue, in the form of a story about an encounter between Elgar and William Gimber. During the first half of the last century, the elder Gimber earned his living as a freelance film cameraman-director-editor, producing his own series of short subjects called 'Around the Town.' Billed as a celebration of 'Beauty, Celebrity and Fashion', each reel consisted of seven 'feature-ettes', each of which devoted approximately sixteen feet of film to the presentation of a well-known person at work. The Gaumont Company distributed the series to local cinemas.

Although no extant reels of 'Around the Town' have yet been discovered, Gimber's files included copies of marketing brochures prepared by Gaumont to advertise the contents of reels 9 to 12 plus 13 to 16. Also among Gimber *père's* papers was a typewritten sheet listing the draft contents of reel 19 in the series that includes a 'feature-ette' entitled 'At home with Britain's greatest composer, Sir Edward Elgar, O.M.'

According to his son, William Gimber approached Elgar, who invited him to Severn House for a filming session. While Gimber set up his camera, Elgar took from his shelves the manuscript of *Falstaff*. He separated six pages for use to simulate the act of composition.

If the film that includes the short subjects listed on the draft contents sheet for reel 19 is ever found, my guess is that it would show the title page plus pages 99 and 100 pinned to a surface above desk level reminiscent of W.H. Reed's description of his first visit to Elgar's lodgings during the composition of the Violin Concerto, when he found pages of score pinned to the walls. That would explain those drawing-pin holes. I am deducing also that the film would depict Elgar writing 'Falstaff' a second time on the title page, this time in letters large enough to be captured by the camera. That would explain why 'Falstaff' is written twice on page 1, the second time in large letters underlined.

According to Bernard Gimber, Elgar handed the six leaves to his father after the filming, saying: 'Here: you had better have these.'

Why would Elgar entreat William Gimber to take away those six pages? Did Gimber tell Elgar that he might need further footage? Did Gimber express a concern that perhaps the developed film might show the score notations indistinctly, in which case he might have to re-shoot that portion of the footage that focused on the manuscript? If so, why would Gimber take the manuscript material with him instead of simply returning to Severn House if further filming were required?

Steve Race wrote to Bernard Gimber, then old and frail, on my behalf. Gimber's reply rather unnecessarily characterizes his father as 'a man of great integrity'. Doth he protest too much?

The answer might come to light if we could fix the filming date. Unfortunately, all the papers from William Gimber's files are undated. Bernard Gimber's letter suggests that the filming may have taken place in 1924, but an analysis of the texts of the marketing brochures suggests a more interesting date.

The brochure for reel 9 includes a visit to Jerome K. Jerome. We know that Jerome died in 1927, so reel 9 could not post-date that year. The brochure's description of reel 12 narrows the field further by announcing that one of its subjects is 'the final portrayal of the character which has made the success of *Tilly of Broadway* ... at the Apollo Theatre. All the characters are shown including ... Mary Glynne as Tilly.' The seventh edition of *Who's Who in the Theatre* tells us that Mary Glynne played Tilly at the Apollo between July 1919 and December 1921.

From year-end 1921, we come closer to the logical date of the Elgar filming session when we note that reel 13 includes a visit to Fay Compton, who was then playing Sylvia in *Summertime* at the Royalty Theatre. According to *Who's Who in the Theatre*, Fay Compton ceased playing Sylvia at the Royalty in January 1920. The description of reel 16 corroborates a first-quarter 1920 date by including an interview with Henry Ainley, then playing in *Julius Caesar* at the St James's Theatre. *Who's Who* confirms that Ainley played Mark Anthony in *Julius Caesar* between January and March 1920.

Further proof of an early 1920 date is offered via the 'feature-ette' list proposed for reel 19. In addition to 'At home with Britain's greatest composer ...' the draft contents sheet lists 'a brief visit with Mr Owen Nares in *Mr Todd's Experiment* at the Queen's Theatre, London'. *Who's*

Who says that Owen Nares played Arthur John Carrington in *Mr Todd's Experiment* at the Queen's Theatre between January and July 1920. If January–July 1920 is the relevant date range, the filming had to have taken place by early April, given Elgar's inconsolable grief at the death of his wife on 7 April.

Alice's diary records that Elgar was filmed twice in March 1920. On 1 March, a Mr Bishop of the 'Art and Film' Company filmed her husband at Severn House. Elgar viewed the results on 5 March at the Denman Street Cinema. The second filming took place on 12 March at a film theatre in London referred to as a 'laboratory cinema' but otherwise unidentified. Elgar returned to see the results on 17 March.

It seems unlikely that the second of these sessions corresponds to the 'Around the Town' film project since the reel 19 draft contents sheet specifically refers to a film with Elgar 'At home ...' Did Alice mistake Mr Bishop for Mr Gimber? Given her rapidly deteriorating health, she could be forgiven for the error. Referring to the 'Art and Film' session, Elgar's letter to Alice Stuart Wortley dated 6 March 1920 ends with this sentence:

> 'I saw myself (?) on the film yesterday & you shd see it some day – it is going to be 'edited' a little.' [18]

If William Gimber came to Severn House to film Elgar during March 1920, his timing was unfortunate. Normally Alice would have organised the visit, and it is unlikely she would have consented to the departure of any pages from her husband's precious manuscript. But in March 1920, Alice Elgar was in no condition to supervise Elgar's rendezvous at Severn House. Having been ill since the previous November, Alice was almost certainly bed-ridden on the day William Gimber arrived. Carice could have stood in for her mother, but in March 1920 she was away in Switzerland acquiring a fiancé, Samuel Blake. If Gimber did carry out his filming on 1 March 1920 – five weeks before Alice's death – it is likely that Elgar would have responded unfavourably to any request for further filming in Severn House. The logical alternative would have been to take away a few *Falstaff* leaves for off-site filming if further footage were required for the 'editing' Elgar mentions in his letter to the Windflower.

If Elgar meant Gimber to have the six pages as a temporary expedient, why did he not contact him at a later date to request their return? If Gimber filmed Elgar in March 1920, it is likely that the errant leaves would have been forgotten in Elgar's post-April period of desolation followed by his departure from Severn House in particular and London in general the following year. By 1920, Elgar had received his copies of the long-delayed published score, so he would have had no need to re-visit the manuscript. Gimber may have intended to return the pages; but perhaps he too moved on, allowing the papers of his past work to pile up with the *Falstaff* manuscript material tucked away obscurely among them.

Elgar may have lost interest in his manuscript, but he never lost his particular love for Falstaff. Basil Maine recounts a telling incident that took place near the end of Elgar's life. After dinner with friends at Marl Bank one night, the composer led his guests to the gramophone and played a recording of Falstaff conducted by himself. During the first 'Dream Interlude', Elgar listened intently, then exclaimed, 'That is what I call music'.

This essay is based on a lecture given to the London Branch of the Elgar Society at Imperial College, London on 9 January 1995.

Notes and References

1   Moore, Jerrold Northrop: *Edward Elgar: a creative life* [Oxford: OUP, 1984] 649–650.
2   *Birmingham Daily Post,* 3 October 1913 in Moore, *op.cit.,* 654.
3   Trowell, Brian: 'Elgar's Use of Literature' in Monk, Raymond (ed): *Edward Elgar: music and literature* [Aldershot: Scolar Press, 1993] 286–87.
4   Moore, *op.cit.,* 652.
5   Elgar to Ernest Newman, 26 September 1913 in Moore, *op.cit.,* 643.
6   Elgar, Edward: *Falstaff by Edward Elgar, Analytical Essay by the Composer.* Reprinted from *The Musical Times* liv [1913] 575.
7   *The Nation,* October 1913 in Moore, *op.cit.,* 656.
8   Monk, *op.cit.,* 83–107.
9   *ibid.,* 92. Elgar also made post-première revisions to his *Froissart* manuscript score but not to the printed score because *Froissart* did not see publication until ten years after the work's first performance."
10 *ibid.,* 96.
11 Notes for the recording of the *Coronation Ode,* conducted by Alexander Gibson made in December 1976 and issued by RCA under RL 25074 (2).
12 Cowles, Virginia: *1913: The Defiant Swan Song* [London,1967] 40.
13 Moore, *op.cit.,* 646.
14 Cowles, *op.cit.,* 39.
15 *ibid.,* 14.
16 Elgar to Lady Maud Warrender, 22 July 1913 in Moore, *op.cit.,* 649.
17 Reproduced by kind permission of the BBC.
18 Moore, J.N.: *Edward Elgar: the Windflower letters* [Oxford: OUP, 1989] 237.

Chapter Eight

Elgar and Shaw

Michael Holroyd

The story of Elgar's friendship with Bernard Shaw starts with the Malvern Festival, which the theatrical manager and impresario, Sir Barry Jackson, founded at the end of the 1920s. After the First World War Barry Jackson found himself caught between the stagnation of his Birmingham Repertory Company and the soaring prices of London's West End. Shaw recognised his predicament very well. The arts and sciences, he believed, would be kept alive, not by the massive rates and rents of central London, but by the half-crowns, florins and sixpences of the suburbs and provinces.

Both Bernard Shaw and Barry Jackson shared a horror of the expensive and trivial West End, which had lowered the standards of the repertory movement in London. All Jackson's London productions had lost him money and he was tired of being an intruder there.

Jackson cherished a dream of founding a pastoral theatre, similar to the Three Choirs Festival of Hereford, Gloucester and Worcester where Elgar presided. It would be a theatre placed in idyllic rural surroundings where he could renew his dramatic inspiration. It was while walking one day with Shaw, near his home at Blackhill,[1] that there came to him the idea of fulfilling his dream in Malvern. The place had much to recommend it: it had transport accessibility, ample hotel accommodation and wonderful country from the Severn Valley on the east to the Welsh mountains on the west. It was all the more attractive, they both thought, for being a spa town, built on terraces, along a steep range of hills. In addition, it had a newly reconstructed theatre.

Having bought the late-Victorian Assembly Rooms the Malvern Urban District Council had raked the auditorium floor, lowered the ceiling and added a circle. It had widened the proscenium arch, erected a stage tower and installed technical equipment and modern lighting. Barry Jackson proposed renting this new theatre, which seated some nine hundred people, and making it the centre of a festival of drama dedicated to Shaw. He pictured the Winter Gardens, Concert Hall and Pump Room, which

1 – Notes and references for this chapter appear on pages 204-206.

were attached to the theatre, as natural rallying-points for festival visitors. Every instinct told him that here was the ideal place for such a venture – and G.B.S. responded to his enthusiasm. In the England of Shaw's dreams, Barry Jackson would have found himself manager of a National Theatre. But despite all Shaw's campaigning, there was no National Theatre in England. So there was nothing for it but to leave London and make a fresh start in the country, where rents were comparatively low. While London's sleazy West End had become one of the worst growths of capitalism, Jackson's private enterprise impressed Shaw as a fine challenge to socialism. So he made a pact. If Jackson went ahead with his scheme for a festival at Malvern, he (Shaw) would write a new play for it.

Barry Jackson went ahead, assembling a company of more than sixty players. The plan was to present a different play each evening for one week at Malvern and then repeat this programme over the second week. It could then be transferred to Birmingham and elsewhere round the country. Tickets were cheap. It was hoped that visitors would stay a whole week and enjoy the extra-theatrical events: the morning lectures, afternoon concerts, donkey rides up the hills – perhaps even gondoliering and night-bathing in the pools. What optimists!

Jackson had made Shaw the figurehead of the Malvern Festival because he realised that, if this venture was to rise above the level of a local flower show, it needed a dramatic patron – or 'patron saint', as Shaw called it. 'We gather here among the hills to perform an act of homage to our greatest living dramatist', Jackson wrote, 'to be amused and quickened by his humour and wisdom.' [2]

Having the previous month laid the foundation stone of the Shakespeare Memorial Theatre in Stratford, Shaw arrived in Malvern on 18 August 1929 and stayed for nearly a month, doing all in his power to catch the tourists between Stratford and Gloucester. 'I always avoid places where my plays are being performed',[3] he wrote. But for Barry Jackson's Malvern Festival he made an exception. He liked the vertical green hills, the air that 'would raise the dead' – though not the famous waters 'one glass of which,' he claimed, 'destroys my digestion for a week'. Over the 1930s he was to be seen performing almost every summer in the swimming pools, striding in his knickerbockers along the terraces and up the hills with his younger companions labouring after him, or planting before the cameras a municipal mulberry tree. He was constantly on view. 'I have created the general impression that I was born there', he wrote in the 1937 Malvern Festival Book. 'In course of time visitors will be shewn for sixpence the room in which my first cries were heard ... As the festival habit grows from the seed down in Malvern I hope to plant many mulberry trees, and end by having as many birthplaces as Homer.'[4]

The atmosphere of the festival was one of an extended and overflowing country house party. There were folk dances, garden parties, even starlight suppers. Shaw was determined to make the Malvern experiment another chapter in the reform of the English theatre. He was determined, also, to make one of its finest attractions the presence of Sir Edward Elgar.

During rehearsals of *The Apple Cart*, the play written specially for Barry Jackson in 1929, Shaw had invited Elgar over from his home near Worcester – adding that Barry Jackson was determined to get from him an overture to the play. 'My own view was that six bars of yours would extinguish (or upset) the A.C. and turn the Shaw festival into an Elgar one', he wrote, 'but that would be a jolly good thing ...'[5]

Over twenty years earlier, and long before the playwright and composer met, Shaw had responded in the *St James's Gazette* to a request for an opera libretto by invoking Elgar's name. 'I wonder whether Elgar would turn his hand to opera?' he enquired. 'I have always played a little with the idea of writing a libretto, but though I have had several offers nothing has come of it'.[6] Shaw had not then appreciated what he later called Elgar's 'hatred and contempt for singers'. They did discuss setting one of Shaw's plays to music, 'but I think we agreed to my view that he could do nothing with a play except what his *Falstaff* did with Shakespeare's',[7] Shaw remembered.

So there was no overture to *The Apple Cart*. But Elgar came to Malvern and, opening the Bernard Shaw Exhibition in the Public Library, told his audience that G.B.S. really knew more about music than he did. Shaw immediately retaliated by admitting that 'although I am a rather conceited man, I am quite sincerely and genuinely humble in the presence of Sir Edward Elgar. I recognise a greater art than my own and a greater man than I can ever hope to be'. Not to be outdone, Elgar warned the press that some people thought his friend Shaw rather fierce. 'Nothing could be farther from the truth. Shaw is a most remarkable man: he is the best friend to any artist, the kindest and possibly the dearest fellow on earth.'[8]

These were more than reciprocal civilities for the press. They represented what each had genuinely come to feel about the other, and gave Elgar the chance to correct his initially hostile opinion of G.B.S. as 'hopelessly wrong, as all these fellows are, on fundamental things ... an amusing liar, but not much more'.[9] That opinion, arrived at following an early performance of *Man and Superman* at the beginning of the century, had not softened much after he saw *The Devil's Disciple* which 'lacks conviction', he decided. 'Shaw is very *amateurish* in many ways.'[10]

They had finally met in March 1919 at a lunch given by a Belgian socialist leader's wife, Lalla Vandervelde – a lunch that also included the Bloomsbury painter and art critic Roger Fry. Elgar's mind was so overloaded with music (which was 'quite inseparable from orchestration',[11] Shaw observed) that he made nothing of other subjects. One subject of which he made nothing that day was painting – 'damned imitation',[12] he called it. Turning from Roger Fry, he appeared to make the wonderful discovery that Bernard Shaw and a music critic who had long ago amused and fascinated him, a critic called 'Corno di Bassetto', was one and the same person.[13] In fact, Elgar had praised Shaw's music criticism during a lecture on Critics in 1905,[14] but seemed to have separated in his mind the musicologist and the dramatist.

Shaw had certainly been an entertaining musical critic – but he had been much more than entertaining. He was professional rather than amateurish, and very far from being a liar. But he pretended to be a liar in a rather amateurish way:

> when people hand me a sheet of instrumental music, and ask my opinion of it, I carefully hold it upside down, and pretend to study it in that position with the eye of an expert. When they invite me to try their new grand piano, I attempt to open it at the wrong end; and when the young lady of the house informs me that she is practising the 'cello, I innocently ask her whether the mouthpiece did not cut her lips dreadfully at first.[15]

Elgar, of course, could see straight through all these paradoxical Shavianisms when they were applied to music. Shaw's music criticism was designed to drive away melancholy – as music itself had driven melancholy from his Dublin home. If there was love during Shaw's childhood and adolescence, it was the love conveyed by the play of musical instruments and the coming together of voices. Opera in particular, a world of fable and romance, became a necessity to Shaw. He depended upon it like an addict. ' Music', he said, 'is the brandy of the damned'.[16] What others found in loving relationships, Shaw believed he experienced in music, describing himself as a voluptuary rather than an ascetic: 'I never deny myself a Beethoven symphony',[17] he said.

Though often laughed at, Shaw's business as a music critic was to be accurate rather than funny, though the two often converged. He believed that solemnity was only a small man's affectation of bigness, and that there was nothing so serious as great humour. Though sometimes spoken of as severe, Shaw spoke of himself as 'almost foolishly good-natured'. For example, he never indulged in the cruel practice of giving misleading flattery.

He had his passions, though. He hated the cornet and the banjo; he hated the interruptions of encores; he hated the old, such as Mendelssohn, when used as an obstacle to the new, such as Wagner; and he hated audiences – the men who beat time and the ladies who wore pitiable corpses of dead birds on their heads. His criticisms were a continual protest against distractions, whether from audiences or musicians; distractions, that is, from good performances. The worse the music, the more he diversified. Readers liked to hear of the voice trainer who hit his pupils, declaring that it was the only method of making them produce the vowel 0; they liked to discover him, after a visit to the ballet, at dawn the next day with a policeman, a postman and a milkman ('who unfortunately broke his leg')[18] attempting *pirouettes* and *entrechats* in Fitzroy Square; they liked, as part of a teetotal campaign, his plea for dancing in church, which barely stopped short of converting Westminster Abbey into a ballroom. They even accepted his socialism when he made Wagner into a vehicle for enlightenment against the dark forces of London.

Shaw's method of judging music, he once stated, was to do with his ears what he did with his eyes when he stared. In one of his most effective debunking feats, he parodied the academic criticism fashionably known as 'scientific analysis', parodied it with a comparable analysis of Hamlet's soliloquy on death, 'To be or not to be'.

> Shakespeare, dispensing with the customary exordium announces his subject at once in the infinitive, *[to be]* in which mood it is presently repeated after a short connecting passage in which, brief as it is, we recognise the alternative and negative forms on which so much of the significance of repetition depends *[or not to be]*. Here we reach a colon; and a pointed pository phrase, *[That is the question]* in which the accent falls decisively on the relative pronoun, brings us to the first full stop.[19]

Shaw was merciless on the pedantry which the oratorio market manufactured for the regular English festivals at the turn of the century. The very word 'oratorio' roused in him a tempest of evil passions. 'Had the oratorio been invented in Dante's time, the seventh circle of his Inferno would have been simply a magnified Albert Hall', he wrote, 'with millions of British choristers stolidly singing in the galleries, and the condemned, kept awake by demons, in the arena, clothed in evening dress'.[20]

Elgar was removed from all this. Shaw judged him to be a great orchestral technician with as irresistible a vocation as Mozart's, and also to have the only original English style on the market. In respect of English music, he told readers of the *Morning Post* in 1911, 'the history of original music, broken off by the death of Purcell, begins again with Sir Edward Elgar'.[21] After a century of imitation Handel and Mendelssohn, Elgar's music had arrived as a new sound, free from the academic pedantry of Parry and Stanford, a sound 'as characteristically English as a country house and stable are characteristically English'.[22] All this had been written before their meeting in 1919.

Elgar invited the Shaws to Severn House, his Hampstead home, a few days after that first lunch, to hear a trial run of three of his chamber works, including the Piano Quintet. 'The Quintet knocked me over at once', Shaw wrote the next day: '... There are some piano embroideries on a pedal point that didn't sound like a piano or anything else in the world, but quite beautiful ... they require a touch which is peculiar to yourself.'[23] It was this peculiarity that Shaw sought to define and celebrate at the end of the year in a eulogistic essay which described Elgar as the man who was carrying on Beethoven's business: 'Elgar's *Cockaigne Overture* combines every classic quality with every lyric and dramatic quality of the overture to *Die Meistersinger*', he wrote. '... You may hear all sorts of footsteps in it, and it may tell you all sorts of stories; but it is classical music as Beethoven's *Les Adieux* sonata is classical music; it tells you no story external to itself and yourself.'

Shaw continued as follows:

> ... Elgar's range is so Handelian that he can give the people a universal melody or march with as sure a hand as he can give the Philharmonic Society a symphonic adagio ...*[Gerontius]* was no literary paper instrumentation, no muddle and noise, but an absolutely new energy given to the band by a consummate knowledge of exactly what it could do and how it could do it ... The enormous command of existing resources, which this orchestral skill of his exemplifies, extends over the whole musical field, and explains the fact that, though he has a most active and curious mind, he does not appear in music as an experimenter and explorer, like Scriabin and Schonberg. He took music where Beethoven left it, and where Schumann and Brahms found it.[24]

This tribute delighted Elgar's wife, hitherto suspicious of what she thought of as Shaw's atheism. Her death three months later seems to have redoubled Shaw's championship of Elgar's work. In the summer of 1922, following a meagrely attended performance of *The Apostles* by the Leeds Choral Union, he erupted in *The Daily News:*

> *The Apostles* is one of the glories of British music: indeed, it is unique as a British work ... I distinctly saw six people in the stalls, probably with complimentary tickets ... The occasion was infinitely more important than the Derby, than Goodwood, than the Cup Finals, than the Carpentier fights, than any of the occasions on which the official leaders of society are photographed and cinematographed laboriously shaking hands ... The performance was none the less impressive, nor the music less wonderful. I apologise to posterity for living in a country where the capacity and tastes of schoolboys and sporting costermongers are the measure of metropolitan culture.[25]

Shaw's Irish disgust merged with Elgar's English disappointment. Approximately the same age, they had both initially been 'discovered' in Germany, and were now beginning to go out of fashion in Britain, the audiences for Elgar's oratorios disappearing in the 1920s, as they were to disappear in the 1930s for Shaw's extravaganzas. Though proudly un-academic, both of them appeared to have read whole libraries and were recognised for their technical dexterity. But while they seemed to take their inspiration from the skies, they continued using structures perfected by their predecessors. Shaw's pugnacious loyalty to Elgar was therefore invigorated by a sense of cultural affinity.

Their friendship ripened in old age when, after the Malvern Festivals began, they saw each other regularly. Elgar, like the artist Wilson Steer, was built on a model very dear to most Englishmen. One would never guess that the one made up tunes and the other muddled along with paint. Both resembled country gentlemen with, perhaps, some military connections. Wilson Steer actually carried his painting materials in a cricket bag, explaining 'I get better service that way'. Elgar, who could talk about every unmusical subject on earth 'from pigs to Elizabethan literature', gave the impression of not knowing 'a fugue from a *fandango*'. And yet, Shaw wrote: 'Music was his religion and his intellect and almost his everything.'[26] Elgar prided himself, however, on being a considerable playgoer. It was true that he had never stuck out *Romeo and Juliet* to the end (he used to leave when Mercutio was slain), but he would travel almost anywhere to see the comedian Jack Hulbert perform, and he came to relish the Shavian productions at Malvern. 'Can't you engineer that I sit with you for the first performance of *Too True To Be Good* – my last chance', he appealed to Shaw in the summer of 1932. 'I remember the glory of being with you for *The Apple Cart*.'[27]

As Master of the King's Musick, Elgar was a martyr to conventionality, insisting on Shaw and his wife Charlotte being very correctly dressed for these occasions and for his own musical performances at Hereford, Gloucester and Worcester. 'The Protestant Three Choirs were the centre of his musical activities, especially Worcester', Shaw later remembered: 'to hear *The Music Makers* conducted by him was a wonderful experience.'[28] Shaw's letters to Elgar are full of music and reveal the extent of his knowledge and admiration of Elgar's work. In 1930 Elgar dedicated his *Severn Suite* to Shaw who, 'hugely flattered and touched', noted in his inscribed copy: 'so my name may last as long as his own'.[29] After hearing the piece 'only eight times' at the Crystal Palace Band Competition in September that year, Shaw wrote to Elgar: 'Nobody could have guessed from looking at the score and thinking of the thing as a toccata for brass band how beautiful and serious the work is as abstract music.'[30]

Shaw tried to get Elgar's co-operation for re-writing the second verse of the National Anthem (for which Elgar had composed an orchestral arrangement in 1902). The second verse read as follows:

> *O Lord our God arise!*
> *Scatter his enemies,*
> *And make them fall!*
> *Confound their politics,*
> *Frustrate their knavish tricks;*
> *On Thee our hopes we fix,*
> *God save us all!*

In Shaw's opinion, this was unacceptable in the twentieth century, and should be changed. In its place he suggested:

> *O Lord our God arise*
> *All our salvation lies*
> *In! Thy! Great! Hand! (à la Elgar)*
> *Centre His thoughts on Thee*
> *Her Let him God's captain be (let her God's handmaid be)*
> *Thine to Eternity*
> *God save the King.*
>   *Queen.*[31]

Shaw argued that the First World War had 'killed Muscular Christianity' and created the opportunity for such a 'glaringly needed change'. This was the sort of brash Shavian statement that had upset Elgar in the old days. But after his wife's death, and as his own religious faith faded, he began to respond to Shaw's bracing scepticism. 'G.B.S.'s politics are, to

me, appalling, but he is the kindest-hearted, gentlest man I have met …
to young people he is kind', he had written in 1921 to Sidney Colvin.[32] But
by the late 1920s, when they campaigned together against a restrictive new
Music Copyright Bill, Elgar was beginning to look at Shaw's politics as the
basis of his kindness. 'If I were King, or Minister of Fine Arts', Shaw had
written, 'I would give Elgar an annuity of a thousand a year on condition
that he produce a symphony every eighteen months.'[33]

Elgar had opened himself up to a Shavian education by rather
nervously inquiring what 'capital' was after the publication of Shaw's
political work *The Intellectual Woman's Guide to Socialism and
Capitalism.* By way of explanation, and turning the subject back to music,
Shaw replied that Elgar's products were infinitely consumable without
limitation or deterioration. He then proposed an Elgarian Financial
Symphony: '*Allegro:* Impending Disaster. *Lento mesto*: Stony Broke.
Scherzo: Light Heart and Empty Pocket. *Allo con brio*: Clouds Clearing.'[34]

Whenever Elgar needed the clouds clearing, the Shaws shone down on
him. 'Don't let yourself think dark thoughts', Charlotte Shaw had urged
him. And G.B.S., who made him a present of £1,000 early in the 1930s
(equivalent to £30,000 now), persuaded the BBC to commission a Third
Symphony for another £1,000. 'He [Elgar] does not know that I am
meddling in his affairs and yours in this manner', he had written to John
Reith, Director General of the BBC, ' … but I do know that he has still a
lot of stuff in him that could be released if he could sit down to it without
risking his livelihood.'[35] Welcoming this commission in a letter to *The
Times* at the end of 1932, Shaw added: 'But is it not a pity that Sir Edward
has had to wait so long for the advent of a public administrator capable of
rising to the situation? The forthcoming symphony will be his Third: it
should be his ninth.'[36]

The Third Symphony of course was never finished, owing to the
collapse of Elgar's health. Shaw and Charlotte had tried to persuade him
to go to an osteopath to manipulate his spine – a rumbustious American
whose 'resemblance to an ophicleide would please you'[37] was Shaw's
choice, though Charlotte Shaw preferred a Chinese virtuoso from San
Francisco who played expertly upon the bones. Alternatively, there was
homeopathy in the person of Raphael Roche, a sensational, unregistered
practitioner from a well-known Jewish family of musicians (including
Mendelssohn). He had a craze for healing which he had successfully
exercised on Shaw, using what appeared to be a grain or two of powdered
sugar. In 'the depths of pain', Elgar seems to have felt that the Shaws were

trying to cure him with laughter. In 1933 he entered a nursing home, and Shaw, resisting the impulse to rush down and rescue him from the 'damn doctors', was left trusting to Elgar's mighty Life Force.[38]

'Having friends like you', Charlotte Shaw had written in 1932, 'is the one thing in life worth having when one arrives at the age of GBS & myself.'[39] The following year Elgar returned the compliment: 'the world seems a cold place to me when you are both away'.[40] Shaw described Elgar's death from cancer on 23 February 1934 as 'world-shaking' and far too early. But there was still the music. At the Gloucester Three Choirs Festival in the summer of 1934, he and Charlotte heard *The Kingdom*. 'I cannot tell you how we all miss Edward Elgar', Charlotte wrote afterwards to Nancy Astor. 'We loved him … & when another man got up into the Conductor's Chair it was hard to bear.'[41]

And that was, or should have been, the end of the story. But there is a postscript. In 1948, when in his ninety-third year, Shaw wrote to Reith, calling his decision to commission the Third Symphony 'magnificent', and reminding him that it was only Elgar's poor health that had prevented him from finishing it. There was nothing wrong in this – except the language Shaw used. Elgar was a snob, he claimed, and would not try out any alternative medicine – indeed any doctor not registered with the British Medical Association. Therefore he died, a martyr to extreme conventionality. As for the Third Symphony, Shaw had heard a few scraps which Elgar and William Reed played at Elgar's house in Worcester. 'I could make neither head nor tail of the stuff', Shaw admitted to Reith. 'There was certainly no big theme in it'.[42]

Then there was the matter of the £1,000 with which Shaw had presented him. Elgar, he recalled, had immediately spent £800 of it on a car which he gave to his 'very attractive secretary', Mary Clifford. Shaw's money was 'nominally a loan', he wrote to Rutland Boughton later that same year, 'but I never got it back'.[43]

Kevin Allen quotes these letters in his recent book *Elgar in Love: Vera Hockman and the Third Symphony* and suggests that they were written by Shaw with 'half an eye' on his own 'posthumous reputation'. If that were so, then Shaw must have been peculiarly anxious to downgrade his generosity and have us think less well of him.

What actually happened was that, when Shaw found out that Elgar had left his daughter Carice a settled income but no ready money, he put in a claim for his £1,000, and when Elgar's estate paid it to him he transferred the money to Carice 'as a birthday present'.[44] His lapse of memory was surely more likely to have been due to his age (his early nineties) than any desire to re-write history to his own advantage.

It is true that Elgar and Shaw had different temperaments – that much is clear from Elgar's early comments on Shaw's plays as well as from the eccentricities of Shaw's medical advice. Inappropriate as it may have been, that advice came from the knowledge that orthodox treatment could never cure his friend, and from the fervent wish to keep his friend alive and composing by any means available. Those who claim that, after his wife's death, Elgar only took up with Shaw because Shaw flattered him, and that there was no real friendship between them at all, must have a most narrow definition of friendship. I hope that the evidence I have assembled will lead to a more positive verdict: for though they were certainly very different kinds of people, theirs was a genuine friendship, Elgar and Shaw.

Lecture given to the London Branch of the Elgar Society at Imperial College, London on 2 April 2001.

Notes and References

WRO = Worcester Record Office (for a time, the Herefordshire and Worcestershire Record Office), whose Elgar collection is now housed in the Elgar Birthplace Museum archive at Broadheath.

1   Jackson's house on Jubilee Drive, high in the Malvern Hills.
2   Malvern Festival, 1929 Souvenir Book, 3.
3   G.B.S to Floryan Sobieniowski, n.d. [assigned to 8 June 1929] in Laurence, Dan H. (ed): *Bernard Shaw: collected letters* [London: Max Reinherdt, 1988] Vol.4 (1926–1950), 147.
4   Malvern Festival Book, 1937.
5   G.B.S. to Elgar, 12 August 1929 (WRO).
6   *St James's Gazette*, 13 December 1907.
7   G.B.S. to Rutland Boughton, 9 August 1932, BL Add.MS 52365 f.41.
8   Elliot, Vivian: 'Shaw and Elgar: Two Famous Friends of Malvern' in Malvern Festival Programme, 22 May–11 June 1978, 3.
9   Malvern Festival Programme, 1977, 5.
10   Moore, Jerrold Northrop: *Edward Elgar: a creative life* [Oxford: OUP, 1984] 519.
11   G.B.S. to Conal O'Riordan, 29 July 1944 (Harry Ransom Humanities Research Centre, University of Texas).

12   Pearson, Hesketh: *Bernard Shaw* [London: Methuen, 1961] 384.

13   For two accounts of this meeting see Pearson, *op.cit.*, 383–384 and letter from
      G.B.S. to Virginia Woolf, 10 May 1940, in Laurence: *Collected Letters,*
      op.cit., Vol.4, 556–557. There is a further account in Laurence, Dan H. and
      Leary, Daniel, J.: *Flyleaves* [Austin, Texas: Thomas Taylor, 1977].

14   See Elgar's lecture on Critics in Young, Percy, M. (ed): *A Future for English*
      Music and other Lectures by Edward Elgar [London: Dobson, 1968] 185.

15   'Fine Strokes of Comedy', *The World,* 15 February 1893 in Laurence, Dan H.
      (ed): *Shaw's Music* [London: John Lane, The Bodley Head, 1981] Vol.2, 809.

16   *Man and Superman,* Act 3. *The Bodley Head Bernard Shaw Collected Plays*
      [1971] Vol.2, 646.

17   G.B.S. to Jules Magny, 18 December 1890 in Laurence: *Collected Letters,*
      op.cit., [1965] Vol.1 (1874-1897), 280.

18   'Knighthood and Dancing', *The Star,* 21 February 1890 in Laurence: *Shaw's*
      Music, op.cit., Vol.1, 933.

19   'Form and Design in Music', *The World,* 31 May 1893 in, Laurence: *Shaw's*
      Music, op.cit., Vol.2, 898.

20   'A Dismal Saturday', *The World,* 19 November 1890 in Laurence: *Shaw's*
      Music, op.cit., Vol.2, 202–3.

21   G.B.S. to the Editor, *Morning Post,* 1911 in Laurence: *Shaw's Music, op.cit.,*
      Vol.1, introduction, 19–20.

22   Shaw, G.B.: 'The Reminiscences of a Quinquagenarian' in *Musical Association*
      Proceedings 1910–11 in Laurence: *Shaw's Music, op.cit.,* Vol.3, 630.

23   Moore, *op.cit.,* 737.

24   Shaw, G.B.: 'Sir Edward Elgar' in *Music and Letters,* I, No.1 [1920] in
      Laurence: *Shaw's Music, op.cit.,* Vol.3, 722–4.

25   G.B.S. to the *Daily News,* 9 June 1922 in Laurence: *Shaw's Music, op.cit.,*
      Vol.3, 729–30.

26   G.B.S. to Conal O'Riordan, 29 July 1944 (Texas).

27   Elgar to G.B.S. quoted in the Malvern Festival Programme, 1977, 25.

28   G.B.S. to Conal O'Riordan, 29 July 1944 (Texas).

29   'Severn Suite' score (Texas).

30   G.B.S. to Elgar, 28 September 1930 in Laurence: *Collected Letters, op.cit.,*
      Vol.4, 201.

31   G.B.S. to Elgar, 2 January 1931 in Laurence: *Collected Letters,* Vol.4, 225.

32   Elgar to Colvin, 13 December 1921 (WRO).

33   Shaw, G.B.: 'Sir Edward Elgar', *op.cit.* in Laurence: *Shaw's Music, op.cit.,*
      Vol.3, 725.

34   G.B.S. to Elgar, 29 June 1932 (WRO).

35   Reith, John: *Into the Wind* [Hodder and Stoughton, 1949] 163.

36   G.B.S. to *The Times,* 20 December 1932 in Laurence: *Shaw's Music, op.cit,*
      Vol.3, 732.

37   G.B.S to Elgar, 2 January 1931 (Elgar Birthplace Museum).

38   G.B.S to Elgar, 5 December 1933 (WRO).

39   Charlotte Shaw to Elgar, 20 September 1932 (WRO).

40   Elgar to the Shaws, 18 April 1933 (WRO).

41   Charlotte Shaw to Nancy Astor, 9 September 1934 (Reading University Library).

42   G.B.S. to Lord Reith, 25 February 1948 in Laurence: *Collected Letters, op.cit.*, Vol.4, 815–816.

43   G.B.S. to Rutland Boughton, 28 May 1948 in Allen, K.: *Elgar in Love* [Malvern, 2000] 119.

44   Carice Elgar Blake to *The Sunday Times*, 25 July 1962 in Allen, *loc.cit.*,119.

Chapter Nine

Elgar's Legacy

Michael Oliver
A transcription of a lecture given on 4 March 1985

I shall begin by considering the opening few pages of a very great movement, the rondo scherzo of Elgar's Second Symphony. Here is Elgar's description of it – and I quote him here because in due course I propose to disagree with him quite radically – he said it was 'very wild & headstrong ... with soothing pastoral strains in between & very, very brilliant'.[1]

The rondo third movement begins in an energetic mood, and the second subject, marked *sonoramente,* might be thought to be one of Elgar's confident and noble themes. But one thing has always struck me about it: when I first heard the symphony I was disappointed by this, in that it soon becomes somewhat uneasy. It fades, it becomes quiet. One is aware of a silence surrounding the tune, and this is still pages away from the famous terrifying interruption to that movement (what Elgar called the 'malign influence' rearing up and threatening to destroy the music utterly). I do *not* find the rondo headstrong or brilliant at all.

Elgar's legacy might be defined as the effect of his music on the English musical scene and the composers who succeeded him, and it may be thought: what has the rondo of the Second Symphony to do with that? It ought to have *everything* to do with it – that movement is an indication of the sheer magnitude of Elgar's legacy. It is the sight that we set when searching for his influence.

Part of the problem is deciding what it is of Elgar that could or should have influenced his juniors. Little passing quotations or backward references do not really count as influences. A large number of Elgar's musical phrases – his manner – have become proverbial, but they do not say anything about his influence, only his ability to compose archetypes, and I do not think it says any more about Elgar's influence to notice that Eric Coates's *Knightsbridge March* is deeply indebted to the *Pomp and Circumstance* marches (and that is not intended as a sneer against Eric

---

1 – Notes and references for this chapter appear on pages 221-222.

Coates). Exactly the same mechanism is just as unmistakably at work in Walton's coronation marches. I predict that when the Coronation of King Charles III arrives and Brian Ferneyhough or Harrison Birtwistle is asked to write a coronation march, they will write one with an Elgarian ring to it. He made the mould.

But then I do not suppose that any of us would suggest that the *Pomp and Circumstance* marches are the essential Elgar. To look for real influences, I ought to say what I mean by 'an influence'. I mean the firm impress of one creative mind on another. To look for influences, we have to look for something much closer to Elgar's essence than *Pomp and Circumstance*. What might that essence be?

It is a matter of interpretation and of how we read Elgar's mind, and the fact that he described the rondo of the Second Symphony as 'wild & headstrong with soothing pastoral strains in between & very, very brilliant' is an indication of how very difficult it is to interpret his music and how hard to read his mind.

I shall start to look for influences where you would most expect to find them. Strauss raised his glass to 'Meister Edward Elgar and the young progressivist school of English composers'.[2] What did he mean by that? It is interesting, and it might be significant, that Elgar had no pupils. John Ireland said that a brief talk with Elgar was the best orchestration lesson he had ever had.[3] Obviously there was no man in England, there was practically no man in the world, who was better qualified to teach orchestration at that period. For a good deal of his life, Elgar complained that his income as a composer was insufficient. He could have supplemented this by teaching composition and orchestration. Did he ever seriously consider it?[4]

If he had, the gentlemen amateurs of the colleges would have sniffed a bit. They would have regarded him as insufficiently qualified to teach, although has there ever been a composer more superbly trained than that self-trained composer? Yet the highly respected Professor Prout[5] had no qualifications whatsoever and Elgar could have taught orchestration, if he had wanted to. He did not because he had a very clear perception of what his 'business' was – he was to become a full-time, freelance professional composer, and that was an enormous risk. England had not had one since Handel, and Elgar decided, early on, exactly what he was going to do. He realised also in whose company he was. Brahms did not teach; Wagner did not teach; Parry and Stanford might teach if they please – but not Brahms, Wagner, or Elgar. He realised what a serious job composition alone was.

Now that in itself could have been an influence, or rather an example. We know that when Holst heard the *Variations* and Havergal Brian heard *King Olaf,* both of them said very much the same thing. Holst's words were: 'I realised it was possible to be an Englishman and a composer'. Havergal Brian 'regarded Elgar as a phenomenon'.[6] Neither of them said that after hearing music by Parry or Stanford. Not that they would not have regarded Parry or Stanford as serious composers, but I think both Holst and Havergal Brian recognised that Elgar was in a different league.

Still, a composer does not have to teach in order to found a school. But those 'young progessivists' that Strauss referred to, do they sound like Elgar's 'school'? After the *Variations* had taught Holst that it was possible to be an Englishman and a composer, you would have expected him to enrol in Elgar's school without delay. But where are the sounds of it? There is evidence, for sure, in *The Hymn of Jesus,* and perhaps elsewhere, that he had heard the semi-chorus in *The Dream of Gerontius.* As a trombonist, he knew all about the *Pomp and Circumstance* marches, and what he knew came in useful whenever he needed to write a march. There is the big tune in 'Jupiter' which has a sort of kinship with one of the tunes in the finale of Elgar's Second Symphony. But as Brahms said of a similar kinship, 'any fool can see that'. It is the differences that are most noticeable. The best of Holst is Holstian – spiritually it is miles away from Elgar, and in fact I would say that the most Elgarian of Holst's pieces is the one that sounds *least* like Elgar, *Egdon Heath,* that evocation of the bleak landscape portrayed in Hardy's novel *The Return of the Native.* Elgar certainly was part of Holst's landscape. He affected the light Holst saw by, but surely by no stretch of the imagination was he a young progressive of Elgar's school. It might be significant that the name 'Elgar' does not appear once in Imogen Holst's study of her father's music and only twice in her biography of him.

I have, incidentally in preparing for this, studied every biography of every composer since Elgar in my library, including foreign composers as well as English ones, and the number of them that make not even the most passing reference to Elgar is really quite extraordinary.

Vaughan Williams is a more curious case. He acknowledged Elgarian influence, especially in the first two symphonies – and as Carlyle said of a New England transcendentalist, 'By God he'd better'. But the interesting influences are the ones Vaughan Williams does *not* acknowledge. Maybe by the time he wrote *Job,* he no longer realised how much of Elgar's Second Symphony and *The Apostles* were lodged in his memory. But as Vaughan Williams himself put it:

> Real cribbing takes place when one composer thinks with the mind of
> another even when there is no mechanical similarity of phrase. When, as
> often happens, this vicarious thinking does lead to similarity of phrase the
> offence is, I think, more venial. In that case one is so impressed by a certain
> passage in another composer that it becomes part of oneself.[7]

It is a very fine distinction and I am not quite sure which of those cases
applies to the apparent quoting of a mood (not a tune) of Elgar in the
finale of *A London Symphony*. It inhabits the same sort of world as the
opening of Elgar's First Symphony and once one hears the two in
conjunction it casts a light on both pieces. The beginning of Elgar's First
Symphony is a *locus classicus* of what he called *nobilmente*, but it acquires
a touch of ambiguity, perhaps again unease, when you set it alongside the
finale of *A London Symphony*. Is this because Vaughan Williams regarded
Elgar's *nobilmente* with dubiety or is it because we know that Elgar's tune
will eventually triumph, that we associate it with triumph from the start?
Does it not rather earn its triumph, does it not earn its *nobilmente* with
some difficulty, through a symphonic process? VW's vision was so intensely
personal that you would not expect it to be marked all through by the
name of another composer – like 'Brighton' runs through the rock. Again,
it is very difficult to think of him as a member of Elgar's school.

Walton looks like surer ground, though he was further from Elgar's time
than either Holst or Vaughan Williams. I have mentioned the Coronation
marches, and there are pages of proud pageantry in Walton. The music for
Henry V is the nearest thing we will ever have to an Elgarian film-score. You
might find traces of Elgar's choral writing in *Belshazzar's Feast*; but a word
of caution. Walton did not hear *The Kingdom* and *The Apostles* until forty
years after he had written *Belshazzar's Feast*; and at that time he said he
preferred both to *The Dream of Gerontius* and that he found all three
inferior to the symphonies.[8] And if anyone listens to *Belshazzar's Feast* and
seems to find that there is an obvious recollection of one of the more
violent passages in *Gerontius,* can one really visualise William Walton,
during his formative years, sitting round the drawing-room fire in Chelsea
with the Sitwells listening to *The Dream of Gerontius?* Osbert Sitwell
described Elgar's music as 'obnoxious, so full of English humour and the
spirit of compulsory games'.[9] Incredibly enough, he was talking about the
String Quartet, the Quintet and the Violin Sonata. We are going to have to
come back to that sort of *massive* incomprehension.

In the circumstances and with the distance of time and differences of
personality taken into account, it is almost surprising to find any Elgarian

characteristics in Walton. But then if you listen to the finale of the First Symphony, you do hear something there, in particular that fugue – it's what Elgar would have called 'a devil of a fugue' – and you can certainly draw a neat line from Elgar's *Introduction and Allegro,* not only to the fugue in the finale of Walton's First Symphony, but also to the fugue in Britten's *Frank Bridge Variations.* And you could say that Walton's First Symphony ends *nobilmente*; but does he sound like a member of Elgar's school? Elgar heard Walton's Viola Concerto – he detested it.

In any case, if you think of those pieces that I have mentioned as having certain Elgarian overtones – Holst's 'Jupiter', RVW's *A London Symphony* and Walton's First Symphony[10] – do any of them sound like overtones, responses to a composer who is still alive; alive and vital?

Here are two voices who seem not to think so:

> … but the aggressive Edwardian prosperity that lends itself so comfortable a background to Elgar's finales is now as strange to us as the England that produced *Greensleeves* and *The Woods so wilde.* Stranger, in fact, and less sympathetic. In consequence much of Elgar's music, through no fault of its own, has for the present generation an almost intolerable air of smugness, self-assurance and autocratic benevolence.[11]

A famous judgment by Constant Lambert. Still, he did at least say 'through no fault of its own' and 'almost intolerable'.

Here is another view – a no less famous attack by Edward Dent:

> Elgar's music is too emotional and not quite free from vulgarity. His orchestral works … are vivid in colour but pompous in style and with an affected nobility of expression.[12]

Now, the thing to remember about both those judgments is that both were written while Elgar was still alive. Take them together with this, written not long after his death – an entry from Benjamin Britten's diary:

> Haircut. Lunch with William Walton. He is charming, but I feel always the school relationship with him – he is so obviously the head-prefect of English music, whereas I'm the promising young new boy. Soon of course he'll leave & return as a member of the staff – [*Vaughan*] Williams being of course the Headmaster. Elgar was never that – but a member of the Governing Board.[13]

So we can summarise. Elgar – through no fault of his own – represents the suffocating smugness of imperial Edwardian England, and we find him almost intolerable. Elgar is vulgar, pompous and even his nobility is phoney. Elgar represents the remote oppressive authority of the school

Edward Dent is rather nastier. Elgar's music is 'not quite free from vulgarity' – it is the sort of phrase that defines the person who uses it, such as the damning 'not quite our class'. Even the accusation 'affected nobility of expression' has rather a snobbish ring to it. Nobility is acceptable provided you are born to it and do not affect it. There is a slight feeling here of settling scores with an upstart. Elgar *was* an upstart. He was a tradesman's son with little education, who married above him. He was a professional upstart too. He achieved what he achieved without the benefit of college, or academy, or university music department or the ecclesiastical musical establishment; and he was a Catholic too. He must have been resented, but he did not shield himself against resentment with tact. He wrote:

> Critics frequently say of a man that it is to his credit that he is never vulgar. Good. But it is possible for him – in an artistic sense only, be it understood, to be much worse; he can be commonplace. Vulgarity in the course of time may be refined. Vulgarity often goes with inventiveness, and it can take the initiative – in a rude and misguided way no doubt – but after all it does something, and can be and has been refined. But the commonplace mind can never be anything but commonplace, and no amount of education, no polish of a University, can eradicate the stain from the low type of mind which is the English commonplace. This applies to other arts besides music. One branch of art never understood and never developed in England is the decoration of the public building. An Englishman will take you into a large room, beautifully proportioned, and will point out to you that it is white – all over white – and somebody will say what exquisite taste. You know in your own mind, in your own soul, that it is not taste at all, – that it is the want of taste – that it is mere evasion. English music is white, and *evades everything.*[17]

'No polish of a University can eradicate the stain from the low type of mind which is the English commonplace': that must have hurt and it must have rankled, and what could be more powerful in the England of the 1920s and 30s than an alloy of snobbery with a long-matured grudge?

There was snobbery about the music as well. Constant Lambert was at least honest when he had to admit that Elgar was the last English composer to retain a real contact with the public, but to some others that would have been further cause for condemnation.

What about Britten's feeling that Elgar was on the board, a member of the establishment? It may be significant that Britten later spoke with great warmth and insight of Elgar. It was not long after writing that youthful diary entry that Britten began to have his first taste of being an outsider – the jealousy aroused by his brilliance, the quiet sneers that he must have known about concerning his sexuality. Perhaps he came to realise how much an outsider Elgar was.

That may seem an odd thing to say about Sir Edward Elgar, Bart, Order of Merit, and Master of the King's Musick. But for how long was he an insider? From the première of the *Variations*, surely, in 1899, when he was in his forties, but for how long did he remain so? Elgar's last major work to be an unqualified success was the Violin Concerto, premièred only eleven years later, at a time of rapid and violent change. 1910 was the year in which King Edward VII died, and six months after the first performance of the Violin Concerto, in November, Diaghilev's Ballet Russe appeared in London. In 1910 Picasso painted his cubist portrait of Ambrose Vollard and Stravinsky's ballet *The Firebird* was premièred in Paris. It was also, if we are talking of clouds no smaller than a man's hand, the year in which Charles Ives began his Fourth Symphony and Webern drafted his *Six Pieces*, Op.6. Exciting things clearly were happening abroad and such a very English voice was bound to sound, can we say, a little dull by comparison. To us Elgar is an Edwardian, but to the Georgians he was a Victorian.

That sends us back to the question: just how English Elgar is? His music is rooted in Brahms and Wagner[18] – Delius and De Conde were right about that – rather less so in Mendelssohn, but firmly in Schumann ('my ideal' he called him). Michael Kennedy has traced one or two French roots in Elgar and I fancy there is a distinct presence of César Franck in the first two movements of the First Symphony.

Then there was Strauss, Elgar's beloved Coeur de Lion; but there was not much in the English past. Handel, naturally, and there were some works of Purcell he admired. He liked only a little of Byrd and Tallis, saying they were of antiquarian interest to him.

I am more inclined to agree with Donald Mitchell, who wrote:

> It has, I must confess, always astonished me that Elgar has been so strenuously claimed as a representative English figure; he has never struck me as such.[19]

Mitchell states that he can perceive no folk influence in Elgar of the kind that so powerfully marked Holst and Vaughan Williams as English. To which Hans Keller, in a useful and provocative article, replied that there *was* an English influence Elgar could not escape – the influence of folk song, but

> ... the reason why Mr Mitchell does not spontaneously hear this specific English flavour which, however faint on the surface, permeates virtually all Elgarian music, is that he was born and bred in England and thus subjected

to the same early folkloristic influences as Elgar himself: they do not strike him as something to write home about, as long as they are sufficiently concealed by a Central European harmonic idiom.[20]

Now this is valuable testimony. It comes from somebody who first encountered Elgar when he was already steeped in the Viennese tradition. Keller goes on to find modal and pentatonic themes, notably in the so-called 'Welsh theme' in the *Introduction and Allegro*, but also in the first subject of the *Allegro* itself, which 'is far more profoundly, though far less obviously, folkish in character'. He suggests that Elgar found a way of naturalising 'undiatonic modes into a diatonic framework', quite the reverse of the 'far more self-consciously national Vaughan Williams' who took 'the opposite course of naturalising diatonicism into his archaic, modal frame of mind.' This is Elgar's unnoticed revolution to which Britten, without probably realising it, owed a great deal.

Once, when rehearsing the middle section of the second movement of his First Symphony, Elgar told the orchestra play it 'like something we hear down by the river.' [21] That has often puzzled me. What did Elgar hear down by the river? Certainly he heard a murmuring of leaves and a rippling of water. Did he hear folk songs across the Severn? I rather doubt it. But what an easy tune that is – and so many others like it – to whistle, to hum. What would Jerome K. Jerome have meant if *he* had said play it like something you hear down by the river? One could write an essay on what 'the river' meant to the Victorians and the Edwardians. It was a place that you went with a couple of friends, your dog and a pipe, to be idle, relaxed and cheerful, to saunter; you probably wore flannels and a blazer, and for one day of the week, a soft collar. You do not have to quote folk songs to bring a popular element into your music, and there is a great deal of 'down by the river' music in Elgar.

Of all composers, it is practically more difficult with Elgar than probably any other composer to sort out the precise dividing line between his great concert music and his light salon music. The two do interpenetrate, and quite often in the midst of a symphony you hear something which you recognise from the other music, and Elgar's mind is not making this division. One of the most important things about him is the way he can draw the vernacular, the popular, into his greatest possible music.

I may have gone a long way from the subject of influences and legacies; I am slowly but surely getting back there. I did say at the beginning that to look for real influences we need to search for Elgar's essence, to read his mind a little. Strolling by the river is not irrelevant to either of those objectives.

He wrote:

> I am still at heart the dreamy child who used to be found in the reeds by Severn side with a sheet of paper trying to fix the sounds & longing for something very great – source, texture & all else unknown. I am still looking for this ...[22]

Now that says a great deal. As a boy, he stole down to the reeds with scores of Mozart symphonies borrowed from his father's shop and already he was sufficiently a musician for the score to be enough. He devoured those symphonies and he longed for something very great. He longed to be a great composer, like Mozart. But for him this appeared to be absolutely impossible, as composers were either gentle folk or foreigners. Yet, he would not accept that, and one of the most astonishing things about Elgar is the enormous courage and the enormous perseverance it took to go in search of that 'something great' he had dreamed of down by the reeds. It meant a long apprenticeship; it meant learning by trial and error. It involved writing works which he knew were not first-rate because, at that moment, he did not have the capacity to write first-rate works, but he knew that by writing lesser works he would achieve first-rate works in due course. It took rebuffs, disappointments and poverty, many a slight, many a humiliation. But by the age Mozart had been dead for a decade, he found it, but – how soon it turned to ashes and how short a time it lasted.

Go back to the river. Elgar walked there with his father as a boy and his father took him into some of the grand houses where he, the father, went to tune the pianos. In later life, Elgar re-traced those riverside walks with a friend and he recited a precisely remembered catalogue of which county family lived in each house fifty years before. By then the owners of those houses would have been honoured to receive a call from Sir Edward Elgar, Bart, O.M., Master of King's Musick. But during the years of striving how many of them were open to him, how many of them were actually *closed* because his wife had married into trade? There is an extraordinary mixture in Elgar of social tension. Rosa Burley was both amazed and amused to find the Elgars in full evening dress for a dinner with one guest;[23] and even such a sympathetic friend as Frank Schuster laughed at Elgar's weakness for white waistcoats and Court dress, even calling him the 'pouter pigeon'. All that makes for a deep social resentment. 'Everything seems so hopelessly & irredeemably *vulgar* at Court',[24] he wrote; and in 1913 he left the Royal Academy banquet in a rage because he was not placed at the top table.[25]

'Dreaming' he said 'of something very great', and that could include having a burning idealism for what music could be in his country. He was a Tory, he was a patriot, and as he said 'there's nothing apologetic about me.' But in 1905 he wrote:

> *Some of us who in [1880]* ... were young and taking an active part in music – a really active part such as playing in orchestras – felt that something at last was going to be done in the way of composition by the English school ... It is saddening to those who hoped so much from these early days, to find that after all that had been written, and all the endeavour to excite enthusiasm for English music – "big" music – to find that we had inherited an art which has no hold on the affections of our people, and is held in no respect abroad.[26]

Obviously he exaggerated, for even by then his own music held the affections of 'our people' and was held in great respect abroad. But imagine how many lamentably slipshod performances he had heard by then of his own music, how much uncomprehending rubbish had been written about it and how much bad music had been played, alongside his own, and accorded not much less respect. Yet even so, how many where there in 1905 who recognised 'big' music when they heard it and how many who valued him for writing 'little' music?

His melancholia – which is often ascribed to the passing of the Edwardian high summer, or to the bitterness of the First World War or to the death of Lady Elgar – goes back much, much further than any of those things. I have suggested some of the reasons for it – disillusionment, regret that things were not as he had once hoped down by the reeds, feelings of betrayal, of idealism mocked by vulgar reality. But why did he feel all this so deeply? It is almost impossible for us to understand, but he had practically no protective emotional shell at all. In August 1914 he wrote:

> Concerning the war I say nothing – the only thing that wrings my heart & soul is the thought of the horses – oh! my beloved animals – the men – and women can go to hell – but my horses; – I walk round & round this room cursing God for allowing dumb beasts to be tortured – let Him kill his human beings but – how CAN HE? Oh, my horses.[27]

Michael Kennedy wrote, in his beautiful *Portrait of Elgar*:

> What manner of man was this, who had composed the death of Falstaff and the cadenza of the Violin Concerto and could consign human beings in wartime to hell?[28]

May I suggest a simple, dreadful answer? This was a man driven close to madness, by imagining (he never saw it, he imagined it, which was much worse) horses maimed and dismembered by shell fire, and who could not, *for his reason's sake*, contemplate the sufferings of men torn to pieces in the same way. He simply could not contemplate it and so he fell to cursing them instead. And it was *that* sensibility, the sensibility that wrote that letter, that composed the death of Falstaff and the cadenza of the Violin Concerto. It is a sensibility in which emotions are experienced with an extreme intensity: Edward Dent would have called it vulgarity. But, these emotions are expressed kaleidoscopically, and iridescently, for seldom is there a *nobilmente* without a shadow, seldom a positive statement without a doubt or some ambiguity. It is a language as expressive as Mahler's, but unfiltered through neurosis.

*

I used to have difficulty with Elgar. In my youth I recognised he was a 'big' composer, but programme notes and descriptions of Elgar's music tended to apply words like 'radiant', 'glorious' and 'resplendent'; I have never liked music that is describable by those words. Elgar also tended to be pigeonholed as an Edwardian – I have suggested that to those in the 1920s and 30s he was probably seen as a Victorian (was he an Edwardian in his own estimation?). In my opinion, the Edwardian period was unquestionably the most vulgar (apart from the present) in our history. Elgar was spiritually not part of that assertive, bombastic vulgarity. There is plenty of evidence of him wincing at it. However, over a period of time, I came to realise that what I was hearing was not adequately described by those words – resplendent, radiant, glorious. Elgar's music has, in my opinion, a great deal of pain in it, a great deal of uncertainty and a great deal of a lack of self-assurance. It has a great deal of feeling that things will never be, not what they once were, but not what he once *hoped* they might be and that is a more essential quality to Elgar's music than *Pomp and Circumstance*, patriotism or even *nobilmente*. All over the world composers are discovering alternative histories to twentieth-century music. Routes from the late nineteenth century to now are being noticed that do not pass through Schoenberg, although they may pass very near him. Looking for descendants from Elgar's music is very difficult in the generations that followed him, as – for one reason or another – they had to turn their backs on him. Elgar is not going to prove a route in the sense that Debussy, Bartók or Sibelius were, because indeed Turina was right, Elgar was a summation – but what a summation! The whole of the nineteenth century was available to him as an expressive resource, still further enriched by the extreme sensibility of his own temperament and yet further enriched by his ability to use popular elements in a subtly, evocative way – marches obviously – haunted marches, hectic marches and something from 'down by the river'.

That is the legacy, and for a very long time composers shied away from it, either out of one or other of those prejudices, or because he seemed wholly of the past, or because the associations attached to his name, whether true or false associations, were unwelcome to younger composers.

But now the position has changed. People are now looking for broader rather than narrower paths. Composers may again be looking for richness and comprehensiveness. If they are looking for formal paths, I do not think they will find much in Elgar. But if it is expressive subtlety, responsiveness to musical means or delicate and grandiose shadings of emotion, then they may find a deal worth pondering on his legacy.

There are signs of composers, whilst not really joining Elgar's school or submitting to his influence, are at least becoming ready to accept his relevance, to accept there can be bridges between his time and ours, bridges between his sensibility and ours – and that those bridges can be valuable ones.

The closing pages of Hugh Wood's Cello Concerto do not sound in the least like Elgar, but the composer does quote him, in order, he says, 'to pay more than one homage'. Wood's awareness of Elgar is obvious and he is aware of him as somebody from the past who is relevant to our present. The same can be said for Robin Holloway; and while I have no idea of his feelings for Elgar, I suspect they are warm ones. His *Romanza* for Violin and Orchestra shows a composer who is certainly not trying to imitate Elgar, or trying to take up where he left off, or pretend there is no time difference between then and now, but who is, at any rate, prepared to regard that epoch which, ever since it ended, has seemed historical. (The Edwardian era was already part of remote history six months after King Edward died.) We are beginning to realise that music of that period may have something to say to us which is not nostalgic, and in that sense I would say Elgar has left a healthy and a very rich legacy indeed.

Edited transcription of a lecture given to the London Branch of the Elgar Society at Imperial College, London on 4 March 1985.

Notes and References

1   Elgar to Alice Stuart Wortley, 16 February 1911 in Moore, Jerrold Northrop
     (ed): *Edward Elgar: the Windflower letters* [Oxford: OUP, 1989] 79.

2   *The Times,* 23 May 1902.

3   Similarly when Herbert Howells once asked him the secret of his writing for
     strings, Elgar told him: 'Study old Handel. I went to him for help ages ago.'
     Kennedy, Michael: *Portrait of Elgar* [Oxford: OUP, 1987] 218.

4   Holst wrote to Vaughan Williams in 1903: 'Don't you think we ought to
     victimise Elgar? Write to him in Worcester and see him *a lot?* I wish we could
     do that together.' Holst, Imogen: *Gustav Holst: a biography* [Oxford: OUP,
     1969] 180. RVW had previously approached Elgar, writing to him in about
     1900 'asking him to give me lessons, especially in orchestration. I received a
     polite reply from Lady Elgar saying that Sir Edward was too busy to give me
     lessons but suggesting that I should become a pupil of Professor Bantock.'
     Vaughan Williams, Ralph: 'A Musical Autobiography' in *National Music and
     Other Essays* [Oxford: OUP, 1963] 188.

5   Ebenezer Prout (1835-1909), largely self-taught composer, organist and
     teacher. Taught theory at the Royal Academy of Music from 1879 and was
     Professor of Music at Dublin University from 1894 -1909.

6   Nettel, Reginald: *Ordeal by Music* [Oxford, 1945] 11.

7   Vaughan Williams, R., 'What have we learnt from Elgar?' in *Music and
     Letters*, XVI, No.1 [1935] in Redwood, C (ed): *An Elgar Companion*
     [Ashbourne: Sequoia Press, 1982] 266–267.

8   Walton to Sir Adrian Boult, 12 October 1975: 'I've been having an interesting
     & enjoyable time with the 'Apostles' & the 'Kingdom' neither of which I had
     heard before. I like them both more than 'Gerontius' – perhaps your new
     recording [of *The Dream of Gerontius*] will convert me! I hope so for I find
     Elgar's choral works rather inferior to the orchestral ones.' Moore, J.N. (ed):
     Music and Friends Letters to Adrian Boult [London: Hamish Hamilton,
     1979] 192.

9   Sitwell, Osbert: *Laughter in the Next Room* [London, 1949] 196.

10   Although the first three movements of Walton's symphony were first
     performed on 3 December 1934, nine months after Elgar's death, and the
     Finale was completed in 1935, Walton's first ideas for the work date from
     October 1931 and composition continued over the next three years:
     Kennedy, M.: *Portrait of Walton* [Oxford: OUP, 1989] 64 *et seq.*

11   Lambert, Constant: *Music Ho! a study of music in decline* [London: Penguin,
     1948] 205.

12   Dent, E.J.: ' Englander' in Adler, Guido (ed): *Handbuch der Musikgeschichte*
     [Frankfurt-am-Main, 1924] 934-48; Michael Oliver adopts the wording given

in Kennedy, M: *Portrait of Elgar, op.cit.,* 316. For a variant translation see Trowell, Brian: 'Elgar's Use of Literature' in Monk, Raymond (ed): *Edward Elgar: music and literature* [Aldershot: Scolar Press, 1993] 286. Trowell translates the conclusion of the quotation as 'chivalresque in their utterance.'

13   Diary of Benjamin Britten, 28 July 1937 partly quoted in Carpenter, Humphrey: *Benjamin Britten: a biography* [London: Faber & Faber, 1992] 110.

14   Frederick Delius to Granville Bantock, 17 December 1908, in Carley. Lionel, ed., *Delius: a life in letters* [London: Scolar Press, 1983] Vol.1 (1862 – 1908), 377.

15   Joaquin Turina, Spanish composer, conductor, pianist and musical critic (1882–1949).

16   Unhappily, despite enquiries at the Westminster Music Library, Bromley Music Library and elsewhere it has not been possible to trace 'Roland de Conde' or this extract. He is not in *Grove's Dictionary of Music and Musicians.*

17   Elgar, Edward: 'A Future for English Music' in Young, Percy M. (ed): *A Future for English Music and other lectures by Edward Elgar* [London: Dobson, 1968] 47– 49.

18   Charles Ives, who did not greatly care for Wagner, gave a short list of composers who, for him out-did Wagner in his list of qualities of 'wholesomeness, manliness, humanity and deep spiritual, perhaps deep religious meaning'. His list consisted of Franck, Brahms, D'Indy (that's the surprising one) and Elgar, 'for all his tiresomeness' – whatever he may have meant by that.

19   Mitchell, Donald: 'Some Thoughts on Elgar', in Redwood, *op.cit.,* 282– 3.

20   Keller, Hans: 'Elgar: The First of the New' in *Music and Musicians* [June 1957] in Redwood, *op. cit.,* 277.

21   Reed, W.H:, *Elgar as I Knew Him* [London: Gollancz, 1936] 141.

22   Elgar to Sidney Colvin, 13 December 1921 in Moore, J.N. (ed): *Edward Elgar: letters of a lifetime* [Oxford: OUP, 1990] 359.

23   Burley, Rosa and Carruthers, Frank C.: *Edward Elgar: the record of a friendship* [London: Barrie and Jenkins, 1972] 59.

24   Elgar to Alice Stuart of Wortley, 16 April 1924 in Moore: *The Windflower Letters, op.cit.,* 290.

25   Elgar to Alice Stuart Wortley, 3 May 1913, *ibid.,* 117.

26   Young, *op. cit.,* 33–5.

27   Elgar to Frank Schuster, 25 August 1914 in Moore: *Letters of a Lifetime, op.cit.,* 277.

28   Kennedy: *Portrait of Elgar, op. cit.,* 261.

Index

Musical and literary works are listed under the name of their composer or author. Urban geographical entries appear under the town or city in which they are located.

The Elgar Society was formed in 1951 with the objective of promoting interest in the composer and his music. With a number of significant achievements to its credit, the Society is now the largest UK-based composer appreciation society with ten regional branches in Britain and about 10% of its membership resident outside the UK. In 1997 the Society launched its own Internet website (http://www.elgar.org) with the aim of spreading knowledge of Elgar around the world and, in the process, attracting a greater international membership. This was followed in 1999 by Elgar Enterprises, the trading arm of the Society, whose purpose is to raise funds for the Society's charitable projects through the publication and sale of books, CDs, CD-ROMs and other material about the composer and his music, and in October 2001 by the launch of the Elgar Society Edition, a scheme to continue the uniform edition of all the composer's music.

All enquiries about membership should be addressed to :
Jon Goldswain, 31 Queen's Road, Marlow, Bucks SL7 2PS
telephone : +44 1628 475897; e-mail : membership@elgar.org

On-line and postal membership application forms can be found on the website at: 'http://www.elgar.org/5memform.htm'

~   ~   ~

The Elgar Foundation was established in 1973. Its objectives include supporting the Elgar Birthplace, the cottage in which Elgar was born in Lower Broadheath, some three miles west of the city of Worcester. The Birthplace now houses a collection of memorabilia associated with the composer, while the adjacent Elgar Centre provides an introduction to the composer's life and music and a meeting place for Elgarian events. They are open to the public daily throughout most of the year.

To check opening times or for further information:
telephone +44 1905 333224; fax +44 1905 333426;
e-mail: birthplace@elgar.org